複数議決権株式を用いた株主構造のコントロール
（令和元年5月28日開催）

報告者　松　井　智　予
（上智大学大学院法学研究科教授）

目　次

Ⅰ．はじめに……………………………………………………………………2
Ⅱ．IPO時点における複数議決権株式の利用と創業者利益……………4
　1．複数議決権株式をIPO時に導入するアメリカ企業の増加　………4
　2．議決権種類株式を用いたIPOに対する学説・投資家の反対　……5
　3．小括・議決権種類株式の利用目的・抑止を可能とする環境………8
Ⅲ．ヨーロッパの長期株主優遇と議決権種類株式……………………9
　1．背景…………………………………………………………………9
　2．フランス法の複数議決権制度……………………………………10
　3．複数議決権株式制度導入の影響…………………………………12
　4．フロランジュ法導入手法の特殊性………………………………14
　5．資本の移動の自由との葛藤………………………………………16
Ⅳ．日本における運用…………………………………………………19
　1．IPO時点での議決権種類株式と創業者利益……………………19
　2．上場会社による種類株式の発行と長期的保有…………………21

討　　議………………………………………………………………23
報告者レジュメ………………………………………………………48
資　　料………………………………………………………………71

金融商品取引法研究会出席者(令和元年5月28日)

報 告 者	松 井 智 予	上智大学大学院法学研究科教授
会　　長	神 作 裕 之	東京大学大学院法学政治学研究科教授
会長代理	弥 永 真 生	筑波大学ビジネスサイエンス系 　　　　　　　ビジネス科学研究科教授
委　　員	飯 田 秀 総	東京大学大学院法学政治学研究科准教授
〃	大 崎 貞 和	野村総合研究所未来創発センターフェロー
〃	尾 崎 悠 一	首都大学東京大学院法学政治学研究科准教授
〃	加 藤 貴 仁	東京大学大学院法学政治学研究科教授
〃	河 村 賢 治	立教大学大学院法務研究科教授
〃	後 藤 　 元	東京大学大学院法学政治学研究科教授
〃	武 井 一 浩	西村あさひ法律事務所パートナー弁護士
〃	藤 田 友 敬	東京大学大学院法学政治学研究科教授
〃	松 井 秀 征	立教大学法学部教授
〃	松 尾 健 一	大阪大学大学院高等司法研究科教授
〃	松 尾 直 彦	松尾国際法律事務所弁護士
オブザーバー	岸 田 吉 史	野村ホールディングスグループ執行役員
〃	森 　 忠 之	大和証券グループ本社経営企画部担当部長兼法務課長
〃	森 　 正 孝	ＳＭＢＣ日興証券法務部長
〃	陶 山 健 二	みずほ証券法務部長
〃	本 井 孝 洋	三菱ＵＦＪモルガン・スタンレー証券法務部長
〃	島 村 昌 征	日本証券業協会執行役政策本部共同本部長
〃	塚 﨑 由 寛	日本取引所グループ総務部法務グループ課長
研 究 所	増 井 喜一郎	日本証券経済研究所理事長
〃	大 前 　 忠	日本証券経済研究所常務理事

(敬称略)

複数議決権株式を用いた株主構造のコントロール

神作会長 まだお見えでない方もおられますけれども、定刻になりましたので、ただいまより第9回金融商品取引法研究会を始めさせていただきます。

　最初に、オブザーバーの方に変更がございましたので、ご紹介させていただきます。

　人事異動に伴い、ＳＭＢＣ日興証券の法務部長に新たにご就任されました森正孝様にご参加いただくことになりました。森様、どうかよろしくお願いいたします。

森オブザーバー 森でございます。よろしくお願いします。

神作会長 また、昨年11月から当研究会にご参加いただいておりました研究所の土井俊範エグゼクティブフェローが、いわゆるＡＭＲＯ（アムロ）、ＡＳＥＡＮと日中韓３国によって設立されたＡＳＥＡＮ＋３マクロ経済リサーチ・オフィスの所長に、今月の26日からご就任され、シンガポールにご赴任されましたので、ご紹介させていただきます。

　本日は、既にご案内させていただいておりますとおり、松井智予先生から「複数議決権株式を用いた株主構造のコントロール」というテーマでご報告いただくこととなっております。

　それでは、松井先生、早速ですけれども、ご報告、よろしくお願いいたします。

［松井（智）委員の報告］

松井（智）報告者 上智大学の松井でございます。本日は、ご出席いただき、本当にありがとうございます。それでは、拙い研究ではありますが、これから発表させていただきます。

　今回は、種類株式を日本が導入したときに、これを使って複数議決権株式のようなものができるかということが議論されたことがありまして、その後、

どのようにいろいろな状況が動いているのかという報告を含め、考えられる弊害についてどんなものが出てきているのか等についてご報告をさせていただければと思います。

I．はじめに

「1．はじめに」として、もう皆さんご案内のことかと思いますけれども、どのような背景があったのかということを簡単にまとめさせていただいております。

日本においては、108条1項8号というところで、種類株主を構成員とする種類株主総会の決議があることを必要とするものを定めることができるとの規定があります。この株式を発行して一部の株式にのみ譲渡制限を課した公開会社を上場すれば、黄金株について譲渡制限を付するというスキームができると考えられまして、一時期、非常に関心が高かったという経緯がございました。

これについて東京証券取引所が、自分の取引所でこういったものを取り扱うべきかどうかということについて考え方を公表しました。これに対して、企業価値研究会の提言というものが一方でございまして、こちらはいろいろな利用パターンがあるということについてメンションし、かつ、ヨーロッパでは議決権型の種類株式が広く用いられていて、黄金株は民営化企業を中心に広く用いられているということが指摘されております。

報告書では、今回、論文の中で立法があったということで取り上げたフランスについては、6割の企業が、一定期間株式を継続保有した場合に議決権が2倍になるという制度を導入済みであるということが報告されております。また、EUは、この時期に1株1議決権原則をどこまで進めるかということを検討していて、それとの関係で外部委員会を組んで調査報告書を出したのですけれども、そこで「1株1議決権原則と企業の経済パフォーマンスやガバナンスと間に相関関係があるとは断定できない」ということになったので、とりたてて何らかのアクションをとることはしないというふうに姿勢

を一度決めたということになっております。ただし、こういったものについては、個別の事例で弊害が起きる都度、ＥＣＪで否定される例も多いということが指摘されておりました。

　こういったことを踏まえて、日本も、さまざまな発行目的を許容すべきという報告書が出たわけですが、実際には、なかなか運用されないという状態が続いたわけであります。

　その後、約10年経過して、どのようなことが起きているかということですけれども、まずアメリカの側は、創業者ＩＴ企業が上場する際に、議決権種類株式を活用して創造性と会社の方針を維持しようという動きが顕著になりまして、こういった株式については主要な機関投資家等が強い反対を表明し、さまざまなＩＴ企業に対して訴訟が提起される状況になっております。また、サンセット条項によって徐々に株式を一本化していくべきではないかというような主張も出ております。一方で、より多くの利益が創業者に分配されるという構造があったとしても、市場へのリターンも高いということで、それを了解の上でより多くの投資機会を求めるというのがあってもいいのではないかというようなことを主張する方々もいらっしゃるという状況であります。

　逆に、ヨーロッパの側がどうなったかというと、リーマンショックを経て、短期間での業績追求を反省する動きが強まる中で、複数議決権株式には長期保有を行う機関投資家の優遇策という一面もあるのではないかというようなことが考えられて、スチュワードシップなどと並べて議論されることもあるという状況になっております。これはＩＰＯではなくて、一般的に権利を再配分するというスキームを考えるべきかどうかという話になるので、何らかの指針なり規制ということになってくるわけです。一時期、欧州の法務委員会で、株主権利指令の改正案の中に中長期株主に対する優遇策の採用を２年以内に各国に義務づけるというようなことを書かれたことがあったのですけれども、これは結局のところ、その後の草案から落ちております。そういった攻防がある状況にあるということです。

ヨーロッパの中でフランスが何をしたかというと、2014年に、国内事業の主要な設備や雇用が国際資本の決定に左右されるのを防ぐことを主眼として、立法によって上場会社における2年以上の長期保有株式を2議決権を有する優先株とするということをデフォルト化して、これを利用して政府保有を進めようとしました。これは統計の上でそれほど顕著に出るような数ではないのですけれども、日本では2018年に日産の関係で非常にニュースになったために耳目を集めて、それも今回こういったことを調べようという気になった一因ですが、この立法に伴って、新規上場における複数議決権の導入も顕著に増加したとされていて、その影響が注目されているところであります。

　また、イタリアやベルギーなども、この動きに倣って、複数議決権株式を法制化したとニュースで言われておりまして、このような制度が広がることがECJの従来判決とどのような関係に立つのかということが、問題として残されているかと思います。

　では、日本ではどのようなことがあったのでしょうか。日本では、2014年に1社、CYBERDYNE社が単元株を利用して複数議決権類似の投資単位制度を導入して話題になりましたが、これがきっかけになって隆盛をきわめているかというと、そういうわけではないということなので、こういったことについてもう一度状況を見ておきましょうということであります。

Ⅱ．IPO時点における複数議決権株式の利用と創業者利益

1．複数議決権株式をIPO時に導入するアメリカ企業の増加

　2．で、アメリカは何をしているのかということですけれども、アメリカではNYSEが1985年に種類株式制度を容認することとし、その後、1988年にSECが1株1議決権制度の会社がその後に複数議決権制度に移行することを制限したので、1988年以降は、IPOについてだけ種類株式制度を採用する余地が残されているという状況であったということになります。

　2004年にグーグルの親会社が複数議決権株式を利用してIPOを行って、

その後、いろいろな著名な創業者が持っているＩＴ会社が、上場するに当たって複数議決権株式というのをかなり多く導入しているというようなことが言われております。こういったＩＴ企業だけでなくて、さまざまな業種の企業もこのタイプの株主構成を採用しております。

２．議決権種類株式を用いたＩＰＯに対する学説・投資家の反対
（１）機関投資家との攻防
　ただし、このようなことで耳目を集めた一方で、創業者がずっと株式を持っているということは、その人たちが高齢化していった場合にどうするのかとか、そこまで長いスパンの話ではなくても、ＩＴ企業であったとしても大規模な増資を行ったらどうするのかとか、そういったことでいろいろな懸念が生じて、機関投資家とか投資顧問、規制庁などの立場にある各リーダーが反対を表明するようになっております。

　グーグルの親会社のアルファベットは、複数議決権株式を導入したという点でも注目を集めましたけれども、訴訟もいろいろ抱えています。種類株式があるせいでガバナンスがおかしくなるのだという論理を使うと、アメリカでは救済という観点から裁判所が柔軟に介入しやすいということもあって、いろいろな契機があって訴訟が起きるたびに、複数議決権株式があるからだということで廃止を求めるという請求が、様々な請求の一部に入るというような状況になっているということです。

　企業が複数議決権を持ったまま上場したときに何が起こりがちかということについては、訴訟になったケースで主張されてはいるものの、実際にどうだったかということはわかっていないのですけれども、一つには役員や幹部に問題があって退陣を促されたときに高額な退職金パッケージを認めてしまうということが起こり得ます。ほかには、議決権株式の増資のようなものを数次にわたって行おうとするとか、そういったことが生じてきております。

　最近の事例では、2017年に上場申請したスナップ社というのが、発行株式を全て無議決権株式とするというようなスキームを採用しましたが、こう

いった弊害への批判が多かったことで、訴訟は起きていませんが、インデックスの中から外されるというリアクションを受けております。

（２）学説における分析と規制の導入

　このように創業者に極端な形で支配権を残すスキームが登場してきたために、2017年に有力な論文が発表されており、種類株式においては支配株主の議決権割合と資本割合との差が大きいほどエージェンシー・コストも大きくなり、会社価値が下がるという分析があるということを1つの証左として、上場会社が同族企業と同様の承継リスクにさらされる例などを挙げつつ、導入時には魅力的な株式に見えたとしても、経時的に弊害が増大していく可能性があるということを指摘しております。

　例えばIT業界では、IPO後に技術革新によって環境が激変し、あるいは支配持ち分が血縁者などに譲渡され、当初創業者に見出されていたリーダーシップが適切に働かなくなる可能性が高い。あるいは、創業者自身もポートフォリオ分散のために持ち分を減少させたいというような動機づけがあったりする可能性もあります。

　一方で、創業者による支配や一定の株主が長期にわたって支配するといった安定性の利点、あるいは株主と比較した場合の経営者の支配の利点、これらはいずれも時間とともに失われるという要素があるので、プレミアム部分というのがなくなっていきます。こうしたことで、経営者による搾取とかインセンティブのゆがみという問題が時間がたつにつれ顕著になってくるということであります。

　では、その弊害をどうやってなくすのかというときに、支配株主は種類株式を自分から廃止した場合、私的な利益は全て失ってしまうのですが、便益は一部しか得られないので、単一株式構造への移行というインセンティブを持たないということになります。この論文は、そこで、さまざまなサンセット条項を考えた上で、支配者と無関係な株主が延長に同意しない限り、種類株式制度を10年ないし15年で終了させるというような制度を入れることを推奨したということであります。

この論文と同じころに、有力な年金基金などもこの種の金融商品に対する反対を表明し、2018年の2月には、ＳＥＣのコミッショナーの1人が、複数の議決権のある株式に期限を設けるような新しい上場規則を課すべきだとの主張をするという状況になっております。
　こうした圧力のもとで、ＩＴ企業も、業績が好調で創業者支配に対する顕著なリスクがない環境のもとでは、訴訟や株主運動によって繰り返し費用が発生するような事態を回避するようになっているように思います。ここ1、2年の話なので、実際どういうトレンドがあるのかということをきちんとチェックしたわけではないのですけれども、ニュースベースの話で言えば、インターアクティブコーポレーションとかフェイスブックといったようなところが議決権株式の発行計画を撤回しているといったことが挙げられると思います。

（3）マーケットによる規律と市場間競争

　そうはいっても、当然、機関投資家側は、リターンが上回る限りは納得して投資をするのだということで反対をすることが考えられるわけで、インデックス除外といったことを、ある一定の投資家がしたとしても、ほかの投資家がこういったＩＴ関連の新規上場株式を組み込んでいるＥＴＦみたいなものを積極的に買っている場合には、なかなか抑止力にはならないのではないかというような見方もあります。創業者が利益の大部分を持っていくのであっても、ＩＰＯを通じた利益参与の機会がもたらされる状態というのは、そもそも上場が起きないという状態よりはいいのではないかということ、あるいは世界のほかの市場で種類株式発行会社の上場を誘致する競争が存在することを考えると、投資機会を狭める必要はないという論拠に基づくものです。
　このように考え方が分かれているため、例えばＭＳＣＩなども、インデックスから複数議決権発行会社を外すべきかということを一度検討したのですけれども、最終的には、そういったものを含まないインデックスと含んだインデックスの2つをつくるという解決策をとるというようなことをしてい

て、必ずしも排除しないという選択肢をとっているわけで、投資家側も対応がいろいろ分かれている状況です。

３．小括・議決権種類株式の利用目的・抑止を可能とする環境

　企業がＩＰＯのときに、なぜこんなに種類株式制度を導入しているのかということについてケーススタディーをしたものを見ると、無形投資の重要性の高まり、アクティビスト投資家の増加、期差式取締役会やポイズンピルのような他の経営手段の減少が理由であるとされております。特に1990年代には、上場しようとする株式会社は、経営者に優しい法律を選んだり、ポイズンピルや期差式取締役会といったようなものを導入するということを装備しておくことができたのですけれども、こういったものの導入率は1990年代から2020年に近づくにつれて急激に減少しているということが見てとれます。

　これは、現在、機関投資家が証券取引所企業の過半数株主となっており、彼らがガバナンスへの参画を強める中で株主提案を可決させることで、こうした敵対的買収策を骨抜きにしてきたという事情があると言われております。種類株式は、期間に制約のある買収防衛策や特定事項についてしか支配権維持を確保できない特別多数決制度などと比べても、より恒久的で裁量性の高い制度として経営陣に期待されていると考えられるということです。

　経営陣に優しく、投資家にとって好ましくない効果は統計上も確認できます。恒久的に種類株式制度を入れていると、株価収益率が低くなるとか、ファンダメンタルズに比べて取引価格が割安になるとか、エントレンチメントの部分が株価を押し下げる可能性が高く、また、価値破壊的な企業買収にもさらされやすいといったようなことを示す研究があるとも言われております。

　株価がこのように割安になりやすいという長期的な構造があるのであれば、ＩＰＯで一時的に強気の相場をつけたとしても、それは単に初期の出資者に新規投資家からお金が移転するのを容易にするという効果を持つ─だけとは言いませんが、そういう傾向が強いということがある─ので、それは必

ずしも望ましいお金の調達方法とも言えないかなということです。

　逆に、2007年から2017年までの期間において、種類株式発行会社の株式のパフォーマンスがマーケット全体の成績を上回っていることから、アグレッシブな成長と家族支配との組み合わせが長期的な成長につながっているという主張も存在するということです。ガバナンスが閉鎖的で搾取が起こりやすい会社であったとしても、投資家が規律を効かせることができるのであれば、そういった不利益は受忍されるのかもしれないということになります。

　先ほど見たとおり、事例ベースではありますが、訴訟であるとか委任状といったような投資家のプレッシャーが活発に動いていれば、議決権種類株式の利用を思いとどまらせるという効果を持つかもしれません。ただ、そういう調整がうまく働いていれば望ましいと必ず言えるのかということもあって、繰り返し起きる訴訟のコストや、訴訟が経営者の経営能力に与える影響を考えると、事後的な調整はプランニング段階における調整と比較して相当程度無駄が多いのではないかということが、1点、考えられるかと思います。

　また、どのようなマーケットでも、投資家が必ず活発に行動してくれるかにも問題があります。株主からの株主提案や訴訟を事前に阻止できないような制度があるとか、株主の側に訴訟を繰り返し起こすために集合し資金を集めることができる制度がある、そういう環境部分も重要なのかもしれないと思います。

　以上アメリカの状況はこのような感じになっているということです。

Ⅲ．ヨーロッパの長期株主優遇と議決権種類株式

1．背景

　逆にヨーロッパの側は、議決権種類株式を違った目で見ているというお話をしましたので、そちらでどのように事態が動いているのかということです。

　ヨーロッパにおける株主権利指令案では、スチュワードシップ・コード、複数議決権株式、株主総会出席への報酬、役員報酬決議への参加などが、短期的視野に基づく投資に対抗する方策という文脈でまとめて整理されており

ました。先ほど出てきた、後で落とされた草案に載っていた株主優遇策の列挙というのは、このような形で並べられていたということです。

　もともとEUは、1株1議決権原則を加盟国に強制するべきかということを検討していたという経緯がありますが、これを断念していたわけです。逆に、2015年の案は、複数議決権株式を推奨すべきではないかという文脈ですから、逆側に振れたという形になっています。そうすると、長期的な参加を促すための手段として複数議決権株式というのは適切なのかという問題があると思われます。

　2007年の外部委員会の調査によれば、構成国は全て何らかの形で種類株式を導入し得る制度を維持していることになっていて、ヨーロッパ各国は、現地では比較的一般的なものなのではないかと思うのですけれども、平均して5つぐらいの、種類株式制度を導入し得る手段を持っているというふうに書かれています。

２．フランス法の複数議決権制度

　EUにおいては、複数議決権株式は長期株主創出制度の1つとして挙げられましたが、EU構成国の中には、複数株式ないし黄金株式が存在しない国、存在する国、かつて導入されたけれども廃止された国など、さまざまな国があります。イタリアはもう一度導入すると政策上決定しましたけれども、現在の1株1議決権原則の普及は、この複数議決権制度が定着し維持されている国かどうかによって大きく差があります。

　1株1議決権原則適用に関する報告書が2005年に出たときには、EU全体では上場企業の65％がこの原則を適用していて、一株一議決権の会社は、ドイツでは97％、イギリスでは88％、スペインでは59％であったのに対して、複数議決権制度を持つ国ではこの割合は低く、スイスでは59％、フランスでは31％、スウェーデンでは25％、オランダでは14％というふうに大きく差がありました。

　では、フランスはどんな制度を持っているのかということですけれども、

19世紀の法律は原則として株式の数と同じ数の議決権を有するとしていたのに対して、20世紀早々に入って優先株の創設を許可するということを法に書いたという経緯があります。この優先株は複数議決権の権利を含むとされていて、銀行などが積極的に導入したと言われておりますけれども、一部でこの株式設計の自由が悪用されたため、金融界でこういったものを導入することへの反対が強くなり、1930年4月26日の金融法で複数議決権を付した株式発行が禁止されました。1933年に1株1議決権という原則を確認し、それ以後、二重議決権を有するタイプ以外の優先株式をつくることは禁止することになりました。

　一方で、受益持ち分と呼ばれる制度があります。これは特定の創設者によってなされた現物出資と引き換えに発行され、その後、株式に転換されるものとして、創設者株式と呼ばれるものです。これは資本金を積む基本となる株式の種類とは別のものというふうに理解されていて、会社の経営権に対しては特に何も決定権を持たない特殊な種類の株式ですが、これも1966年以降は新規発行が禁止されています。総括すると、複数の種類の制度が導入されては、以後発行してはいけないと禁止され、輻輳的にさまざまな種類株式が残っているという状態です。

　現在はどうかというと、現在は、公開有限会社は複数議決権株式を設計する自由を制限されており、商法典においては、一番最初にL.225-122という条文で1株1議決権原則というのを規定した上で、その例外として、1人の株主が株主総会で行使する票の数にキャップをはめるということが認められる場合がある。それから、ロイヤリティ株式として、長期保有の株主に二重議決権が認められている。こんな形になっております。

　そのほかに、複数議決権のカテゴリーとは別に、2004年に商法典が改正されて、議決権の有無を優先株の内容として定めることができ、無議決権株式も会社資本の過半数を超えない範囲で認められるというふうになっております。これと、従来黄金株と認識されているものは別のもので、拒否権付株式というものが1986年の民営化に関する法律で導入されて、これにより、

国益保護の要請によって国有の株式の権利が特別の権利に転換され得るということが認められております。

　こういうふうになっているのですけれども、冒頭でご紹介したフロランジュ法というのが導入されたときに、先ほどの L.225-123 という条文で、ロイヤリティに報いるための二重議決権というのが認められました。もともとの L.225-123 は定款で定めればそのような株式を置くことができるとして、定款変更を条件にしていたのに対し、フロランジュ法というのは、明示の反対をしない限りそのような規定があるとみなすという方法をとった法律であります。これは資料２として１枚紙で入れておりますので、ご興味があれば読んでいただければと思います。

3．複数議決権株式制度導入の影響

　フロランジュ法の分析に当たっては、長期保有による議決権付与という構造も関係するのですが、その導入手法が非常に特殊なものだったので、どちらかというと導入手法の特殊性による弊害が大きいのではないかと思うので、そういったこともあわせてここでは議論したいと思います。

　長期保有による議決権の付与という構造は、どの株主に保有されていても、保有期間が長くなればその株主に複数議決権をもたらすという優先株主制度が、投資家及び経営陣の行動にどのような影響を及ぼすかということが問題になります。

　学説により、長期保有で複数議決権を獲得した株式は優先株式として扱われると解されております。しかし、この株式も取得段階では普通株式なので、転換するという形になるわけです。投資家側は投資価値を判断して株式を購入するわけですが、取得時点では、より低い価値しかないので、長期、短期、いずれの保有を目的とした取得だったのか説明するかによって取得判断の経済的合理性が分かれることに、どうもなりそうな気がします。また、ほかの株主が常に長期株主に該当したり資格を失ったりし得るので、結局、自分が何％株主になったのかがわからないという問題もあり得ます。

しかし、どのような問題があるにせよ、複数議決権株式制度自体は従来から存在する制度なので、これらの問題は法律を導入したことで急に生じた問題というわけではなくて、投資家の株式の保有期間というのはずっと同じトレンドをたどっていると言われております。資料３として出しているものの49ページあたりに、この法律を入れたことで保有期間にどのような変更があったのかを示している表があるので、これを見ていただければ、一番上の非常に激しい減少傾向を示している線が、２倍議決権に移行した会社の線です。

　つまり、少なくとも複数議決権が与えられる会社で株式保有期間が延びるという影響は見られず、アメリカで投資家が無議決権株式を積極的に買うのと同様、フランスでも、議決権が増えるか減るかというのは、投資家の取得・売却の判断に影響を余り与えていないのではないか。そうだとすると、複数議決権が存在すること自体にはそれほど弊害はないのかもしれないというような議論があり得るかもしれないということです。

　一方、投資家の行動に変化をもたらさないとしても、この制度は経営陣の側には大きな変化をもたらす可能性があると思います。この制度がＩＰＯにおいて導入される場合には、支配権争奪に際して既存の種類株主に時間と手段を与え、支配権維持を強固にするという効果を持つからです。投資家が支配権の獲得を目的として株式を取得したとしても、取得初年度には２倍の議決権は持てないので、既存の支配株主と協力しないと買収防衛のための対抗策をとられてしまうことになります。特にフランスの会社は、株式を買い上がっている株主がいるときに、その背後に誰がいるのかを会社が納得するまで究明する権限が与えられているので、支配権をとろうと思っている株主は早々に見つけ出されるということがあり、会社は対抗策をとりやすい環境にある。したがって、買収のリスクが高い企業は、この制度を積極的に用いるのではないかと思います。特にＩＰＯをする会社においては、２倍議決権制度の導入率は37％だったのに対して法導入後の導入率は54％になったと言われていて、ＩＰＯをする会社はこの制度を以前より高い頻度で用いている

ことがわかります。

　一方、既存の企業が新たにこの制度を導入する場合には、違う分配が恐らく実現するのだろうと思います。フランス法上、通常、ある種類株式の名義人の権利を変更し得る株主総会の決定は、当該種類株主の種類株主総会による承認の後にのみ確定することになっているので、議決権種類株主制度は導入すれば廃止が困難になり、同制度の導入は気軽に試せるようなものではないということになります。

　また、株主が上場会社の議決権の3分の1以上を保有した場合は株式の強制買付制度の対象となるが、長期保有で3分の1以上に至った場合もこの対象になるというのが、一応原則になっております。

　フランスの上場会社における議決権の分布は、この制度があるため、ほとんどは創業者などが最初から多くの長期保有株式を有しており、長期保有に利益を有しているのが明らかな場合と、分散した株主が多くて目立った利益を長期保有株主が持っていない場合とに二分される形になっていると思います。

　そこで、あえてこういった制度の導入が闘われる場合としては、支配株主に近い株式数を有する少数株主がいるといった形の状態ではないかと思います。資料3の実証分析によれば、既存の上場会社45社中31社が単独議決権を選び、14社が2倍議決権制度導入会社となり、当初から導入していた58社はそのままであったと言われております。

4．フロランジュ法導入手法の特殊性

　2倍議決権制度それ自体については、目立って言うことはないのですけれども、この制度を導入するときに、どうもいろいろと弊害があるような導入の仕方をしているのではないかと思われるので、まず導入手法の特殊性についてお話ししておきたいと思います。

　従来、2倍議決権制度を導入できなかった45社中7社が同制度の導入阻止に失敗したという数は、少なくないように思われます。こうした会社の業

績面での特色として、TobinのQの値が低いことが挙げられていますが、より大きな要因は導入当時に株主構成がどうなっていたかにあるのかなと推測いたしました。フロランジュ法の導入直後には、少ない資金で拒否権を手に入れることができるチャンスが生まれていたので、少数株主が長期保有株主となることを新たに選んだという可能性もあるかもしれないし、現在の支配株主が少数株主と妥協することを選んだこともあるかもしれません。

どうしてそういうことになるのかというと、定款変更を阻止するためには、出席株主の議決権の3分の1を取得することができればいいわけです。そこでルノーの事案が出てくるわけですが、フランス政府は証券会社と一緒になってルノー株式を追加取得するという合意を結んで、保有比率を20％近くまで引き上げました。3分の2というのは出席株主の議決権の3分の2ですので、出席割合というのを合理的な割合であると考えると、相当の割合で否決が可能な状況に持っていったわけですが、その後にプットオプションを用いて最低価格を保証した上で、持ち株比率を再び15％に引き下げるということをしております。

そうすると、一定の株式を保有している少数株主が、この時期に限って非常に少ない負担でプレゼンスを拡大できる、そういう状況が生まれていたということが示唆されます。これはフランス政府の狙いの1つとして、財政赤字の削減のためのお金の捻出ということがあったと言われているので、そういう事情があるのかもしれませんが、そういうことができる構造が存在していたということです。

また、本来であれば、ほかの優先株式が存在する場合の優先株主による反対、あるいは買付提案を強制されるリスクがふえることなどの他の要素も、実は機能できない状況になっていたと思います。

先ほど言ったとおり、ある優先株式の名義人の権利を変更し得る株主総会の決定に先立っては、種類株主総会の承認が必要ですが、フロランジュ法による複数議決権株式の導入は、法律でみなしで導入されてしまうので、特段の株主総会がないという状況になります。

また、議決権の3分1を超える持ち分となることについては、証券取引の一般規則の中に、2014年から2018年の間に2倍議決権を割り当てられる状態になった場合については公開買付義務を免除するという特別規定が存在するので、とりたてて資金負担について心配する必要がないという状況になっていたということです。

5．資本の移動の自由との葛藤

　この制度が、長期の一般株主を創出するという効果を持っておらず、一部の株主の利益を創出するだけというような制度であったならば、そういった制度は一般投資家に対して大きな不利益を及ぼすだろうと思います。

　最初に2倍議決権株式を保有することになった支配株主がその株式を手放さない限りは、その構造はアメリカで問題とされる議決権種類株式と結局同種のものになるので、同じようにこれは規制すべきだといった批判が起きてもいいように思われるわけですが、フランスでは、政府が大企業の長期保有株主なことも多く、たまたま受益者でもあったりするので、規制庁側は、この制度に問題があるというふうに言う立場にはないことになって、では、一体どこが投資家の心配をするのかということになると、ＥＣＪではないかと考えられるわけです。

　では、今までＥＣＪがこういったものについてどのように介入してきたかということですが、従来は、このような典型的な株式制度の一部に組み込まれた種類株式としてではなく、黄金株制度に対してさまざまな判例法による制限が行われてきたわけです。ＥＣＪの判例法は、2002年の時点で出された3つの判断で確立したと一般的には説明されております。

　どのような制限かというと、ＥＣＪの判決の基本的な構造としては、規制が形式的には非差別措置であっても他の加盟国からの投資を萎縮する効果を有するならば、資本の自由移動の規定に抵触する。しかし、当該措置が正当化され得る場合としては、除外事由に当たる場合、あるいは一般的利益保護について不可避的な要請がある場合であって、比例性原則を満たし、かつ客

観的基準と救済措置が用意されている場合が挙げられます。

　フランスも2002年に出されたこの3つの判例で対象となった国の1つですけれども、特別法があるというお話を先ほどしましたが、特別法の適用というのが、TFEU65条の除外に該当するのかどうか、あるいは資本の自由移動を定めた条約の規定に違反するのかどうかといったことが問題になりました。

　フランスの規定は、結局のところ、比例性原則を満たさず、資本の自由移動の原則に反するという結論になったのですけれども、これはなぜかというと、比例性が否定された根拠は、介入関連規定は大臣の承認の基準を明文で設定していないので自由に裁量権を行使できる。したがって、投資家が承認を得られるかどうかについて見通しを持つことができず、ある会社の業務執行を事前に承認するかどうかの権利を経済大臣に与えるものであっても、あるいは、ある行われた業務執行について後から異議申立権を与えるタイプの法律であったとしても、そのどちらであっても侵害に当たるというふうにされました。

　3つの判例の1つとしてベルギーの規制があって、これは違反ではないとされたのですが、これは主務大臣のイニシアチブで異議申立手続が開始されるわけではなく、開始できるための要件があることによります。かつ、エネルギー大臣は、自己の決定について書面により理由書を作成して取締役会に通告しなければならず、かつ当該決定は司法審査に服するという要素によるというふうになっていたわけです。

　したがって、2002年の段階で、ＥＣＪの判決については、以下のように分析されておりました。

　第1に、エネルギーや通信などの国家安全保障にかかわる事業とは関係ない経済的・経営的性質の事業については、一般的利益という言葉の対象にそもそもならないのではないかというふうに考えられておりました。また、第2に、優先的権利というのは、株式譲渡、議決権取得、役員の選任、その他の例えば合併とか事業譲渡といった会社の決定について与えられるのです

が、これらの決定に際して、どういう手続によって特定の株主に拒否権などの権利を与えるかということについては、ＥＣＪ判決は、個別に権利内容を吟味し、それが許容されるかどうかを判定してきました。第三に、事前予測が可能な介入については認めるということになっているので、裁量権の広いような介入に対しては抑制的に判断しているという了解があったということになります。

そうすると、例えば従業員が多いからという理由で介入対象を選定するとか、雇用が維持されるように状況に応じて議決権を行使するということは、ＥＣＪの考え方からは何となく正当化されにくいのかと思われるわけです。

しかし、フランスはそういったことを非常に警戒して、立法趣旨説明においては、ＥＣＪ判決は黄金株に関するもので、種類株式は一般的な株式制度の一部であって、これに対してＥＣＪが入ってくるというのは認められないのだというようなことを主張しております。

もっとも、2014年のフロランジュ法の前年にフォルクスワーゲン事件というものに対して判決が出されており、こちらの判決は、今まで言ったようなＥＣＪの態度に若干の変更を加えているものではないかとも言われております。どういうことかというと、ドイツではフォルクスワーゲンに介入するドイツ法というものが存在していて、連邦及びザクセン州が20％ずつ株式を支配し、10人の取締役のうち２人ずつを選任し、また、他の株主の投票権を20％までに制限し、決議要件は５分の４に引き上げるということで、結局のところ、他の株主がどれだけ頑張っても決議をひっくり返すことができないという法律をつくっていたわけですが、これが2007年にＥＣ条約に違反するというふうに言われておりました。

その判決が出た後、ドイツ政府は、他の株主の保有上限についての20％キャップは外したけれども、議決権要件は維持しました。また、フォルクスワーゲン社の定款にも同じ規定が置かれていて、法律が20％キャップを外した後も、９カ月間はフォルクスワーゲン社は同様の20％キャップの規定を定款上に残していたという状況があったので、再度提訴が行われて、2013

年に判決が出ました。

ここでは、2007年の判決の射程は法に関するもので定款には関係しないというふうに言っています。また、議決権要件は20％キャップと相まって制限的効果を生じたものであって、議決権要件だけで資本の移動の侵害になるかどうかについては判決していないというふうに言っております。つまり、どれだけ少なくても、議決をひっくり返す可能性があるような環境があれば、しかも、そういった環境を定款に書くことで認めていれば、ＥＣＪは介入しないと言ったのではないかというふうにも言われております。

また、オランダがＥＵ指令に基づいて電気やガス事業を分割してパイプラインは民営化するのではないかと言われていたわけですが、輸送の側も国営化するというふうに法改正をしたときに、分割をしろとは言ったけれども、別にその部分を民営化しろということまでは言っていないというようなことを言ったことがありました。正当化事由や相当性についてはかなり広く認めていて、公益として正当化根拠となり得るとしました。

こういったことを考えると、株式会社法ないし定款に深く埋め込んで黄金株制度というものを導入すると、ＥＣＪも追いかけられないという状況になっているのではないかと推測されるということです。

Ⅳ．日本における運用

1．ＩＰＯ時点での議決権種類株式と創業者利益

結論を全然出さずに比較法的なことをやっていって申しわけないのですが、では、日本で何をしているかということです。

日本では、古くからＩＮＰＥＸ（国際石油開発株式会社）が上場会社として拒否権付株式を入れているということで有名だったわけですけれども、そのほかにサイバーダイン（CYBERDYNE）社というところが、創業者の保有割合を高く保った株式を発行したということで注目されました。この方法は、単元を用いて創業者側の議決権を10倍にすることができるというものです。

東京証券取引所は、この弊害防止措置をどうやって制度に落とし込むかについて、ずっといろいろ議論してきたわけですけれども、現在のところどのようになっているかというと、「上場会社が備えるべき基本的かつ重要な権利が著しく損なわれる状態となった上場会社が、6か月以内に当該状態を解消しない場合には、上場を廃止する」となっており、その一部分として、「拒否権付種類株式のうち、取締役の過半数の選解任その他の重要な項目について種類株主総会を要する旨の定めがなされたものの発行」をこれに該当するとし、買収等を困難にするような拒否権付種類株式ないし取締役選任付種類株式を発行するような場合も同等に扱う可能性があると言い、かつ、既上場株式会社で同様の制度を導入するときには、より慎重にチェックするということを述べているわけです。

　このように、世の中の流れ的にはＩＴ企業の上場を促そうという方向にあるので、東京証券取引所がどういった防止措置を入れていればオーケーを出すのかということが問題になっていて、より強く規制すべきだとか、緩和すべきだとか、いろいろな考え方があるとは思います。

　ただ、ガバナンスを是正するというような環境が、例えばアメリカでかなり乱用的な発行が行われそうになっている状態を押しとどめている背景にもしあるのだとすれば、日本の株主がどういうふうに分布していて、どういうふうに動くのかとか、分散保有し過ぎていて協調できないのではないかとか、いざというときの議決権として何を持っていれば効率的に動けるのかというようなことを考えると、個別のスキームを誠実に見ていくしかないのかなというふうには思うのですけれども、株主による監督・是正権を最初から奪うような種類株式や支配株主に付される議決権の割合を高く維持し過ぎるスキームには問題があり得ることになります。非常に漠然としていて申しわけありませんが。

　こうした問題があるということを指摘しつつ、その規制を証券市場に委ねることについて、最初から非常に健全な種類株式しか上場させないことで証券取引所の機会を奪っているという批判もあり得るとは思うのですけれど

も、今言ったような環境次第で不当になり得る条項とか、一律に最適な期限を定めることができないサンセット条項みたいなものは、会社法では扱うのがなかなか難しいものだろうと思うので、やはり個別の事案を見ていくしかないのかなということで、余り慌てて緩和するべきという話をする必要はないのかなと思います。

　また、市場間の競争があるとはいっても、ほかの市場がこういった議決権種類株式を非常に積極的に取り入れているとは言えないと思います。今日になってアリババが香港証券市場に上場するという話が出てまいりましたけれども、2018年4月に香港、同年6月にシンガポールの証券取引所が議決権種類株式の上場を許可する方針を発表しました。これらの証券取引所は、今言ったような経緯をずっと見てきているので、どのような制限をかけるのかについて、そういった経験をもとに意見を収集していると思います。

　シンガポールの場合は、2017年7月にプライマリー・リスティングが先行していることを条件にセカンダリー・リスティングを認めており、独立取締役や監査役の選解任、定款変更、リバース・テイクオーバー、清算及び上場廃止において、1株1議決権の原則を復活させること、セーフガードとして取締役会に委員会構造を入れることやサンセット条項の挿入ということを求めています。

　そして2018年に新たな上場も許可したわけですが、これに加えて、複数議決権の発行先の明示、複数議決権株式の許された対象以外への譲渡や責任のある理事の退任の際の複数議決権の強制転換、資本増加の際の複数議決権株式増加は特別決議によるべきこと、複数議決権株式の割合を普通株式との比較で増加させることの禁止、総会開催や議決権行使の要件などについてのルールも定めているということです。

２．上場会社による種類株式の発行と長期的保有

　上場会社と株主との間の長期的関係を構築しようとする場合、法律によって種類株式制度導入のハードルを一律に下げると、そのときに会社にどうい

う株主が分布していたか次第で、望ましくない利益移転が伴う可能性があるように思われます。しかし、逆に分散が進んだ会社が自主的に種類株式を導入して長期株主をつくり出そうというのは、これはこれで結構難しいのではないかと思います。十分に議決権が分散した上場会社においては、極端な議決権種類株式を発行しない限り、支配権プレミアムは発生しがたいわけです。

そうすると、支配株主の持ち株割合が経営に批判的な長期的投資家と余り差がない場合に、そういった投資家の持ち分が同時に強くなるような仕組みは副作用が大きいので、結局のところ、長期的な株主をつくろうという意図で分散した株式会社で複数議決権株式を入れようというようなことを考えることは余りないのかなと思います。

今の会社法は、株主権の相対的な地位関係を維持することには十分注意を払っていると思います。定款変更とか、株主総会による有利発行承認決議を経る手続とか、株主の意見が事前に反映され得る仕組みが存在するし、322条によって一定の拒否権が設定されています。ただし、拒否権は定款で排除が可能だというところをどういうふうに料理するかということで大分変わってくるというのはあります。

また、実務においても、上場審査において既上場会社による種類株式発行は慎重に審査するとされております。なので、現在、上場会社が種類株を創出して長期株主をつくろうというふうになった場合には、議決権というよりは、配当とか譲渡制限といったものを組み合わせた種類株式を考えるというのが現実的になってくると思います。

これは加藤先生からも以前にご報告があったかと思いますが、ＡＡ種類株式を導入した場合であっても、そういったものについての賛成割合は顕著に低かったというような指摘がございます。ということで、長期的な関係を構築するときに、何が、どういうふうに望ましいのかということを判定するとか、導入手法としてどういったものがあるかということについて、全ての企業が創意工夫してくださいというふうに本当に言っていいのかということについては、引き続き注意して見ていく必要があるかなと思います。

非常に雑駁で、どこに行くのかよくわからない報告になってしまって恐縮なのですが、以上になります。ご指導、ご指摘いただければと思います。

神作会長　松井先生、大変貴重な報告、特にＥＵやフランスの状況についてもくわしくご紹介いただきまして、まことにありがとうございました。

討　議

神作会長　それでは、ただいまの松井智予先生のご報告に対しまして、どなたからでも結構でございますので、ご質問、ご意見をよろしくお願いいたします。

大崎委員　大変興味深いご報告、ありがとうございました。
　１点確認したいのですが、フロランジュ法について、長期に保有した場合に議決権が２倍になるというのは、そういうことを選択できるというのではなくて、自動的に２倍になるという理解でよろしいんですね。

松井（智）報告者　いえ、デフォルトルールを変えたということで、今までは定款規定を導入すれば２倍議決権だったんですが……。

大崎委員　それはわかるんですけれども、保有している人の議決権が２倍になるのは、保有者の意思によるのか、自動的になるのかということなんです。

松井（智）報告者　これは、法律によれば、２年間以上の期間を定めて、その登録によって２年以上と判定された株主に保有されているすべての発行済み株式に対して、２倍の議決権を与えるという定款規定を定めることができるとなっているだけということです。

大崎委員　そうだとすると、かつ、これは2018年12月31日までの２倍議決権割り当ての場合は公開買付義務は免除ということになりますと、事実上、ことしに入ってからは15％以上の議決権を積極的に取得して、完全に経営支配をするというのではないんですが、いわば物言う株主として行動しようとすることを抑制する効果を生んでいると思うのです。
　この法律は、もちろん非差別的に適用されるということ、また国にだけ適用されるわけではないので、何となくＥＵ法上は、余り大きな問題がなさそ

うにも見えるんですけれども、そうなると、事実上、ファンドがある程度の買い集めをするときの上限を15％にしてしまっているというふうにも見えてくるので、ＥＣＪでも問題にされそうな気もするんですが、その点についてご見解をいただければと思います。

松井（智）報告者 資料3の38ページを見ていただきますと、ディストリビューションがこの法律の前後でどう変わったかというのがあります。この法律の効果として、Stateがふえているのはほんの微々たるものでありまして、Dispersedがふえているんです。やっぱり警戒して、高い割合の株式を持てなくなるという株主が一定程度出てくるのではないかという効果はあると思います。

　警戒して一定程度持てなくなるということについて、ＥＣＪが何か言うことができるのかということについてですが、この法律が導入されたときに、憲法との関係で個人の利益みたいなものを収奪しているんじゃないかということをフランス国内で幾つか提訴されたんです。でも、その主要な部分は工場の閉鎖に関する部分だけであって、株式については出てこなかった。ＥＣＪについても、これが継続されているという事実は今なくて、私は最初にこれを調べ始めたときに、この法律について、ＥＣＪはなぜ何も言わないんだろうと思ったんですが、今のところないんです。

大崎委員 そうすると、もしかすると29％ぐらい買い占めた人が1年11カ月たったところで売らざるを得なくなったといって何か訴訟でも起こすと、新たな判断が示されるかもしれないということですね。

松井（智）報告者 ただ、先ほどお話ししたとおり、当初の状況として、30％の公開買付の義務に抵触する前の時点で、株主が単独であれ、あるいは協力してであれ、株式を買い上がっていると、フランスの経営陣の側が誰が買い上がっているのかというのを会社が納得するまで究明することができる制度があるので、そもそも分散が非常に進んでいると言われているんです。なので、この時点でそういう微妙な数の株主がどのくらいいたのかはわからないんですが、そういった株主がいれば、確かに出てくるとは思います。

武井委員 私からも議論が深まる前に事実関係の確認で。細かいことですが、「10対13」で可決ということですよね。13対10で可決されたけど、施策には進まなかったということですね。

松井（智）報告者 そうです。ごめんなさい。

武井委員 「10対13」と、ひっくり返されていることに何か意味があるのかなと思って。

松井（智）報告者 いえいえ。

武井委員 あと、脚注43ですが、会社の気が済むまで、誰が持っているのか知れるという箇所ですが、これは2001年改正のフランス会社法で？

松井（智）報告者 2011年の早稲田法学で……。

武井委員 2001年改正以降と。

松井（智）報告者 はい、そうですね。そうなっています。

武井委員 2001年のフランスの会社法改正で入った。

松井（智）報告者 そういうふうになっていました。

武井委員 こういう制度があることは驚きなのですが、「気の済むまでわかる」というところ、会社の気が済まないうちに、保有者側が答えなかったときの法的効果はどうなっているのでしょうか。議決権停止とかそんな効果まであるのでしょうか。

松井（智）報告者 確かに、これは定款に規定して権限を与えているので、その場合は、私もフランスの会社法の解釈論が、この後、効果についてどう書いているかはよくわからないんですけれども。

武井委員 あとでわかれば教えてください。

松井（智）報告者 はい、わかりました。

　※228-2条は、企業が中央預託機関等に対して情報を求めることができると定める（反する合意は無効であり、同条第3項により不完全あるいは誤った情報が提供された場合にはペナルティのもとで裁判所判決のもとコミュニケーション義務の履行を請求できるとされている）。

武井委員 ちなみにここでいう受益者というのは、経済的受益者と議決権行

使を決めている人の両方の意味を含んでいるという感じなのですかね。
松井（智）報告者　「真の受益者」と書かれていますので、そうだと思います。経済的にこれで受益をする人間は誰かというところまで発見できるということだと思います。

　※228－2条は、中央預託機関のほか金融法L.211-3に規定する仲介者に対するインタビューも可能としており、同条の仲介者は、同法L.542-1に定めるフランスの金融機関・投資会社・資産管理会社などを指す。

武井委員　なるほど。わかりました。

　すいません、あともう1点。その上のページの「45社中31社」という、45社って何でしたっけ。上場会社が45社しかないわけではなく・・。

松井（智）報告者　いえ、単独議決権をそもそも最初から選んでいて。

武井委員　最初から選んでいた上場会社が45社しかないということですね。

松井（智）報告者　はい。当初から2倍議決権を導入していたのが58社と。

武井委員　フランスの上場会社が100社しかないというわけではないですよね。

松井（智）報告者　一番トップの部分について。

武井委員　この調査結果は、時価総額の大きなところについて調べたということですね。

松井（智）報告者　はい。もともと資料3のものですので、それからとっているんだと思います。

河村委員　104社ぐらい調査して、そのうち45社がもともとシングルというような話ではなかったでしょうか。

武井委員　104社はどうやって選ばれたのでしょうか。時価総額が大きいとか。

河村委員　それはそうです。フランスの株式市場のインデックスの中から選んだということだと思います。

武井委員　S&P500みたいなことで100社を選んだ。主要な代表的な上場会社を選ぶとこうだという感じの調査ですかね。

松井（智）報告者 資料3の12ページにありますが、SBF120というインデックスがありまして、取引高が多い上位120社に対して調査を行ったと。

武井委員 なるほど、SBF120のところですね。ありがとうございます。

大崎委員 これも感想みたいな話なんですけれども、このフロランジュ法は何となく買収を困難にする効果が大きいようにも思えるのですが、他方で、15％買っておいて、2年待てば30％になるということを考えると、時間をかければ、逆に買収しやすくなるような気もちょっとしたんですが、その点、どうなんですかね。

松井（智）報告者 確かにそのような側面はあるのではないかと思います。どういうふうに対応するのかという部分は、15％買っておけばというんですが、そうすると、支配株主の側が何の対策も打たないかというと、支配株主の側はそれに応じて買い上がっておけば恐らくほとんど差がなく、株式は2倍議決権の分がふえていくという形になるのではないか。

大崎委員 既に2倍議決権を持っている人は、買い増した分も全部2倍になるんですか。

松井（智）報告者 株主名簿に2年以上名前が載っている人間に2倍議決権を与えることができますので。

大崎委員 1株買えば2株になるということ。

松井（智）報告者 そういうことです。打ち出の小づちのような不思議な話かと思いますが。

神作会長 ほかにご質問、ご意見、いかがでしょうか。

　私から1つご質問してよろしいでしょうか。ご報告の中でも言及されたEUの第2次株主権指令は、スチュワードシップの考え方を基本的にはコンプライ・オア・エクスプレインのベースで導入しています。対象となっているのは生命保険とか年金とか、中長期的な運用および保有を目的とする株主に限っています。スチュワードシップの主体として、そのような機関投資家は、経営陣との建設的な対話によって企業価値を高めていくことが期待できるという考え方に立っていると考えられます。これに対し、本日の報告の対

象である長期保有株主は、どのようなメカニズムで、企業価値の向上あるいは会社の利益等につながると考えられているのでしょうか。

　先ほどの株主権指令におけるスチュワードシップ活動についての考え方の背後には、中長期の保有目的の機関投資家は、スチュワードシップの責任を課せばその専門性や最終投資家に対する責任を根拠として、エンゲージメントにより企業価値を向上させる方向に持っていく可能性があるという期待があると思いますけれども、フロランジュ法のように、長期的に株式を保有していればそれだけで議決権が倍になるという制度の根本にある考え方というのが何か教えていただければ幸いです。

松井（智）報告者　この制度がそもそも何で入ったのかというところを本当はきちんと調べておけばよかったのですが、ご指摘がありましたとおり、長期保有をして、会社ときちんと対話をしてくれそうな株主を特定した上で義務を課すのか、ある株主に義務を与えてしまって、その人が長期的関係を築いてくれることを期待するのかでは、かなり雲泥の差があるとは思います。

　今言っていただいたように、変なアクティビズムを持っている株主が２年以上という保有要件を満たして優先議決権を持った株主になってしまった場合には、やはりガバナンスにゆがんだ影響を与えるというリスクは否定できないと思います。それはスチュワードシップ・コードの話をする前に、株主指令をつくるときに長期保有株主といっても変なアクティビズムが増長されるような形で環境を築くのはよくないという議論が一般的にあったのと同じ話がフランスにもあるのだと思います。ただ、そういった人たちを排除して、いい株主だけに長期保有をしてもらうという構造にはなっていないので、そこはご指摘のとおり、やはり問題があるところかとは思います。

飯田委員　レジュメの注の９の、アメリカで代表訴訟などで定款変更を求める救済について記載があるのですが、このような救済はあまり見なれないものなので、代表訴訟で定款を書きかえるという判決を出せるということなのでしょうか。また、ご報告の最後のほうで、松井先生が、日米の状況を比較したときに、日本ではガバナンス是正を求めるような代表訴訟の利用は活発

とは言えないということをおっしゃったと思います。その比較の対象となるのは、アメリカの定款変更を求めるような代表訴訟のことを指していらっしゃるのでしょうか。

松井（智）報告者 そもそも日本でガバナンスに直結するような改善を求める株主代表訴訟というのはないわけです。間接的に株主が経営陣の責任を問うことで是正を促すぐらいしかできないわけでありますから、そこは大きな違いですし、そもそもアメリカでこういう訴訟ができるのかという問題がもう1つあると思います。

ここでは代表訴訟を起こしているんですけれども、訴訟というのが本案は損害賠償だと思うのですが、それに対して裁判所のリリーフを求めているというのが附帯でくっついていて、これが集団訴訟のどこの部分に入ってくるのかというのをちゃんと見ておけばよかったのですが、この訴状を精査しておりませんので、どの法律のどういったところに基づいて可能になったのかというのは、申しわけありませんが、後でまた確認をさせていただければと思います。

※アルファベットに対する訴状は、訴えがカリフォルニア州裁判所に対するfiduciary duty違反（法令違反ないし会社法違反による。81段落参照）に関する派生訴訟であることを示している。訴状226－8段落で、会社が議決権の集中をリスクファクターとして認識しており、性差別的報酬支払に対して助言会社が反対を助言しても有効でなかったこと等を指摘しており、経営陣による内部統制構築やリスクマネジメントを整えられなかったことによるfiduciary duty違反の論拠となっている。これにより、原告は損害賠償等のほか、差し止め、コーポレートガバナンス改革を含む救済を求めている（16段落）。

飯田委員 そうしますと、アメリカの場合は、そういう直接的な救済が認められるかどうかはともかく、支配株主が権限を乱用したようなことがあると、すぐに代表訴訟が起こってくる可能性が高いので、そのこと自体に抑止力とか、影響力があるのではないかというご趣旨でしょうか。

松井（智）報告者 和解などでどのくらいお金が払われたかということについては明らかにならなくて、報道ベースで見るしかないんですけれども、裁判所が、例えばフェイスブックの事例では、無議決権株式を発行するということを後で取り下げますと言った。そもそも理由があって最初に無議決権株式を発行したはずなのに、何で途中で突如として発行するのをやめると言い出したのか説明しろという、今度は追いかけで主張が来ました。その理由を開示しないことに対して、訴訟費用を支払うことに合意したという報道があったりしまして、訴訟ではっきりした何かが出たという感じではないんですけれども、裏でお金が動いている事例は相当程度あるのではないかと推測されます。こういったものが実質的な圧力になっているということは考えられるかなと思います。

後藤委員 最後の結論は慎重に留保されたように思ったので、そのことをわかった上であえて伺わせていただきます。

　最後のほうにシンガポールを少しだけ言及されていまして、その前に市場間の競争があるとはいっても、ほかの市場も積極的に認めているわけではないんだというふうに評価された上で、例えばシンガポールではいろんな制限がついているということで、こういう読み方なのですが、こういう制限をつければ複数議決権の乱用が制約されているので、ここまでやれば十分だというご評価なのか、そこの松井先生の見方、逆に言うと、ここまでやれば日本でもいいのかということにつながるのかというところをちょっとお伺いしたい。

　もう１点は、これは果たして松井さんにお伺いするのがいいのか、実務の方に伺うのがいいかわからないんですが、結局、日本でニーズが全然出てこないような感じがしていまして、何でなんだろうと。単純に東証が余りいい顔をしないからということなのか、政府がやるかどうかというフランスみたいなものは、ちょっとまた別かもしれませんけれども、日本のＩＴ系のスタートアップはいろいろ出てきている中で、ニーズがあるのかないのかというところが気になっております。もしニーズがあるのにできていないんだとする

と、それは一応考える余地はあるのかもしれませんけれども、ニーズすらないんだとすると、逆にそれはそれで何でなんだろうかというところで、もしお考えがあればお聞かせいただければと思います。

松井（智）報告者　後半についてはなかなか私も、それがわかっていればすばらしい投資家になれるのですが、できないのかなと。

前半に関しては、シンガポールのこの条項を見る限り、強制的な議決権原則の復活のような制度を入れることを条件にしていたりしまして、どちらかというとニューヨークのサンセット条項のようなもの、事項について、よりはっきりと、こういったことやこういったことについては、1株1議決権でやってくれというはっきりした態度を示しているように思いまして、そういう意味ではかなり踏み込んだ投資家保護という姿勢を見せているのかなと思います。なので、シンガポールの保護というのは、議決権種類株式の上場を許可するという方針をとる中で、1つのバランスを見せているのだろうと思っています。

ただ、これをすれば、どの市場、どういう会社でもいつでも大丈夫なのかと言われると、そこはよくわからないのですけれども。というのは、シンガポールの条項は結構厳しいということがあるので、どちらかというと東京でCYBERDYNEが上場されたときよりも、もう少し踏み込んだことを言っているような気がするので、例えば日本の東証がこういったことを全部入れなさいということをすると、印象としては、追随するような企業はさらに減ってくるかなという気がします。

河村委員　先ほどの45社のところに戻ってしまうんですけれども、45社のうち31社はもともとシングルのストラクチャーで、それが引き続きシングルのままであると。14社はダブルのストラクチャーに移っていくのだけれども、本当はそれをしたくなかった会社も7社あったということで、案外シングルというか1株1議決権原則を維持したい会社も多いように思うのです。

それは結局、先ほどおっしゃったように、一旦入れてしまうと、いいこと

ばかりではなくて、廃止が困難になるであるとか、神作先生とのやりとりの中でも出てきましたけれども、必ずしも長期保有する株主が会社の持続的な成長にとって望ましい株主であるとは限らないというところを考えて、あえてうちの会社はシングルのままでいきたい、こういうふうに考えたからであると理解してよろしいのでしょうか。

松井（智）報告者 そうではないかと思います。シングルをずっと維持することを決めた会社というのは、恐らく最初からオーナーシップが分散していて、誰の手に支配権が落ちるかわからないような不確かな状況で2倍議決権を入れるのはリスクが高いというふうに理解した可能性が高いと思います。

　資料3だと、この改正がある前の最大株主の議決権保有量というのが45、46、47ページのあたりで書かれているんですけれども、スイッチをした側を見ると、30％よりも安定した保有をしている会社は大手を振ってというか、自分の会社のイニシアチブで2倍議決権にスイッチしているのですが、そこを下回っているところは、抵抗しているのに無理やり入れさせられるという形をとっているのが47ページの図でわかると思います。one share-one vote の場合については、30％より下のほうに数としては多目に入っていると思うのです。そうではないところ、30％より上に分布しているのもかなりあるので、ここで第2位以下の株主がどんな感じで分布しているのかというのは45ページの図からはよくわからないんですけれども、少なくとも47ページの Figure 3 を見ると、支配株主の持ち株比率が余り安泰でないときには入れたくないと思う傾向があるのかなと思います。

河村委員 もう1点よろしいでしょうか。例えば複数議決権株を入れている会社で、先ほど言ったような弊害あるいは副作用みたいなものに対して、そういう会社はどのように対応するのでしょうか。対応するための制度が何かあるのでしょうか。

松井（智）報告者 もともとダブルで持っているダブル・ダブルの会社でどういうふうに運用がされているかという……。

河村委員 例えば、本当は廃止したくなってきたのだけれども困難だとか、

長期保有株主が２倍議決権を持っているけれども、どうも望ましくないというときに、そういう会社はどうやってその状況に対応していくのでしょうか。それはもうしようがないということになってしまうのでしょうか。

松井（智）報告者 普通に考えると定款変更なので、その定款変更の前に種類株主総会が入るので、ブロックされてしまえばもう終わり。支配株主がやめたいと思ったときだけやめられるという形にならざるを得ないのだと思います。

河村委員 とても危険な感じが。

松井（智）報告者 はい。

河村委員 なるほど。わかりました。

松井（秀）委員 幾つか前提をお伺いしたいのですけれども、複数議決権株について、時代なり場所なりによって、結構そのあらわれ方が違う気がしております。まず、アメリカでの議論が紹介されていますが、これは、主に創業者が一定の支配を持ち続けるという文脈で問題になってきた。アメリカではそれ以外の問題意識は余りないという理解でよいのでしょうか。

松井（智）報告者 創業者が支配を持ち続ける以外というのは、例えば……。

松井（秀）委員 私もイメージできないのですけれども、たとえば、フランスは長期保有を促す方向での議論になりますね。これに対して、きょうご紹介くださったアメリカの議論というのは、たとえばグーグルの例のように、創業者が支配権を持ち続けるために特殊な株式を持っている。でも、一方で普通株式は上場しておく。こういう形で複数議決権株を用いて、特定の株主に議決権を寄せるということが許容されるかどうか、という形で議論が進んでいるものと理解しました。つまりアメリカでは、この種の議論をするときに、創業者のようにある特定の支配株主に対して議決権を与えるための種類株を使い、他方でそれ以外の株式の上場が許されるか、こういう形での議論がなされている。それ以外の複数議決権株の利用、ないし種類株の利用の仕方は余り議論がない、ということなのでしょうか。

松井（智）報告者 先ほどの経緯からもわかるとおり、ＩＰＯのときしか、そもそも複数議決権を分配するという社会環境がないので、そのときに誰が持つかとなると、創業時から深くかかわっている人しか持たないという形になるのだと思うのですけれども。

松井（秀）委員 アメリカの議論はそのようなものとしてさしあたり見ていくこととして、今度はフランスなのですけれども、11ページで過去の変遷をたどってくださっていて、フランスは複数議決権の歴史がものすごく古いですね。1903年からあるのですけれども、これはどのような背景で入っているんですか。

松井（智）報告者 特に銀行、金融業界の支配権に関して非常に批判が出ましたというふうになっていたのですが、どうもその業界を念頭に置いて優先株創設を許可するという制度をつくったらしいということまではわかったのですけれども。

松井（秀）委員 これはちょっと古い言い回しですけれども、金融の産業支配みたいなものがあって、そのツールとして必要性が認められて出てきた制度であるけれども、余り行き過ぎると意思決定に非常にゆがみが生ずる。なので、1933年に２倍という形だけが許容されて、それが現在に引き継がれているという訳ですね。そうすると、フランスの制度は、21世紀に入って、長期保有のために流用されてきたというような理解をすればいいですか。

松井（智）報告者 そういうことです。

松井（秀）委員 そうすると、そこに特殊フランス的な固有の事情があるのか、気になるところです。ヨーロッパでは、株式の長期保有を求めるトレンドがある中で、もともとこういう制度が入っていたフランスは、制度が２つの意味を持つ、あるいは複数の意味を持つようになってきた、と理解すればよろしいでしょうか。

松井（智）報告者 これと同様の制度をイタリアとベルギーが立法しているという情報がありまして、それはどういうことかというと、歴史的にはどのような背景・政策があって、どういう法によるかというのは国によってさま

ざまではあるものの、いろんな国が何らかの複数議決権制度を持っていた。ただし、それが20世紀の終わりごろにＥＣＪ判決が相次いで出されたことで、ストレートにそこに反する法律を維持するのが難しくなったという背景がある。これに対して、例えば定款に入れておけばいいとか、株主が挽回できる余地があればいいみたいなことを判決も言っていますし、会社法一般則でそれを導入すると、まだ自国としての独自の運用ができるのではないかという思惑があるのではないかと思うのですが、そうすると、それはかなり弊害というか、1つの制度をいろんな目的で使ってしまうという傾向があるのかなとは思っています。

松井（秀）委員 実は、質問したい内容の答えを半分ぐらいいただいたのですけれども、ヨーロッパ、特にフランスの例では、複数議決権の話、その前提となる政策判断の話が完全に会社法の文脈で出てきていますね。これに対して日本では、会社法が種類株式の仕組み方について規定していますけれども、その具体的な方法は各会社が考えればよく、積極的に複数議決権ができますとも言っていないし、できないとも言っていない。その意味で、日本は、その点の政策的判断についての会社法の態度はニュートラルだと思います。その結果、日本でこれを実現しようとすると、東証の話になって、市場規制のほうで考えることになる。けれども、フランスは会社法で正面からやっているのはなぜなのか。このことと、先ほどの背景がどう結びつくかを伺おうと思っていたのですけれども、今の松井（智）先生のお話で、何となくわかってきたところもある。それはヨーロッパにおいて、ＥＵとしての規制との関係が1つあるということなのでしょうか。

松井（智）報告者 先ほどの話で、定款自治で会社が自分の意思もしくは投資家の総意としてそれを入れるというのであれば、ＥＵ統合が進む中でも自分の国の中でまだ独自の運用ができるという政策的思惑はあるのだと思うのです。それを証券取引所の上場審査において、このような定款規定を入れることというふうに要件づける方法をとるのか。それとも、フランスの定款規定を入れられますよというデフォルトルールをひっくり返すことで入れるの

かという2つの選択肢において、フランスは後者をとったわけなんですけれども、入れられますよではなくて、デフォルトルールをひっくり返したというところに多分意味がある。

松井（秀）委員 そこに非常に強い政策的な意思を感じるというのはあります。

　最後にコメントですけれども、日本は買収防衛策の文脈でこの問題が出てきましたので、アメリカともフランスともまた違う意味合いを持つのかなと思いました。私自身、まだうまくまとまっていないのですけれども、似たように見える制度が、それぞれの国でそれぞれの背景を持って議論されているので、そういう意味で並べて見ていくと、純粋に興味深いなと思った次第です。

松井（智）報告者 アメリカもやはりこの種類議決権株式を導入している理由として、買収防衛策を恒常的に入れていることに対して機関投資家からの圧力が強いからというのがあったと言われていますので、そういう意味では、同じような動機が裏にあるということはあります。

弥永会長代理 2つほど質問させていただきます。アメリカでは複数議決権タイプの株式がかなり使われているというご報告でしたが、私が昔、アメリカのものをちょっと調べたときには、アメリカでは議決権付株式と無議決権株式の両方を上場している会社が、他の国に比べるとかなり多く存在していたと記憶しております。なぜ、無議決権株式の発行という形で支配権を維持するのではなくて、複数議決権タイプがＩＴ産業などにおいて非常に好まれるようになったのか、おわかりだったら教えていただきたいというのが1点目です。

松井（智）報告者 例えば1株10議決権というのだけを使っているわけでもなくて、株式公開の際にほかの株式を全部無議決権にするというスキームを使った会社もあるので、会社、会社でいろいろ違うんですけれども、確かに1株につき10議決権とか20議決権といったタイプの株式が多用されています。決して規制でできないからとかそういう理由ではないのだと思うので、

先例があって使いやすいからというのが一番はっきりした理由なのかなという気はするのですけれども、判断の理由については、はっきりわからず申しわけありません。

　※スナップ社は2017年の自社無議決権株式のIPOを初めてのケースと説明している。

弥永会長代理　もう1つは、かなり古い話なのですけれども、レジュメの3-2のところで紹介していただいているように、黄金株が伝統的に非常に多く使われている国の典型は北欧だと昔聞いたことがあります。北欧の場合には、創立者の一族が20倍とか10倍という株式を持っていることが一般的と言われてきたと思うのです。北欧でそのような制度が用いられていたのに対して、他方、ほかの国ではさほど使われていなかったか、あるいは廃止されたか、そのような傾向があるということが、先生のご紹介からうかがえるのです。イタリア、オーストリアあるいはスペインで、廃止された理由はどのようなところにあると言われているのでしょうか。

松井（智）報告者　これもフランスの立法の趣旨説明の中で、背景について書かれていたというのを読んだだけでありまして、どういう事情を経て廃止に至ったということまでは紹介されていなかったので、申しわけないのですけれども、もう少し調べて何か出てくるようであれば……。

　※たとえばスペインでは、Telefonica、Repsol YPF、Endesa、Argentaria、Tabacalera.ECJの黄金株がECJ判決により違法とされており、ECJ判決の影響が無視できないものと考えられる。

加藤委員　複数議決権株等の種類株は何らかの目的を達成するための手段にすぎないと思います。本日の報告では明確な形では触れられていなかったかもしれませんが、松井（智）先生は、日本の現在の状況に何か問題があって、それを複数議決権株等の種類株式を利用して解決できるのではないかという問題意識をお持ちなのでしょうか。別の言い方をすれば、種類株の制度を見直すことによって、例えば日本の上場企業が抱えるガバナンス上の問題を良い方向に変えることができるのではないかという問題意識をお持ちでしょ

か。

松井（智）報告者 変えなければいけないというか、もしこういった形で上場するとなったときに、どちらかというとアメリカの状況と似てくると思うのですが、世界でどういう弊害が起きているかということを考えると、例えば日本の会社法の制度をそのまま使っていくと、いざというときの議決権を排除するというのが単元株の形でも種類株の形でも広く設計の自由が認められているということがあるので、これについて、どこら辺に制限をかけるのかというところに落ちついてくるのかなと思っております。

先ほどアメリカの話をしたときには事後的な訴訟の話がありましたが、日本でガバナンスを効かせようとすれば、事前に議決権をどうやって行使するかというところで調整をすることになるのかなと。先ほど後藤先生に挙げていただいたシンガポールの事例のように、議決権が一定の場合に復活するというルールを入れている証券取引所があるわけで、東証がきちんと運用して、ガバナンスが効くかどうか見ていますということであれば、実際に一律のルールで決めるということは必要ないかもしれませんけれども、議決権が最初からありませんとか、どういう場合にも復活しませんというようなスキームにならないように気をつけるというのがあるかなと思います。

ちなみにそれは、どういう問題を解決しようというよりは、日本ではそもそも余り上場がされていないので、もしそれで上場を考えることになったときには、そういったことを考えるということかなと思います。

加藤委員 そうすると、例えば現在の東証の上場審査に何か問題があるといった認識をお持ちではないのですね。

松井（智）報告者 そういうことではないです。

加藤委員 私の個人的な評価になってしまいますが、現在の東証の上場審査は非常に厳格だと思います。ご報告でも指摘があったように、最近、アメリカで複数議決権株が問題になっている理由の1つは、複数議決権株を発行している会社が上場することに対してNYSEは特別な審査をしていないということにあると思います。複数議決権株の利用を対象とした証券取引所によ

る特別な審査が存在しないので、創業者が保有するキャッシュフローに対する権利の割合と議決権の割合の間に非常に大きな乖離が生じてしまっているようです。ただ、このようなアメリカの状況と比較すると、東証の規制は上手く機能しているという評価もあり得るかもしれませんね。

松井（智）報告者 加藤先生のご認識だと、東証が指摘しようとしている問題点は理論的には非常に正しいが、きっちりやり過ぎているというようなことになるのでしょうか。

加藤委員 きっちりやり過ぎているか否かはともかく、東証が対処しようとしている問題は現実に存在するのだと思います。東証による規制は、上場会社が複数議決権株を発行する場合だけではなく、可能な限り、複数議決権株を発行した会社が上場することも制約すべきであるという基本的な方針に基づいていると思います。このような方針は、制度整備が行われた当時の上場会社のコーポレートガバナンスや株式保有構造を前提とすると、事後規制に多くを期待することはできないため、合理的であったように思います。しかし、例えばスチュワードシップ・コード等によって、上場会社のコーポレートガバナンスが機能するようになってくると、上場審査の段階、すなわち、入口の段階で厳格な規制を設ける必要性に対する評価が変わってくると思うのです。本日の松井（智）先生のご報告でも指摘されていましたが、上場時の審査でなすべきことと、上場後に複数議決権株を採用する若しくは採用しようとする会社に対してどのような規律が働くことを期待できるかという問題との間には相関関係があると思います。

　日本の現在の制度はアメリカに倣って作られていると思いますが、少なくとも、上場後の会社及び支配株主に対する規律が機能するか否かという点について、現在でも、日本の状況はアメリカほどこのような規律に期待できないという評価が妥当であると思います。ですから、現在では、東証が上場審査を通じて複数議決権株の利用を厳格に規制することは正しいと思います。その一方、このような評価は、上場会社のコーポレートガバナンスの発展によって変化する可能性があることも意識した方が望ましいと思います。

1点、松井（智）先生のご意見を伺いたい点があります。レジュメの最後で、長期的な関係の構築については、各会社の自助努力に任せることには限界があるというご指摘がありましたが、この指摘は長期的な関係を構築したほうがいいということが含意として含まれているのでしょうか。

松井（智）報告者　長期的な関係を構築したほうがよいかということについては、私個人としては、そのほうが望ましいのではないかと思います。これは日本の株主がどういう人かということを考えたときに、非常に不安定な株主構造になっていると、日本の市場に余りよくない影響があるのではないかとか、そのほか、例えばステークホルダーの意見を会社の経営に反映させることができるのではないかとか、いろいろと議論はあるので、なぜ望ましいのかについては、いろいろと根拠があり、同様に、それによる弊害もあり得るという議論があることはよく承知しているのですが、個人の結論としては、やはりあったほうがいいかなと思っています。

　先ほどの、日本が厳し過ぎるのかどうかということですけれども、市場間である程度足並みをそろえる必要があるのかなと思っています。きょうかきのう、アリババの上場のニュースがありましたが、結局、複数議決権株式でアメリカの投資家から資金を調達した後、香港でもまた資金を調達してみたいなことになってきたときに、複数議決権株式と普通株式との割合をどう維持するのかとか、問題がいろいろある気はしていて、プライマリー・リスティングのところで全部統一しますというふうにするのか、あるいはそこは話し合って均衡をとるのかみたいな話も出てき得るかなとは思います。

松尾（健）委員　脚注の10がついているあたり、資料1の論文の内容のご紹介で、アメリカのデュアル・クラス・ストックについての評価があります。創業者の支配の利点というのは失われていくとか、あるいは特に業績がどうとか企業価値がどうという実証研究がたくさんあることは承知しているんですけれども、一方で、a、b、cのcで指摘されている搾取が顕著になった事例そのものは余り報告されていないようにも思うんです。

　業績がどうとか規律が緩むからというようなことは、上場されなくて投資

機会がなくなるよりはましだという意見が一方であるということもご紹介されていましたけれども、そういう人たちからすると、そこは放っておいてくれ、別に構わないということになりそうです。搾取（利益移転）が起こるとなると、これは放っておけないということで、取引所等が介入する、禁止する、あるいは一定の制限をかけるということもあり得るのかな。そこは違うようにも思います。理論的には搾取（利益移転）が起こりやすそうだという指摘は目にしたことがあるのですが、実際に搾取的なことが起こったということは聞かないと従来から思っていまして、そのあたりのご事情を何かご存じであれば教えていただきたいということです。

松井（智）報告者 ここでエントレンチメントという名前を持って何を指そうとしているのかということもあると思うのですけれども、経営者が個人的な利益を求めて、例えば退職金パッケージとか、そういう利得部分を必要以上にとりますよという話なのか、経営者と投資家の取り分を大きく見たときに、普通の会社と比べて、そっちのほうが顕著に多いという状況がずっと続いていますよという話なのかというのがあると思うんです。前者の問題だとすると、それが法的に問題となるケースとして出てくるのだと思うので、分析というより、そもそも余り望ましくない状況だと考えられるのではないかと思います。

　そういう意味で、これについての実証分析とかそういった形ではないのですけれども、これは基本的なエージェンシー・コストの議論に乗っかる部分というのが半分くらいはあるのかなと。あと、その後半部分、この会社が、投資家に対してより経営者に対して分配を多くする結果として、会社のパフォーマンスが下がっていますよという話については、会社価値が下がるという一般的な、よくある分析に入ってくるのかなという気がします。済みません、お答えになっているかというところはありますけれども。

尾崎委員 会社と株主が長期的な関係を持つのが望ましいという話で、想定しているのがどういう株主なのかなというのを、もう既に質疑応答の中で一部出ていますけれども、改めてお伺いしたいです。今の日本だと、種類株と

か議決権をふやすという形で長期的な株主に報いるというのは基本的にはしていないわけです。他方で、個人株主相手であれば株主優待とか、あるいはトヨタの種類株も、一応、個人株主をターゲットにしているみたいな話がされていたと思うのですが、そういう状況は、先ほど来の議論から見ると、どう見えるのかなというのを少しご教示いただければと思います。

松井（智）報告者 日本の現状が、スチュワードシップ・コードが考えているような、大き過ぎて退出できなくて協力的になる投資家とはかなりかけ離れているというのはご指摘のとおりかと思います。したがって、そのときにどう望ましいのかという議論についても、長期的な関係を、投資家とウィン・ウィンの関係を築きますという話よりは、多様なステークホルダーみたいな話に入ってきて、それはスチュワードシップ・コードの話で目指されているガバナンスの状態とは少し違う話というのが日本の現状では動いているのかなと思います。

　それがいいのかどうかという判断ですが、責任を持って対話をする大きい株主の存在があるのが望ましいかなというふうには思うのですけれども。AA種類株式のようなものを汎用的に使って、そういった人たちの割合を大きくふやせということではなくて、私個人としては、これは株主を多様化する一環という程度のものということであればわかるかなというぐらいの評価をしております。

藤田委員 単なる感想と、1点だけ質問があります。

　まず感想の方ですが、1株1議決権原則とか種類株式という抽象的な問題の立て方が有効性を失ってきているということが分かった気がします。松井（智）先生が最初に触れられたことですが、アメリカで最初に Dual Class Capitalization が話題になったのは1980年代終わりから1990年代の初めごろではないかと思います。そのときは、IPOのときの創業者のインセンティブ等というコンテクストは抜きに、およそ種類株式あるいは Dual Class Capitalization がいいか悪いかという議論の仕方をしていました。有名な Easterbrook and Fischel の Economic Structure of Corporate Law の中の1

章がVotingで、そこでは種類株式について割と厳格に規制していたニューヨーク証券取引所の立場をサポートするような方向で書かれていたのですけれども、本当に抽象的な議論で、要するにキャッシュフローとコントロールが比例しないことがエージェンシー・コストを増加させるという抽象的な議論なのです。つまり、そこではコンテクスト抜き、環境抜き、かつ手法抜き――ここで手法というのは、議決権の種類を設ける手法という意味ですが――の検討だったわけです。それに対して、その後は、そんなに単純ではないということで、例えば、一株一議決権からの離脱は一方でエントレンチメントというか、経営者自身のプライベート・ベネフィットを確保するために用いられる危険もあるかもしれないけれども、他方で積極的なインセンティブ効果もあって、たとえば創業者等にインセンティブを与えるために必要なこともあるのではないかとか、しかし、それでもＩＰＯのときにそれが濫用されていないかという形で、具体的なコンテクストを与えた上で、いろいろ実証的な検討がなされるようになる。

　種類株式をめぐる環境も、国によって全然違っていて、たとえば大崎さんの質問で出てきましたが、ヨーロッパ型の公開買付規制――一定割合以上の議決権を取得すれば他の株主の株式を全部買い取れという特殊な義務がある制度――を前提とすると、買収するつもりはないけれども、ある程度以上の議決権を持ちたいという人に対してすごく抑制的に働きます。特定の人に特定のインセンティブを与えるわけです。しかし、これは特定の市場規制という環境がもたらすゆがみで、そういう環境がない場合には同じことになるとはかぎらない。

　さらに、種類株式を導入する際の手法も、単純な複数議決権株式なのか一定期間持つとふえるものか、ふえるというのも、長期保有している株式分についてふえるのか、一定以上の期間で持っていた人なら、次から買う株式も全部複数議決権がもらえるということなのかで全然違ってきます。

　だから、このようなコンテクスト、環境、手法といった変数を加えて緻密に検討していかないと、意味のある議論ができないということがだんだんわ

かってきたのが、近時の状況ではないかと思います。ＥＵの2007年のレポートの難点も、コンテクストを捨象したまま１株１議決権原則から離脱しているか否かという観点だけでパフォーマンスの影響を見たために、特に意味のある結果がでなかったことにあり、そのためもうちょっと細かな分析をする必要があることを教えてくれた気がします。これが感想の部分です。

　それで、質問ですがフランスのフロランジュ法のような形で、特定の人に対する特権という形で与えた場合、具体的にどんなインセンティブ効果を与えるのかというのがよくわからなくないので教えてください。まずそもそも内容の確認ですが、１株を２年間持っていれば、その後取得する株式は複数議決権となるということでしたでしょうか。

松井（智）報告者　申しわけありません。恐らくこれは２年間持っていると確認された株式について２倍議決権。

藤田委員　議決権が増えるのは２年間持っている株式なのですね。

松井（智）報告者　はい。

藤田委員　そうすると、与える効果としては、２年間持っている株式は売るときには１議決権に戻ってしまうということですが、株式の売却を抑えるという意味での買収防衛効果は一般的にあるということでしょうか。

松井（智）報告者　これは売ってしまうと損になるのかどうかというところなのですが、買うときの金額も１議決権のものとして買い、出るときも１議決権のものとして売るので、その個人にとって買う正当化ができるだけの額かどうかという点についてはいろいろ影響があり得るものの、市場としては変わらないのではないかという気がします。

藤田委員　無議決権株が余り値引きされないのと同じことで、売買価格は余り変わらないとすると、長期的に持っている多くの株主にとっては影響ないことになり、買収防衛効果は大きくないことになる。そうなると長期保有というのをどういう観点から促しているという理解になるのでしょうか。

松井（智）報告者　短期保有株主は持っていても余りいいことがないということで分散が進むと思うのですが、長期の株主にとっては、一時的に長期保

有株主の持っている期間だけは延びているんですけれども、絶対的な議決権を確保した上で売れるという余剰利得が存在するので、そこの閾値を超えて持っている人には逆にそれを手放すというインセンティブが生じていると思います。あとは、かなり接近した感じで株式を保有している株主たちは、自分が手放してしまうと一気にほかの株主の議決権が大きくなるので売れないというのはあるんですけれども、これは前からそうだったかなという気がします。

　そうすると、先ほど一番最初に、結局のところ、これで長期保有が促されたのかということについては、49ページのFigure 5でしたけれども、かえって顕著に短期化しているのではないかという指摘もあったりとかするんです。

藤田委員　ガバナンスに対して複雑で、結局よくわからない影響を与えているという印象が強いですね。買収防衛的という観点から、一番有効なのは複数議決権株じゃなくて、長期保有したら配当がふえるというタイプで、これなら一定期間以上持っている株主は売らなくなるので、そのほうが有効な気がします。フロランジュ法は、ガバナンスの影響というのは複雑過ぎてわからない制度をつくったのかなという印象です。

　そうすると、アメリカにおけるＩＰＯの議論とも、全然違うことになる。あちらは確実に特定の人の行動に影響を与えるため、その是非という形で問題は問いやすいけれども、フランスの場合は、そもそものインセンティブ効果の内容自体がよくわからない、そういうふうな理解でよろしいでしょうか。

松井（智）報告者　ご指摘のとおりですね。かなり一般的な制度の中に埋め込んでしまって、しかもかなり広く入れてしまっているので、何かを狙っていたのだとしても、それに対する副作用みたいなものがかなりあって、どっちを向いているのかというのが、実は、設定した目標を達成できているのかという点については疑問の多い制度ではないかと思います。

武井委員　すいません、質問ばかりで申し訳ないのですが、フランスの上場会社の今の株主構成ってどんな感じなのでしょうか。たとえば日本だと、国

内機関投資家は３割、外国機関投資家３割、企業２割、個人２割とかと言われます。フランスでは個人株主が案外多いということも聞いたことがあるのですが。

松井（智）報告者　先ほど38ページをお見せしたと思うんですけれども、2016年の割合です。企業の持ち合い部分が19％くらい、金融機関と分散株式の割合が35％、創業者である同族ファミリーないし国家が持っているのがそれぞれ30％超と12％という形になっております。これはいろんな企業を横断的に見た結果で、創業者のところとStateのところが結構大きくなっていて、それがかなりミックスされてしまっているので、こんな数になっていると思うんですけれども、そこがない会社であれば分散はかなり進んでいるというふうには聞いています。

武井委員　分散というのは個人株主のことですかね？

松井（智）報告者　Dispersedのところですね。あとはFinancialが15.38％なので、余り大きくはないというか、Dispersedのほうが上になっている。

武井委員　創業者の保有株式まで含めると個人株主が相当多そうですね。他方で、機関投資家の保有比率は日本よりも低そうですね。Dispersedは個人の意味ですね。

松井（智）報告者　個人です。

神作会長　そろそろ定刻になりますが、よろしゅうございますか。

　それでは、まだご議論もあろうかと思いますけれども、定刻になりましたので、本日の研究会の質疑を終了させていただきます。

　松井智予先生、本日は貴重な報告ありがとうございました。

　ここで１点、お願いがございます。この研究会では、長年、ご報告の内容を改めて論文集として取りまとめて、単行本として刊行してきております。前回のセッションから、委員の方々のご報告を前半部分と後半部分に分けて、上下２分冊として刊行しておりまして、今回も同様にお願いしたいと存じます。

　委員の先生方は現在17名いらっしゃいます。本日の松井先生で８名の委

員の方々にご報告をいただきました。そこで、これまでご報告していただいた先生方に原稿のご執筆をお願いし、単行本の上巻を刊行したいと存じます。

　つきましては、これまでご報告いただいた委員の先生方には、大変ご多忙とは存じますけれども、来年3月末を締め切りといたしましてご執筆をお願いいたしますので、何とぞよろしくお願いいたします。

　また、執筆に当たっての体裁等、詳細につきましては、別途、事務局からご連絡をしていただきますので、どうかよろしくお願いいたします。

　次回の研究会は、お手元の議事次第にございますように、7月31日の午後2時から、学習院大学の小出篤先生にご報告いただく予定です。会場は、本日と同様、太陽生命日本橋ビル8階の日証協の会議室で、午後2時からの開催でございます。

　それでは、本日の研究会はこれで閉会とさせていただきます。長時間にわたってありがとうございました。

報告者レジュメ

複数議決権株式を用いた株主構造のコントロール

上智大学　松井　智予

内容

複数議決権株式を用いた株主構造のコントロール 1
1．はじめに 1
2．IPO 時点における複数議決権株式の利用と創業者利益 3
　2－1　複数議決権株式を IPO 時に導入するアメリカ企業の増加 3
　2－2　議決権種類株式を用いた IPO に対する学説・投資家の反対 4
　　1　機関投資家との攻防 4
　　2　学説における分析と規制の導入 5
　　3　マーケットによる規律と市場間競争 6
　2－3　小括・議決権種類株式の利用目的・抑止を可能とする環境 8
3．ヨーロッパの長期株主優遇と議決権種類株式 9
　3－1　背景 9
　3－2　フランス法の複数議決権制度 10
　3－3　複数議決権株式制度導入の影響 13
　3－4　フロランジュ法導入手法の特殊性 15
　3－3　資本の移動の自由との葛藤 16
4　日本における運用 19
　4－1　IPO 時点での議決権種類株式と創業者利益 19
　4－2　上場会社による種類株式の発行と長期的保有 22

1．はじめに

　日本においては、議決権について何らかのアレンジメントを行う種類株式のうち、とくに会社法 108 条 1 項 8 号が、株主総会または取締役会で定める事項のうち、その決議のほか、その種類株主を構成員とする種類株主総会の決議があることを必要とするものを定めることができるとしており、このような種類株式を拒否権付株式（＝黄金株）という。一部の株式にのみ譲渡制限を課した公開会社（108 条 1 項 4 号・2 項 4 号・5 号）が上場した場合、黄金株に譲渡制限を付することができると考えられたため、取締役選解任等について拒否権を設定した黄金株を友好な関係先に発行するなど、敵対的買収に備えて企業が導入する防衛策としての使途が強く認識され、関心が高かった。

　これに対して、平成 18 年（2006）年 1 月にこのような黄金株発行会社の上場を認めるべきかどうかについて東京証券取引所が「買収防衛策の導入に係る上場制度の整備などについて」を公表した。また、2007 年に企業価値研究会において「上場会社による種類株式の

発行に関する提言」¹が取りまとめられている。

　この提言は、種類株式のアメリカでの使われ方について、創業時の事業者・被用者や出資者である公開前株主が複数議決権株式を持って経営陣の長期的アプローチを可能にするという利用パターンを紹介する。一方、ヨーロッパでは種類株式のうちキャッシュフローを維持するための条項ではなく議決権型の種類株式が広く用いられ、特に黄金株は民営化企業が中心であることが指摘されているが、フランスでは、上場企業上位 120 社のうち 6 割の企業が、一定期間株式を継続保有した場合に議決権が 2 倍になる制度を導入済みであると報告されている。また、EU が一株一議決権原則に関して 2007 年 5 月にまとめた調査報告書²において「一株一議決権原則と企業の経済パフォーマンスやガバナンスの間に相関関係があるとは断定できない」と結論付けているものの、個別の黄金株事例に対しては ECJ で否定される例も多いことも指摘されている。こうした調査の上で、報告書は、種類株式発行について弊害と無関係な制約を設けるべきではなく、様々な発行目的を許容すべきとしたが、一方で上場会社における発行には弊害が考えられるとした。この報告を受けて、東京証券取引所は、拒否権付株式の発行が上場株式が備えるべき基本的かつ重要な権利が著しく損なわれる状態となる内容を含む防衛策となりうる場合を明示した。

　その後約 10 年が経過し、この間に 2008 年のリーマンショックを経て、現在の世界の市場では種類株式の導入について方向性の異なる動きが見られる。

　アメリカにおいては、創業者 IT 企業の上場において、議決権種類株式を活用して創造性と会社の方針とを維持しようとする動きが顕著になり、このような株式については主要な機関投資家等が強い反対を表明し、冒頭にあげて様々な IT 企業に対して訴訟が提起される事態となっている。また、サンセット条項によって徐々に株式を一本化すべきではないかという学説・規制庁の主張も有力となっている。一方で、創業者により多くの利益が分配される構造を了解の上でより多くの投資機会を求める自由を主張する投資家もいる。

　アメリカにおいて創業者が自ら自分に複数議決権を割り当て、機関投資家に議決権を配分しなかったのとは逆に、ヨーロッパでは、短期間での業績追求を反省する動きが強まるなかで、複数議決権株式は長期保有を行う機関投資家の優遇策—スチュワードシップなどを含み、各国が独自に設計できる—の一種と捉えられている。投資家への権利の再配分は自発的に生ずるものではないので、何らかの指針なり規制が伴うことになる。2015 年 5 月 7 日には、欧州法務委員会において、株主権利指令の改正案に、中長期株主に対する優遇策の採用を 2 年以内に各国に義務付ける 3ea 条が 10 対 13 の僅差で導入されるという出来事が耳目を集めた³。ただし、長期株主優遇策が実際に投資家に有利に運用されるとは限ら

1　企業価値研究会「上場会社による種類株式の発行に関する提言　平成１９年１２月」
https://www.meti.go.jp/policy/economy/keiei_innovation/keizaihousei/pdf/joujouteigen2.pdf
²　Report on the proportionality principle in the European Union – ISS Europe, ECGI, Shearman & Sterling - 18 May 2007
³　福本葵「長期保有株主に対する優遇策」証券経済研究第 94 号(2016.6)　77 ページ。同 80

ない。フランスは、国内事業の主要な設備や雇用が国際資本の決定に左右されることを防ごうとしており、立法によって上場会社における2年以上の長期保有株式を2議決権を有する優先株とすることをデフォルト化し、これを利用して逆に政府保有を進め、投資家を排除した。この立法に伴って、新規上場における複数議決権の導入も顕著に増加したとされており、その影響が注目される。また、イタリアやベルギーもフランスの動きに倣って複数議決権株式を法制化したとされる。このような制度が広がることは、資本移動自由の原則に関するECJの従来判決とどのような関係に立つのかが、問題として残されていよう。

　日本は、複数議決権株式について証券取引所・企業が謙抑的な運用をしてきたためか、企業側がIPOにおいて限界を探り、投資家がアクションを起こす応酬の中でバランスを探る動きは生じていない。2014年に、CYBERDYNE社が上場をした際、複数議決権類似の投資単位制度の導入が話題となったが、これに続く例も特にみられない。逆に、国が一定の政策に基づいて複数議決権株式制度を強制的に導入する状況も生じていない。長期株主を積極的に作り出そうという思想に基づく自発的な株式発行については、本研究会において、平成28年7月20日に「上場会社による種類株式の利用」について報告がなされている[4]。

2．IPO時点における複数議決権株式の利用と創業者利益
2－1　複数議決権株式をIPO時に導入するアメリカ企業の増加

　アメリカの会社は種類株式を発行できるが、証券取引市場が種類株式を歓迎をしているわけではない。1985年に市場間競争を通じてNYSEは種類株式制度を認めることを余儀なくされたが、1988年にSECがRule19c－4を新設して1株1議決権制度の会社が複数議決権制度に移行することを制限し、当該ルール導入の権限を裁判所に否定されつつも、主要な証券取引所に同様の制限を導入するよう説得したという経緯から、IPO時の種類株式制度採用と流通市場株式の種類株式制度への移行との間に差が生じた[5]。

　2004年のGoogle親会社のAlphabetが複数議決権株式を利用したIPOを行って以降、

頁によれば、長期保有株主の優遇策として、追加議決権，税制上の優遇措置，ロイヤルティ配当（loyalty dividend）やロイヤルティ株式（loyalty share）のいずれか一つ以上を付与すること，そして，EU構成国に対し、2年以上の任意の期間、株式を保有する株主を長期保有株主として取り扱うこととし、これらの措置は2年以内に行われることが述べられていたが、この後各方面からの質問，議論が盛んとなり、最終的に欧州議会はこの修正案を受け入れず、2015年7月8日に本会議において採用された改正指令では、3ea条は削除され、同指令前文において，機関投資家や資産管理会社がしばしば，不適切に短期的なリターンを注視しすぎるあまりに、会社のガバナンスやパフォーマンスを不適切な方向に導くとし、役員の報酬の方針を中長期のパフォーマンスに寄与するものとすることや、従業員や地方当局，市民社会などのステークホルダーを考慮したコーポレート・ガバナンスを適切に関与させる必要性について触れるにとどまったとされる。

[4] 加藤貴仁「上場会社による種類株式の利用」金融商品取引法研究会研究記録第57号
[5] Lucian A. Bebchuk & Kobi Kastiel, The Untenable Case for Perpetual Dual Stock, 103 Va. L. Rev. 597(2017)

創業者等が支配権を維持するために用いられる複数議決権株は、NYSE でも増加していった。Facebook、LinkedIn、Alibaba、Samsung、または Snap（Snapchat 親会社）のような IT 企業の IPO では導入率が高く、IT 企業の 3 分の 1 はこれらを利用しているとの報道もある。楽天を筆頭株主とする Lyft も上場に際して 1 株 20 議決権と 1 議決権の議決権種類株を利用した[6]とされている。こうした IT 企業だけでなく Visa、Mastercard、Berkshire Hathaway、Roche といった企業もこのタイプの株主構成を採用している。ウォール街では、2015 年に公開された 133 社のうち 14％が複数の議決権を共有し（2014 年 12％、2005 年 1％）、現在複数議決権株発行会社の株式は時価総額 5 兆ドルにのぼるという。

2－2　議決権種類株式を用いた IPO に対する学説・投資家の反対
1　機関投資家との攻防

2004 年の Google 親会社の Alphabet の IPO を契機として、機関投資家・投資顧問・規制庁などの立場にある各リーダーが IPO における種類株式使用に反対を表明するようになった（ただし、ビジネス誌では one share one vote から脱却すべきだという主張も頻繁にみられる[7]）。

Alphabet は、種類株式導入を計画した結果株主との間で訴訟問題に発展した最初の企業となった。訴訟が起きた 2012 年 4 月から約 1 年後の 2013 年 6 月、同社は、最終的に 5 億ドル以上の和解金を支払ったという[8]。しかも、紛争はそれで終わりではなく、同社はさらに今年に入ってから役員や幹部の性犯罪疑惑およびセクハラの隠蔽や退職金の承認などを理由に提訴され、複数議決権株式の廃止を求められている[9]。

---

[6]「米リフト、ＩＰＯを正式申請　楽天が筆頭株主」ロイター通信 2019 年 3 月 2 日
https://jp.reuters.com/article/lyft-ipo-filing-idJPKCN1QI5C4
[7] Simon C.T. Wong, "Rethinking "One share, One Vote"" Jan. 29,2013 Harvard Business Review; Steve Johnson,"Mantra of 'one share, one vote' is under fire Can short-termism be tackled by rewarding shareholders who hold stock for longer?"　Financial Times Feb. 22, 2015; Peter Clapman and Richard Koppes, " Time to Rethink 'One Share, One Vote'? The shareholder-rights agenda has been largely achieved since it began in the 1980s" WSJ June 23, 2016.
[8]"Google settlement clears way for new Class C stock", Reuters June 18,2013
https://www.reuters.com/article/us-google-stockplan-settlement/google-settlement-clears-way-for-new-class-c-stock-idUSBRE95G0MU20130617
[9] "Shareholders file lawsuit against Google over payouts to executives accused of sexual harassment" https://www.theverge.com/2019/1/10/18177445/ 同時期に二つの訴訟が提起されている。一つの訴訟の原告は 2009 年 10 月以降アルファベットの株主である個人であり、提訴の内容は、取締役の一人が人身売買に関わっていたことを把握しつつ不問に付して退職金パッケージを承認したと主張し、これについて過失による監督責任違反でなく誠実・忠実義務違反を問うている。また、こうした点についての改善を行うために、現行 B クラス株式によって創業者 6 人が合計 60％の議決権を有している点が障害となっていることを指摘し、裁判所に対し、1 株 1 議決権制度を採用するような定款変更を含むガバナンス改善を Alphabet および Google に指示するよう救済（Relief）を求めた（訴状は https://assets.documentcloud.org/documents/5682121/19-CIV-00164.pdf 参照）。この訴訟

最近の事例では、2017年1月に上場申請したスナップ社は、株式公開時に発行した株式がすべて無議決権株式とするという非常に極端なスキームを採用した（2人の創業者所有率が30%を下回るとすべての株式が普通株に転換され、どちらかの創業者が死亡すればその株式は譲渡不能となるとされた[10])。同社は訴訟には直面しなかったものの、主要インデックス提供会社による、種類株式発行企業を指数構成銘柄から除外する方針に則り、ラッセル3000指数やS&P500指数に採用されないこととなった。

2　学説における分析と規制の導入

このように創業者に極端な形で支配権を残すスキームが登場してきたため、2017年にBebchukらが発表した論文は、ある株主に支配的割合の議決権数を割り当てる種類株式においては支配株主の議決権割合と資本割合との差（wedge）が大きいほどエージェンシー・コストが大きくなり、会社価値が下がるとの分析をもとに（P603)、上場会社が同族企業と同様の承継リスク（高齢で意思能力の点でも疑問が残るような創業者の支配が続くなど）にさらされる例などを挙げつつ[11]、弊害が経時的に増大することを指摘した。まとめると以下のとおりである。

a. ①IT業界ではIPO後に技術革新によって環境が激変し、あるいは支配持分が血縁者などに譲渡され、当初創業者に見出されていたリーダーシップが適切でなくなる可能性が高いこと、②創業者ら自身もポートフォリオ分散のために持ち分を減少させる可能性が高い、

b. 一方で③創業者による支配や長期支配の利点、さらには株主と比較した場合の経営者の支配の利点のいずれも、時間とともに失われる、

c. こうしたことで経営者による搾取と、インセンティブの歪みの問題（602頁）が顕著になるにもかかわらず、支配株主は種類株式廃止によって私的利益をすべて失う一方単一株式制度のもとで得られる便益の一部しか得られないため、単一株式構造へ

と時を同じくして、2つの年金基金が類似の主張による別訴を提起し、現在カリフォルニア高裁に係属中である（LR Trust, et. al. v. Larry Page, et al., and related actions, Case No. 19CV341522, Superior Court of the State of California in and for the County of Santa Clara、訴状は
https://www.cohenmilstein.com/sites/default/files/Alphabet-Complaint%20-%20Stamped%2001092019.pdf 参照)。

[10] https://oneboxnews.com/articles/snapchat-ipo-founder-control-2017-1

[11] ただし、例えば昨年度離婚により財産を分与したAmazon創業者のベゾス氏の事例においては、逆にAmazonが創業者という属性に多くの議決権を付与する株式を発行していないことがリスクとなり、もし離婚相手が相当規模の株式を持てば会社支配が不安定になるとの懸念から、成長株投資家の間でアマゾンの持ち分を減らす動きが出てくると予想された。"Jeff Bezos' 'beauty' of a divorce probably won't derail Amazon juggernaut" The Sydney Morning Herald Jan.18,2019
https://www.smh.com.au/business/companies/jeff-bezos-beauty-of-a-divorce-probably-wont-derail-amazon-juggernaut-20190117-p50rwj.html

の移行には強い負のインセンティブが働き、事後的な私的調整によっては種類議決権株スキームは消滅しない。

同論文はマーケットの調整により最適な条項が挿入されるはずである、会社により最適な条項は異なる、IPO を抑制する、などの様々な反論を想定しつつ、様々なサンセット条項を検討し、結論として、支配権者と無関係の株主が延長に同意しない限り、種類株式制度を 10 年ないし 15 年で終了させることを推奨した[12]。

この論文と軌を一にして、2017 年春、米国の年金基金、ノルウェーのソブリン資産ファンドおよびシンガポールの GIC に裏付けられた世界最大の資産運用会社（BlackRock、Vanguard State Street）が、株主民主主義の原則を侵害するものとしてこの種の金融商品に対する反対を表明した。また、2018 年 2 月には SEC（証券取引委員会）のコミッショナーの一人である Robert J. Jackson が複数の議決権のある株式に期限を設けるような新しい上場規則を課すべきことを主張した[13]。

こうした圧力を受けて、IT 企業も、業績が好調で創業者支配に対する顕著なリスクがない環境のもとでは、訴訟や株主運動によって繰り返し費用が発生する事態を回避するようになっているようである。同年 2017 年 6 月、米ネット複合企業 InterActiveCorp（IAC）が、訴訟にともなう負担や騒動を理由に無議決権株式発行を取りやめた。同様に同年 9 月、フェイスブックが、提訴されていた無議決権株式の発行計画を撤回すると発表した[14]。その後、フェイスブック株主らは議決権種類株式制度の撤廃を提案し、委任状を集めている[15]。2019 年の Uber の上場に際しては[16]、議決権種類株式スキームは採用されなかったという。

3　マーケットによる規律と市場間競争

だが、このような規制強化の提言は一様なものではなく、機関投資家側からの反対も存在する。Alphabet 訴訟や Snap のインデックス除外といった措置も、IT 関連新規上場株式

---

[12] Bebchuk & Kastiel *supra* note 3 at 585.
[13] "Perpetual Dual-Class Stock: The Case Against Corporate Royalty" Commisshoner Robert J.Jackson Jr. Speech on Feb.15, 2018
https://www.sec.gov/news/speech/perpetual-dual-class-stock-case-against-corporate-royalty．
[14] ザッカーバーグは裁判所において無議決権株式の発行を取りやめた理由を証言することをまぬかれるために、結局 6750 万ドルの訴訟費用を支払うことに合意したと報道されている（"Facebook to Pay $67.5 Million in Fees in Suit Over Shares"　Boomberg Oct. 25 2018）
[15] Facebook Shareholders to Vote on Eliminating Dual-Class Shares "proxy filing(https://www.sec.gov/Archives/edgar/data/1326801/000132680119000025/facebook2019definitiveprox.htm　より proposal five 参照）
[16] 共同創業者カラニック氏やその他創業当時からの出資者を議決権上優遇しないと報道されている。もっとも、2017 年 6 月にカラニック氏は同社の CEO を辞任したが、同年 10 月 1 日、同氏は取締役会の他のメンバーの意見を聞かずに自ら任命権を行使し、新たに 2 人の取締役を任命したとされており、保有株式数を超える議決権の付与は火種となる可能性が高い状況といえた（https://www.esg.quick.co.jp/research/807）

の利益率が高く、そうした株式から組成される ETF が発足するといったトレンドの中では、議決権種類株式を用いた上場を抑える効果はないのではないかとの見方もある[17]。

　創業者が利益の大部分を持っていくのであれ、IPO を通じた利益参与の機会がもたらされる状態は、創業者が支配を失うことを恐れてそもそも上場しない状態よりはよいのであり、マーケットの力が議決権種類株式の行使を正しい水準に調整をすることも期待できる、また世界の他の市場において、種類株式発行会社の上場を誘致する競争が存在することを考えれば[18]、投資機会を狭める必要はないとの論拠に基づく。例えばインデックスについても、2017年7月に S&P1500 の構成企業に種類株式発行会社を含めないことを決定した S&P に対し、例えば MSCI が 2018 年 1 月に複数議決権株式発行会社をインデックスに含めるべきかについて議論を行った際には、排除は実現しなかった[19]。

---

[17] Anita Balakrishnan, "Start-ups go public to get your money — your input on how it's spent is now o ptional" CNBC Aug 5 2017,
https://www.cnbc.com/2017/08/05/snap-exclusion-from-sp-500-wont-stop-multiple-share-classes.html

[18] Alibaba の上場においては、議決権種類株式の上場を認めない香港ではなく NYSE が選ばれたことで、香港取引所が意見募集を行ったこと、シンガポールやイタリアなども同スキーム解禁にうごいていることが報告されている。(「シンガポール取引所、種類株を容認 3月までに規則策定、スタートアップ誘致で競争激しく」日経新聞 2018/1/22 17:00、小阿瀬達彦「シリコンバレー流、日本上陸」大和総研コンサルティングレポート 2015 年 3 月 26 日 https://www.dir.co.jp/report/consulting/governance/20150326_009585.pdf、中国での制度導入について WANG XI & LIU YANG "A Study on the Dual－Class Share Structures of Overseas Listed Companies—Taking Alibaba Group as an Example" European Journal of Business, Economics and Accountancy Vol. 6, No. 2, 2018 など。

[19] MSCI は 2017 年の投資家調査を行ったが、大多数は複数の議決権のある株式に反対する一方、インデックスからの除外は規制当局が義務付け決定した場合のみだとの意見もあり、一定の溝が見られたという。2018 年の同社のディスカッションペーパーにおいては、完全な除外よりも急進的でない解決策として、それまでインデックスの加重の際考慮されていた規模と資本流通量に加え、投票権基準を追加する方法が提唱された（この新しい基準を取る場合、MSCI All Country Weigthed Index を構成する複数議決権発行会社 253 社のうち、12 社は除外され（Snap、CME Group、または Porsche）、209 社のウェイトが全体で 4.26％減少する。たとえば、クラス A のアルファベット株式の場合、流動資本は 100％であったが、調整後の流動率は 43.9％になる）。結局、2018 年 10 月には、インデックスはそのままに据え置いたうえで、複数議決権株式を考慮した新しいインデックスを発足させるとアナウンスした。"Should Equity Indexes Include Stocks of Companies with Share Classes having Unequal Voting Rights?" MSCI consultation discussion paper Jan. 2018 https://www.msci.com/documents/1296102/8328554/Discussion+Paper_Voting+rights.pdf/d3ba68f1-856a-4e76-85b6-af580c5420d7;
"MSCI Will Retain the MSCI Global Investable Market Indexes Unchanged and Launch a New Index Series Reflecting the Preferences of Investors on Unequal Voting Structures" MSCI press release, Oct. 30 2018
https://www.msci.com/documents/10199/238444/PR_Voting_Results.pdf/0b548379-fbe7-71c7-b392-7140b2215cc9

2－3 小括・議決権種類株式の利用目的・抑止を可能とする環境

　IPO 時の種類株式制度の導入動機に関するケーススタディでは[20]、無形投資の重要性の高まり、アクティビスト投資家の増加、期差式取締役会やポイズンピルのような他の経営権手段の減少が理由であるとされている。特に最後のものについては、1990 年代には、上場しようとする会社は①設立時点で敵対的買収防衛を法制化している法律や、敵対的買収の文脈ですべての関係者の利益を考慮することを行政裁判所に許し、あるいは義務づけている法律を選択することができ[21]、さらに②最近のほとんどの会社は取締役の 3 分の 1 ずつの期差式解任や、ポイズンピル（ライツプラン）の導入、合併その他の形態の企業結合に関する投票について、3 分の 2、4 分の 3 あるいは 85％といった特別多数決制度を採用するなどの手段を取ることができた。しかし、S＆P500 指数構成企業をみると、敵対的買収防衛策としての期差取締役会は 1998 年には 60％、2008 年の 34％から 2017 年の 10％に、ポイズンピルの導入は 1998 年には 59％、2008 年の 20％、2017 年の 2％へと減少している。これは、①機関投資家の資金は現在証券取引所企業の過半数株主となっており、②彼らはガバナンスへの参画を強めるなかで、株主提案を可決させることでこうした敵対的買収策を骨抜きにしてきたという事情が大きい。種類株式は、期間に制約のある買収防衛策や、特定事項についてしか支配権維持を確保できない特別多数決制度などと比べてもより恒久的で裁量性の高い制度として経営陣に期待されているといえる[22]。

　また、統計上も、恒久的な種類株式制度の存在は、業績の長期的向上を意味するものではなく、株価収益率が低いこと、ファンダメンタルズに比して取引価格が割安となること、経営陣による収奪や報酬がより高額なものにつくこと、価値破壊的な企業買収が起こりやすいことを示す研究があるとされ[23]、企業の業績への負の効果のほうが大きいことが示唆される。株価が割安となり、また長期的にも企業価値が毀損されやすい構造があるならば、IPO が一時的に強気の相場をつけたとしても、それは単に新規投資家から初期の出資者への移転を容易にするだけであり、起業家は他の方法で支配力の集中と会社全体の価値向上を図るべきように思われる。

　だが、2007 年から 2017 年までの期間において種類株式発行会社の株式のパフォーマンスはマーケット全体の成績を上回っているとの分析から、アグレッシブな成長と家族支配

---

[20] Vijay Govindarajan, Anup Srivastava "Reexamining Dual-Class Stock" Harvard Business publishing May 1, 2018 BH903-PDF-ENG.
[21] デラウエア法を選択する場合、取締役会に敵対的買収の試みに対して単にノーをいう可能性を認める判例法が確立しつつある（Air Products & Chemicals, Inc. v. Airgas, Inc. 16 A.3d 48（2011））ため、株主が魅力的と感じ交渉の時間が与えられたケースでも、買収を中断させることができる可能性が高い。
[22] "Le pouvoir des actions à droit de vote multiple" LeDevoir 1 avril 2019
https://www.ledevoir.com/opinion/idees/551124/pourquoi-les-uber-lyft-et-les-autres-se-sont-ils-entiche-des-actions-a-droit-de-vote-multiple
[23] Vijay GovindarajanShivaram RajgopalAnup SrivastavaLuminita Enache "Should Dual-Class Shares Be Banned?" Harvard Business Review, Dec. 03, 2018

との組み合わせが長期的成長をもたらすという主張も存在する[24]。ガバナンスが閉鎖的で、搾取が起こりやすい会社であっても、新規 IPO 企業が他の企業よりよいパフォーマンス水準を保つように投資家が規律をきかせることができるなら、そうした不利益は受忍されるのかもしれない。先ほど見た通り、訴訟圧力や委任状合戦が IT 企業に議決権種類株式の利用を思いとどまらせているという現象を見れば、マーケットによる調整はうまく機能しているといえそうにもみえる。

　ただし、繰り返し起きる訴訟のコストや訴訟が経営者の経営能力に与える影響を考えれば、事後的な調整はプランニング段階における調整と比較して相当程度無駄が多いように感じられる。また、どのようなマーケットでも投資家のアクションによる調整がうまくいくとは必ずしも言えず、①株主からの株主提案や訴訟を事前に阻止できない制度があること、②株主の側に訴訟を繰り返し起こすために集合し（あるいは特定の投資家に十分株式が集中しており）かつ資金を集めることができる制度があること、といった前提条件が重要であるのかもしれない。

３．ヨーロッパの長期株主優遇と議決権種類株式
３−１　背景

　ヨーロッパにおける株主権利指令では、ステュワードシップ・コード、複数議決権株式、株主総会出席への報酬や役員報酬決議への参加などが短期的視野に基づく投資に対抗する方策の文脈でまとめて整理されているという点が特徴的といえる。もともと、EU は１株１議決権原則加盟国に強制すべきかを検討していたが、2007 年の報告書で企業のパフォーマンスと関係がないとされたことでこれを断念した経緯がある[25]。逆に、2015 年５月 12 日に、欧州法務委員会に提出された株主権利指令の改正案は、中長期株主に対する優遇策の採用を各国に義務付ける 3ea 条を含んでおり[26]、これが 10 対 13 の僅差で可決された（ただし、

---

[24] "Cimitris Melas, "Putting the spotlight on Spotify: Why have stocks with unequal voting rights outperformed?" MSCI Blog Apr3,2018

[25] 岩谷賢伸（2007）「一株一議決権原則は貫徹されるべきか〜欧州委員会による『EU 上場企業の資本と支配の均整』に関する調査報告〜」『資本市場クォータリー』2007 年 Summer p96 以下。当時は非公開中小企業において、コンプライアンスコストを減らす策として複数議決権株式が捉えられていた。（Commissioner Charlie McCreevy speech to Parliament Legal Affairs Committee on 3 October 2017）

[26] "on the proposal for a directive of the European Parliament and of the Council amending Directive 2007/36/EC as regards the encouragement of long-term shareholder engagement and Directive 2013/34/EU as regards certain elements of the corporate governance statement" (COM(2014)0213 – C7 0147/2014 – 2014/0121(COD)), May 12.2015 p33.
(http://www.europarl.europa.eu/doceo/document/A-8-2015-0158_EN.pdf)
　　Article 3 ea　　Support for long-term shareholding
Member States shall put in place a mechanism in order to promote shareholding on a long-term basis and foster long-term shareholders. Members State shall define the qualifying period in order to be considered a long term shareholder, but this period shall

多くの質問を集め物議を醸したため、その後の草案および 2017 年 3 月 14 日欧州議会本会議可決の株主権利指令（SRDⅡ）からは落とされた）という出来事が耳目を集めた。長期株主によるどのようなガバナンス参画が望ましいか、そして長期的な参画を自由に実現させてよいかに自体にもいろいろな議論があるが[27]、長期的な参加を促すための手段として複数議決権株式が適切なのかという問題もそれはそれとして存在しうる。

3－2　フランス法の複数議決権制度

上記のとおり EU においては、複数議決権株式は上記のとおり長期株主創出制度の一つとして挙げられたが、EU 構成国は複数株式ないし黄金株式が存在しない国（イギリス）、存在する国（デンマーク、フィンランド、オランダ、スウェーデン、デンマーク[28]）、かつて導入されたものの廃止された国（イタリア、オーストリア、スペインおよびドイツ）に分かれる[29]。現在の 1 株 1 議決権原則の普及は、この複数議決権制度が定着し維持されている国かどうかによって大きく差があり、2005 年 3 月の ヨーロッパでの「一株一票」の原則の適用に関する報告書で、Deminor キャビネットは、上場企業の 65％がこの原則を適用していると述べるが、これはドイツでは 97％、イギリスでは 88％、スペインでは 59％であるのに対し、複数議決権制度を持つスイスでは 59％、フランスでは 31％、スウェーデンでは 25％、オランダでは 14％であった。

このうちフランスでは、近年話題になったフロランジュ法により商法典を改正し、定款による排除がない限り上場会社においては複数議決権株式制度をデフォルトとしている[30]。

---

not be less than two years.

The mechanism referred to in the first subparagraph shall include one or more of the following advantages for long term shareholders:
- additional voting rights;
- tax incentives;
- loyalty dividends;
- loyalty shares

[27] Alessio M. Pacces, "Hedge Fund Activism and the Revision of the Shareholder Rights Directive" ecgi Law Working Paper No.353/2017, April 2017.

[28] フィンランドでは、この方式による議決権の上限は資本株式（普通株式）の 20 倍に達しうる。多くの加盟国はまた「特殊株」または「黄金株」を導入しており、それによって加盟国は民営化された会社の資本に 1 株を保有することによって、資本提携を承認し、社会的組織の中心に国家の代表者を任命し、あるいは資産の譲渡に反対することができる。

[29] La bataille des centres de décision : promouvoir la souveraineté économique de la France à l'heure de la mondialisation (rapport)　ⅡA２c *at* note 340.
http://www.senat.fr/notice-rapport/2006/r06-347-1-notice.html

[30]　Code de Commerce Article L225-123
　　Modifié par LOI n°2014-384 du 29 mars 2014 - art. 7 (V)
Un droit de vote double de celui conféré aux autres actions, eu égard à la quotité de capital social qu'elles représentent, peut être attribué, par les statuts à toutes les actions entièrement libérées pour lesquelles il sera justifié d'une inscription nominative, depuis deux ans au moins, au nom du même actionnaire.

フランスは伝統的に複数議決権を認めるかどうかについて激しい変遷をたどってきた国である。1867年7月24日の法律第27条は、株式の数は議決権の票の算定の基礎であり、原則として各株式は同じ数の議決権を有するものとしていたが、1903年11月16日法は、「定款の規定に反しない限り、優先株式やその他の株式は株主総会において平等な議決権を有する」とし、企業に優先株創設を許可し、この優先権には複数議決権の権利が含まれうるとされていた[31]。この制度は銀行などによって導入されたが、一部でこの株式設計の自由が悪用され、複数議決権株式に対する反対が金融界で生じたため、1930年4月26日の金融法が優先議決権を付した株式発行を禁止し、1933年11月13日法は、「株主総会において、株式に付着する議決権はその株式が表章する資本の割合に必ず比例しなければならない」という原則を確認したうえで爾後二重議決権を有する株式を以外の優先株式の創設を禁止した[32]。この無議決権株式および2倍以外の複数議決権株式[33]の禁止の原則が1966年7月24日商事会社法174条を経て現在に引き継がれたという[34]。

　また、1929年1月23日の法律により導入された「創設者持分」または「受益持分」（parts bénéficiaires / parts de fondateur）という制度がある[35]。会社の特定の創設者によってな

En outre, en cas d'augmentation du capital par incorporation de réserves, bénéfices ou primes d'émission, le droit de vote double peut être conféré, dès leur émission, aux actions nominatives attribuées gratuitement à un actionnaire à raison d'actions anciennes pour lesquelles il bénéficie de ce droit.

Dans les sociétés dont les actions sont admises aux négociations sur un marché réglementé, les droits de vote double prévus au premier alinéa sont de droit, sauf clause contraire des statuts adoptée postérieurement à la promulgation de la loi n° 2014-384 du 29 mars 2014 visant à reconquérir l'économie réelle, pour toutes les actions entièrement libérées pour lesquelles il est justifié d'une inscription nominative depuis deux ans au nom du même actionnaire. Il en est de même pour le droit de vote double conféré dès leur émission aux actions nominatives attribuées gratuitement en application du deuxième alinéa.

[31] 嘉野敏夫「フランスに於ける議決権株に就て」法学新報56巻，2頁（1949年）
[32] 「フランス法における株式と議決権をめぐる 近時の展開」118頁。
[33] 1966年法175条1項は、「同一株主の名義で少なくとも2年間の記名登録が証明される全ての全額払込済株式（les actions entierement lib à erá ees á ）に対し、定款またはその後の特別株主総会（une assemblee g á ená erale extraordinaire á ）により、その表章する資本の持分を考慮し、他の株式に与えられた議決権の2倍の議決権が付与され得る」と規定する。
[34] Raport supra note 29 footnote 335、斎藤雅代「フランス法における株式と議決権をめぐる近時の展開について」山梨学院大学法学論集80号　P118
[35] 第1条
1　株式事業会社は、創設時または後日に、「創設者株式」または「受益権 」の名の下に、譲渡性のある有価証券を作成、割り当て、および発行することができる。
2　株式資本の範囲外にあるこれらの証券は、その所有者に組織のパートナーとしての資格を与えるものではない。しかし、所有者はそれら証券によって会社に対する残余財産請求権、利益に対する固定的または比例的権利を与えられることができる。
3　同じ会社内に、平等でない権利を持つ、異なる種類の創設者株式または受益者株式を

された現物出資と引き換えに発行され、その後株式に転換されるものとして、創設者株式は特定の受益者に権利を与えるが、最終的な清算の際の残余財産を除き、資本に対する所有権を構成するものではなく、また会社の経営に対する何らの決定権も持たない。異なる権利を持つ異なる種類の創設者株式が発行され、付与される可能性がある。だがこれもまたその後に 1966 年商事会社法 264 条が新規発行を禁止したため、絶滅の危機に瀕しているという[36]。

現在、SAS という簡略な会社形態においては複数議決権が認められているが、そうした形態の会社は公募を行うことが禁じられている[37]。一方、公開有限会社は複数議決権株式を構築する自由を制限されており、商法典 L.225-122 条第 1 段落は、「資本株式または享益株式（actions de jouissance）に付着する議決権は、それらの株式が表章する資本の割合に比例し、かつ、各株式が少なくとも議決権をともなうものとする」ことを規定する。その例外は、定款によって一人の株主が株主総会で行使する票の数を制限することが認められる場合（L.225-125）[38]、および特定の客観的基準を満たす株主のロイヤリティに報いるために、優先株として、2 重議決権のみが認められる場合である（L225-123）。近年では議決権種類株式を容認する改正が行われ、法に定める条件を順守することで優先株を作成することが認められているなか、2004 年 6 月 24 日のオルドナンスによる商法典の改正により、議決権の有無を優先株の内容として定めることができるようになった。現在では無議決権株式も、会社資本の過半数を超えない範囲（上場会社においては 4 分の 1 を超えない範囲）で認められる（L.228-11、L.228-12）[39]。

一方、拒否権付き株式は、1986 年の民営化に関する法律[40]により導入され、同法律によればデクレによって国益保護の要請により国有の株式の権利が特別の権利に転換されることが決定され、それ以降当該証券保有者にその特別な権利が与えられることが規定されていた。商法 L.225-96 および 98 において公序良俗に反しない限り認められており、ここか

存在させることができる。各種類は異なる集団を形成する。
4 株式の所有者の権利は、株式会社の定款またはその後の株式創設にかかる株主総会の審議において決定される。
[36] 現在、このタイプの証券が発行できるのは公開有限会社のみであり（Art.483,453）、SPRL では禁止されている（Art.232）。
[37] SAS に関する商法の L.227-1 条は、SAS に適用される同法の L.225-122 条（上記参照）を明示的に除外している。
[38] 斎藤・前掲注 34・117 頁
[39] 2004 年 6 月 24 日の改正以前の優先株式（actions de priorité）の「優先」の内容は多様であったが、議決権の制限に関しては、議決権のない優先配当株式（actions à dividende prioritaire sans droit de vote）という形のみ認められていた。2004 年 6 月 24 日のオルドナンスによる改正で新たな優先株式（actions de préférence）が導入され、この優先株式は「議決権を有しまたは有さない」ものと定められた（商法典 L.228-11 条第 1 項）。斎藤・前掲注 34・114 頁。
[40] loi n° 86-912 du 6 août 1986 relative aux modalités des privatisations, modifié par l'article 3 de l'ordonnance n° 2000-912 du 18 septembre 2000

ら支配を維持する要請がある国家のみがこれを利用できるとされていた[41]。後述する ECJ 判決で問題となった民営化企業ではこの制度が用いられている。

3－3　複数議決権株式制度導入の影響

　フロランジュ法の分析に当たっては、長期保有による議決権付与という構造自体の影響と、その導入手法の特殊性による影響を分けて考えなくてはならない。前者については、どの株主に保有されていても保有期間が長くなればその株主に複数議決権をもたらす‐それとともに議決権総数をも恒常的に変動させる‐優先株式という制度が、投資家の行動（株価、投資規模や期間、ガバナンスへの参加態様）および経営陣の行動（ガバナンスの充実度、リスク水準、事業成績）にどのような影響を及ぼすかが問題となる。

　長期保有により複数議決権を獲得した株式は優先株式となると解されている。しかし、この株式も、流通市場での取得段階では普通株式である。投資家側は投資価値を判断して株式を購入するが、取得時点ではより低い価値しかない（議決権数が少ない）ので、長期短期いずれの保有を目的とした取得だったと説明するかによって取得判断の経済的合理性が分かれる事態になりそうである。また、他の株主が長期株主に該当したり資格を失ったりしうるので、買った株式が結局何パーセントの議決権を構成するのかが恒常的にわからないという問題もありうる。

　しかし、この制度は従来から存在しており、またフロランジュ法導入に際して投資家の保有期間の短期化トレンドに変化は生じていないとされる[42]。つまり、米国で投資家が無議決権株式をも積極的に買うのと同様、フランスでも議決権の数は投資家の取得・売却の判断に影響を与えておらず、ガバナンスへの参画態様も変わっていない可能性がある。

　投資家の行動に変化をもたらさないとしても、この制度は、経営陣の側には大きな変化をもたらす可能性がある。この制度が IPO において導入される場合には、支配権争奪に際して既存の支配株主に時間と手段を与え、支配権維持を強固にする効果を持つからである。投資家が議決権（支配権）の獲得を目的としていても、取得初年度に既存の支配株主との協力に失敗すれば、買収防衛のための対抗策を取られてしまう[43]。したがって、買収のリス

---

[41] David BABIN et Guillaume CLUNIAT "Action et pouvoir dans les sociétés cotées" p23.(http://memoire.jm.u-psud.fr/affiche_memoire.php?fich=7934&diff=public)
[42] Loyalty Shares with Tenure Voting - A Coasian Bargain? Evidence from the Loi Florange Experiment (April 2018). European Corporate Governance Institute (ECGI) - Law Working Paper No. 398/2018. Available at SSRN:
https://ssrn.com/abstract=3166494 or http://dx.doi.org/10.2139/ssrn.3166494 figure 5.
[43] フランスの公開買付制度は、通貨金融法典（Code monétaire et financier）L433-1 条から L433-4 条にその大枠が規定され、これらの規定の委任を受けた AMF の一般規則（Règlement Général de L'autorité des MarchésFinanciers）第 2 分冊（Livre II）第 3 章（規則 234 各条）や商法典において、その詳細が規定されている。内容についてはヨーロッパ M&A 制度研究会報告書（2010．日本証券経済研究所）15 頁以下参照。振り分けとして、一般規則 234-1 により閾値の算定方法は商法典 L233-7 および 233－9 に定められるとしており、商法典のこれらの条文が閾値を超えた場合に a.株式取得者が取得目的を告知

クが高い企業はこの制度を積極的に用いるであろう。二倍議決権制度導入率は 37%であったのに対し、法導入後は 54%になったといい、IPO をする会社はこの制度を以前より高い頻度で用いていることがわかる[44]。

　一方、既存の企業が新たにこの制度を導入する場合には、まったく違う分配が実現する。フランス法上、通常、ある種類株式の名義人の権利を変更しうる株主総会の決定は、当該種類株主の種類株主総会による承認の後にのみ確定する（L. 225-99 条）。従って、議決権種類株式制度は導入すれば廃止が困難であり[45]、同制度の導入は気軽に試せるようなものではないことになる。また、株主が上場会社の議決権の 3 分の 1 以上を保有した場合は株式の強制買付制度の対象となるが[46]、長期保有による議決権増加の場合も（除外期間を除いて）例外ではない。フランスの上場会社における議決権の分布は、この制度があるため、ほとんどが創業者などが最初から多くの長期保有株式を有しており、長期保有に利益を有している場合か、分散した株主が多く各々にとって長期保有に目立った利益がない場合かに分けられることになろう。あえて議決権種類株式制度の導入が戦われる場合としては、支配株主が議決権の 3 分の 1 を持たず、支配株主に近い株式数を有する少数株主がいるような場合が考えられる[47]。実証分析によれば、既存の上場会社 45 社中 31 社は単独議決権を選んでオプトアウトをし、14 社は 2 倍議決権制度導入会社となり（うち定款変更に失敗したものは 7 社）、当初からこれを導入していた 58 社はそのままにとどまったとされる[48]。

する義務やb.会社による実質的権利者の追求などを定めている。前者に続いて取られる対抗策としてはそれほど強力なものは認められておらず、株式無償割当てが行われるが買収者側の買付撤回が認められうるという。後者については、運用においても、ほとんどのフランスの上場会社では、定款により、無記名証券の背後に誰がいるのかを調べる権限を会社に与えているという（2001 年改正以降、商法典 L.228-2 により、会社が最初に見つけた受益者が真の受益者ではないと思われる場合には会社が真の受益者を発見するまで調査を続ける。（「フランスにおける企業買収ルールの解釈と運用──市場慣行との相克・買収防衛策に関する論点を中心として（フランス M&A 弁護士との対話）──」早法 86 巻 4 号（2011）P306）。結果的に潜在的買収者はかなり早い段階で洗い出されると思われる。
[44] Becht, Kamisarenka and Pajuste, *supra* note40, table 8.
[45] 相続等については、1933 年法以降、1966 年法を通じても当然に 2 倍議決権の継承または期間の継続が認められると解され、一方吸収合併の場合については従来は継続が認められないと解されていたが、2008 年 8 月 4 日法により、2 倍議決権は会社分割・合併による移転に際しても、会社の定款に反対の定めがあるときを除いて消滅しないとされたため、2 倍議決権を保有する株主は、成立すれば処分以外では権利を失うことはない（L225-124）横沢恭平「複数議決権制度に関する一考察」法学研究論集 49 号（2018.9）152 頁。
[46] AMF（Autorite de Marches Financiers）一般規則　Article 234-2 により、最低買付数を定めずに公開買付の提案を行うことが義務付けられている。
[47] たとえば、支配株主が 6/20 株、少数株主が 4/20 株、短期株主が 10/20 株を有しているような会社では、株式制度変更後の保有の分布は各 12/30 株、8/30 株、10/30 株となり、特別多数決の成立が以前に比べて困難となる。
[48] Becht, Kamisarenka and Pajuste, *supra* note 40 figure 3.

3－4　フロランジュ法導入手法の特殊性

　従来 2 倍議決権制度を導入できなかった 45 社中 7 社が同制度の導入阻止に失敗したという数は、少なくないように思われる。こうした会社の業績面での特色として Tobin の Q の値が低いことが挙げられるが[49]、より大きな要因は導入当時の株主構成にある[50]。フロランジュ法の導入直後には少ない資金で拒否権を手に入れることができるチャンスが生まれていたことで、少数株主が長期保有株主となることを新たに選んだといった可能性もあるだろう[51]。

　定款変更を阻止するためには出席株主の議決権の 3 分の 1 を取得することができればよい。そこでたとえば、2015 年 4 月にフランス政府は証券会社とルノー株式を最大 1400 万株追加取得するという合意を結び、2015 年 4 月 8 日までに約 8 億~12 億ユーロかけて 956 万株を取得し、保有比率を一時的に従来の 15.01%から最終的に 19.74%まで引き上げた（基準日は総会の 2 日前[52]）。株主総会後にプットオプションを用いて最低価格を保証したうえで持株比率を再び 15%に引き下げたという[53]。この事例は、政府に限らず一定の株式を保有している少数株主は、この時期に限り非常に少ない負担で自己のプレゼンスを拡大できたことを示唆する。フランス政府の狙いの一つとして、財政赤字を削減するために 50~100 億ユーロ規模の政府資産を売却しつつ企業に対する発言力を維持することが挙げられている[54]。短期株主の層の厚さが不変であれば、2 倍議決権さえ一度成立すれば、従来同様の議決権割合はより少ない持株数で維持できるので、複数議決権制度はその導入時点で企業の支配株主および有力少数株主に余剰部分の売却というプレミアム（このプレミアムは事業のシナジーではなく、他者に分配されることはない）を手にすることができる。

　また、本来であれば、他の優先株式が存在する場合の優先株主による反対、あるいは買付提案を強制されるリスクが増えることなど、少数株主が 2 倍議決権制度の導入に動くのをためらわせるはずの他の要素も、同法の施行時には機能を停止させられている。フランス商法典上、ある優先株式の名義人の権利を変更しうる株主総会の決定は、当該優先株式の種類株主総会の承認の後にのみ確定する（L 225-99）。しかし、法による 2 倍議決権導入の場合は、そのための株主総会決議が存在しないし、その後の長期保有による優先株式の株主の数の変動も承認の対象とならない。また、前述のとおり資本または議決権の 3 分の 1

---

[49] *Id.* Table2.
[50] *Id.* Table7.
[51] *Id* Table 9
[52] EU 法（2007 年の株主権利指令）の要請にもとづく 2014 年 12 月日のデクレにより商法典 R.225-85 条が改正され、基準日を株主総会 2 就業日前と定めた。斎藤・前掲注 34・128 頁。
[53] 「仏政府がルノー株買い増しで発言権拡大狙う、日産連合にも影響か」ロイター2015 年 4 月 8 日 https://jp.reuters.com/article/france-idJPKBN0MZ0MU20150408; 松本惇「2 倍議決権を義務付けたフランス」みずほ総研　みずほインサイト・欧州　2015 年 6 月 17 日
https://www.mizuho-ri.co.jp/publication/research/pdf/insight/eu150617.pdf
[54] *Id* at p2.

を超える持ち分を有することとなる株主は、資本・議決権への権利を有する全証券に対して買付を提案する義務がある（AMF 一般規則 Article234-2）。しかし、フロランジュ法により 2014 年 4 月 3 日から 2018 年 12 月 31 日までの間に二倍議決権を割り当てられた場合については、公開買付義務は免除されているし[55]、すでに会社を支配している株主が複数議決権導入により議決権を維持しつつ資本参加を減らすような持株割合変動に際してもこの義務は適用されない[56]。

3－3　資本の移動の自由との葛藤

　この制度が、長期の一般株主創出という正当化根拠に欠け、一部株主の利益（支配株主の持株割合を高めたり有力株主に余剰の売却機会や支配株主を阻止する発言力）を与えるだけであるならば、そのような制度は一般投資家に不利益を及ぼす。最初に 2 倍議決権株式を保有することとなった支配株主がその株式を手放さない限り、その構造はアメリカで問題とされる議決権種類株式と結局同種のものとなるから、アメリカにおけると同種の批判が起きてもよいように思われる。しかし、この制度を導入する政府はたまたま受益者でもあるため、規制庁側にこうした法の導入に反対するインセンティブは生じにくい。そこで、投資家が特定の国への投資において自由を制約されるようなことがないように配慮する EU なかんずく ECJ が何らかの介入を行う可能性が考えられる。

　従来、EU 構成国の政府が特定の企業の経営に介入しようとする場合には、よりストレートに目的を達成することができる黄金株制度を特別法によって作り出すのが一般的であった。各国が民営化を進めた結果として 1990 年代から多数の黄金株に関する紛争が生ずることとなった。ECJ はこうした事件を審理してきたが[57]、とりわけ 2002 年 6 月 4 日に、欧州委員会が資本移動の自由の観点などから[58]問題があると考えて提訴した各国の規制に対する 3 つの判断により、「黄金株」を設定することのできる上限を明確に定めたと理解されている[59]。第一は Le décret français n° 93-1298 号がフランス政府に Elf アキテーヌ会社にお

---

[55] AMF 一般規則　Article234-9 no10 により、強制公開買付の例外とされている。
[56] Raport *supra* note 29 footnote 345
[57] 以下で取り上げる事案も含め、ECJ 判決の分析は上田純子「EU「黄金株」事件・再考」（EYIJ-Kyushu Review, Issue1 －2011）による。
[58] 黄金株に関する判例では、資本の移動の自由に関する判断基準のもととなる 1997 年コミュニケーション基準（Communication of the Commission on certain legal aspects concerning intra-EU investment［1997］OJC 220/06）違反、かつ、それを法制化した EC 条約 52 条（TFEU49 条、差別的措置の禁止）ないし 58 条（TFEU54 条）、および、73b 条（TFEU63 条　資本移動制限を禁止する。ただし同規定は加盟国の公序・公共の安全の見地から正当化される措置を取る権利を侵害するものであってはならない）違反が主張される。また、同 55 条（TFEU51 条）、56 条（TFEU52 条）、73d 条（TFEU65 条）の除外事由に該当せず、また不可避的要請や政府裁量権の範囲に関する周知の基準によっても正当化できない旨が主張される。
[59] 341 CJCE, 4 juin 2002, Commission CE c/République française ; Commission CE c/République portugaise ; Commission CE c/Royaume de Belgique.

ける特別な株式を認めたもの、第二はポルトガル法 n° 11/90 がポルトガル政府に民営化会社における外国人投資家の影響を軽減することを認めたもので、これらの法は、資本の自由な移動に対する侵害と見なされたのに対し、第三の判決においては、国立パイプライン運輸公社と Distrigas について国に特別な株式を認めた2つのベルギーの規制は資本の自由な移動と両立すると考えられた。

ECJ は、こうした事例においては、①規制が形式的には非差別措置ではあっても他の加盟国からの投資を委縮させる効果を有するならば資本の自由移動の規定に抵触する、②①にもかかわらず当該措置が正当化されうる場合として、a 除外事由にあたる場合または b 一般的利益保護についての不可避的要請がある場合であって、比例性原則を満たしかつ当該事業に知悉される非差別的・客観的基準と当該措置から不利益を受ける者すべてに法的救済措置とが用意されている場合が挙げられる、とする。

フランスの黄金株に関しては、非差別措置である 1993 年第 1298 号デクレ 2 条 1 項について、国家の危急存亡時の石油供給の確保は不可避的要請としての正当な公益保護にあたり、また 73d 条（判決時 58 条；TFEU65 条）1 項 b の列挙する除外事由に該当する、②資本の自由移動を凌駕しうる「公共の安全」は厳格に解釈されなければならず、共同体諸機関の介入なく加盟国が一方的に定めうる性格のものではなく、社会の基本的利益への「真の（genuine）」「十分に重大な（sufficiently serious）」危険があるときに限り援用され[60]かつ③比例性原則を満たさなければならず、これらに反する場合には資本の自由な移動を定めた EC 条約 56 条（当時）に違反するとし、フランスのデクレ規定は、比例性を有しないと判示した。ポルトガル事件では、資本の自由移動への制限の直接的帰結として開業の自由に関する諸規定の違反がもたらされるとしており、フランスの事例でも同様のことが言えるであろう。

フランス事件で比例性が否定された根拠は、介入関連規定は大臣の承認の基準を設定しておらず経済大臣は自由に裁量権を行使でき、その結果、投資家は、承認が得られるか否かについての見通しを持つことができず、このことは、経済大臣の事前承認権であろうと、異議申立権であろうと変わるところはない、というものであった。逆に、ベルギーの規制が違反でないとされたのは、主務大臣のイニシアチブで異議申立手続が開始されるわけではなく、介入できるのは国のエネルギー政策に重大な危険が迫ったときであり、かつエネルギー大臣は自己の決定について書面により理由書を作成して取締役会に通告せねばならず、かつ、当該決定は司法審査に服するという要素による。

多数の判決を通じて定式化された ECJ の判例法は、加盟国に民営化された事業の支配権を与えるすべての国内規定に影響する。だが、この判例法は、以下の点で歴史的経緯[61]や国

---

[60] ECJ 判例法における Cassis de Dijon 原則により、「一般的利益保護」のための政府の介入は直接公共の利益に関係するものでなければならない。
[61] ルノー社は、もともと第 2 次世界大戦までは軍事産業を含めた国策企業として発展し、ドイツへの協力という経緯を経て、戦後（1945 年）にその資産を国に没収され行政命令で「ルノー公団」として国有化されたという歴史を持っている。その後、経営の効率化を目

内雇用[62]などの要請により事業会社の経営に介入しているフランスの態度には一致しない。

① ECJ は、エネルギーや通信などでなく純然たる経済的・経営的性質の事業（タバコ・銀行など）については、EC 条約上の基本的自由への制限を正当化しうる一般的利益をそもそも有しないとの解釈を示している。エネルギーや通信など国家のインフラに関わる基盤産業であったとしても、かかる民営化会社が、単体または子会社やグループ会社等を通じていわゆる多国籍企業化している場合にも、加盟国経済に関する戦略的役務提供の維持に関わらないので、正当化の前提を欠くという[63]。

② 優先的権利は、大きく、a）株式譲渡および議決権取得に関するもの、b）役員の選任に関するもの、ならびに、c）b）以外の会社の基本的意思決定に関するもの、の３つに分けられるが、ECJ 判決は個別の権利内容を吟味してそれが許容されうるかどうかを判定しており、優先権が異議申立権などのような形で与えられているかによる画一的判断はしていない。

③ 特定の企業のガバナンスに政策的な目的から介入すること自体を認める場合も、具体的な介入行為に対しては、どのような理由・基準に基づいてどの程度その介入権が行使されるのかの事前予測が可能である必要があるとされている。

　以上からすれば、従業員が多いからという理由で介入対象を選定することも、雇用が維持されるように状況に応じて議決権を行使することも、ECJ の考え方からは正当化される可能性は低い。フロランジュ法制定時の元老院の趣旨説明は、特に、欧州議会において ECJ の黄金株に関する判例法を、資本移動の自由を制限する効果を持つ複数議決権株式に拡大することについて賛成する声が提起されていることに触れ、警戒を示している。そのため、フロランジュ法制定にあたり、元老院は、EU 法・公開買付指令が、ECJ 判決を黄金株に関する分野を超えて拡張することを認めていないと強く主張している。また、一般的な枠

指して 1996 年に民営化されるに際しても、フランス政府が持株を維持してきたという経緯がある。

[62] 「閉鎖される事業所の売却先探しなどの義務を強化 ―フロランジュ法による大統領公約の法制化」労働政策研究・検収機構　海外労働情報　国別労働トピック 2014 年 4 月
https://www.jil.go.jp/foreign/jihou/2014_4/france_01.html
　もともと、フロランジュ法は 2011 年に鉄鋼最大手アルセロール・ミッタル社のフランス北東部モーゼル県フロランジュ製鉄所の閉鎖が発表された際に、オランド大統領候補（当時）が大統領選キャンペーン中に従業員の解雇問題が生じていた同製鉄所を訪問して対処を約束したものであり、工場閉鎖に関する介入は株主たる地位を介してのものではないため、黄金株に関する判例には含まれないが、同法については、制定時に企業の自由な事業活動を大幅に侵害する内容だとして野党により憲法評議会への審査請求がなされた。憲法評議会の判断は 3 月 27 日に下され、企業が経営環境の悪化への対応を柔軟に行えなくなる懸念があり、企業経営の自由という原則に抵触するとの判断に基づき、制裁条項の削除命令を下した。ただし、「売却先を探す義務」と「従業員代表に通知する義務」は残されており、労組はこれを根拠として商事裁判所に提訴することができるため、新法の施行によって事業所閉鎖の手続きは従来よりも複雑になると懸念する見方もある。
[63] 上田・前掲注 55・40 頁参照。

組みとしての公開買付の強制制度が存在すること、支配株主が当該株式を売却する意思があれば支配権獲得は成立するので、支配構造は固着化していないこと、無条件に長期保有の株主に対して 2 倍議決権を与えたり、特定の株式を複数議決権付のものとすることではないので、特定の株主グループを優先しているわけではないこと、SAS やアメリカ[64]でも許容されていることを挙げている[65]。

　もっとも、その前年に出された判決は、ECJ による介入の緩和を示唆するかもしれない。2007 年にフォルクスワーゲンに介入するドイツ法（連邦およびザクセン州が 20%ずつ株式を支配し、10 人の取締役のうち 2 人ずつを選任する。また、他の株主の投票権を 20%までに制限し、決議要件を 5 分の 4 に引き上げる）が EC 条約 56 条（TFEU63 条）1 項に違反するとされた（ちなみにもし 4 分の 3 であれば政府の支配に干渉できる余地があるとされている）のに対し、判決後もドイツ政府が VW 法上議決権要件を維持し（VW 社が定款に同等の規定を置き）、さらに 20%キャップについては VW 法上の同内容の規定が削除されたあと 9 か月の間 VW 社が定款の規定を置いていたという状況に対して再度提訴が行われ、2013 年に判決が出された[66]。それによれば、2007 年判決の射程は法に関するもので定款には関係ない（para 26）、また議決権要件は 20%キャップと相まって制限的効果を生じていたもので、以前の判決は議決権要件が単独で資本の移動の自由の侵害になるかどうかについて判決していない（para 45）とされている。また、オランダが EU 指令に基づくガス・電気の輸送事業の分割に際して、輸送企業側をも国営化するよう法改正したことについても、条約は民営化・国営化のいずれの選択をも排除しておらず（para30）、ただし資本の移動の自由を侵害しないという要件は満たす必要があるため（para36）、正当化事由及び相当性について判断するとした。そのうえで、立法根拠としてのエネルギー供給の安定性・消費者保護といった目的はガス電気指令に沿うもので公益として正当化根拠となりうる（para66）とした[67]。

　複数議決権株式自体は定款により選択されたものであること、導入に際して政府の支配が完全になるよう保証されていたわけでもないことなどからすれば、フランスが導入したタイプの複数議決権株式について、ECJ が黄金株に対するのと同様の分析を行うことは困難かもしれない。

4　日本における運用
4－1　IPO 時点での議決権種類株式と創業者利益

我が国においては、上場会社が種類株式を発行する例として、古くから石油公団参加の特殊法人であった国際石油開発株式会社（INPEX）が民営化後上場の際に拒否権を設定され

---

[64] デラウェア一般法人法§§ 151 (a)、221 (a)「不均衡投票株式」や NASDAQ と NYSE もセクション 5640 および 313.00 を援用している。
[65] Babin et Cluniat, *supra* note 41, at p20.
[66] Commission v Germany (C-95/12)
[67] Commission v Essent (C-105/12)

た例が挙げられてきた[68]。また、創業者が自発的に創出した議決権種類株式制度として、日本発のロボットメーカーであるサイバーダイン（ＣＹＢＥＲＤＹＮＥ）社が 2014 年 3 月 26 日にマザーズに上場を承認された際、他企業に買収されるリスク回避などをも念頭に創業者山海氏の保有割合を高く保った（発行済株式総数ベースでは合計約 43％、議決権ベースでは約 88％）ことが注目された[69]。この株式においては、普通株式に決議事項制限はないが、種類株主保持者間での株式譲渡は普通株式への転換のトリガーとならないことや、普通株式・種類株式ともに追加発行についての制限がなく両者の相対的割合が変動しうることなどが注目されよう[70]。

東京証券取引所は、弊害防止措置を制度に落とし込むにあたり[71]、「上場株式が備えるべ

---

[68] この拒否権は、ＩＮＰＥＸの普通株式議決権の２０％以上を第三者が保有していた場合のＩＮＰＥＸの取締役の選任・解任、ＩＮＰＥＸまたは子会社の重要な資産の処分等、議決権の付与に関する定款変更、ＩＮＰＥＸ普通株式議決権の２０％以上を第三者が保有することになる合併・株式交換・株式移転、ＩＮＰＥＸ株主への金銭の払い戻しを伴うＩＮＰＥＸの資本の額の減少、ＩＮＰＥＸ株主総会決議による当会社の解散　に対して行使できるものとされている。

[69] CD 社の 2014 年 2 月 19 日付け有価証券届出書及びその添付書類たる定款によれば、同社が投資家向けに売り出す普通株式及び創業者ならびにその設立した財団に割り当てる B 種類株式の概要及び異同は以下のとおりである。

剰余金の配当及び残余財産の分配については、普通株式と B 種類株式は同順位かつ同額である。株式の分割や併合、株式無償割当て、単元株式数の変更等は、普通株式及び B 種類株式ごとに、すべて同時に同一の割合で行う。一方、普通株式も B 種類株式も、全ての株主総会決議事項について議決権を行使できるが、議決権数は、普通株式 100 株につき 1 議決権に対し、B 種類株式 10 株につき 1 議決権である（※単元株式数を、普通株式につき 100 株、B 種類株式につき 10 株とすることで、これを実現している）。会社法 322 条 1 項各号に掲げる行為については、法令又は定款に別段の定めがある場合を除き、普通株主を構成員とする種類株主総会の決議を要しないこととしている。（B 種類株式についてはそのような定めはない）。

<u>譲渡性について、B 種類株主間の譲渡でない限り（株主変動抑制条項）、譲渡には取締役会の承認を要するとされる</u>。普通株式は公開市場で流通するため制限はない。転換については、B 種類株主は、いつでも、会社に対し、B 種類株式 1 株と引き替えに、普通株式 1 株の交付を請求できる（普通株式には取得請求権はない）。

また、①会社が消滅会社となる合併や完全子会社となる株式交換などの M&A、②公開買付による買付者所有株式数が 75％を超えるとき（ブレイクスルー条項）、③創業者である山海氏退任後最初の年度以降 5 年以内ごとに行われる「株主意思確認手続」において、確認手続基準日に議決権を行使することができる株主の議決権の 3 分の 1 以上を有する株主の意思が確認でき、意思を確認した当該株主の議決権（いずれの種類株式も単元株式数を 100 株とみなして計算）の 3 分の 2 以上に当たる多数が B 株式から普通株式への転換に賛成したとき（サンセット条項）、④<u>B 種類株式の譲渡承認請求がなされた場合</u>、⑤B 種類株主死亡後 90 日の経過の各場合について、B 種類株式 1 株と引き替えに、普通株式 1 株が交付される（取得条項）旨が定められている。

[70] 松尾拓也「議決権種類株式を用いた我が国初の上場事例の登場～強制公開買付規制の種類株式への適用について望まれる解釈の明確化～」
https://judiciary.asahi.com/outlook/2014033100002.html

[71] 2006（平成 18）年 1 月 24 日　「買収防衛策の導入に係る上場制度の整備等について」

き基本的かつ重要な権利が著しく損なわれる状態となった上場会社が、6か月以内に当該状態を解消しない場合には、上場を廃止する」とし、「拒否権付種類株式のうち、取締役の過半数の選解任その他の重要な事項について種類株主総会の決議を要する旨の定めがなされたものの発行（会社の事業目的、拒否権付種類株式の発行目的、割当対象者の属性及び権利内容その他の条件に照らして、株主及び投資者の利益を侵害するおそれが少ないと当取引所が認める場合を除く）」場合はこれに該当するとしたうえ、さらに①「持株会社に該当する上場会社の主要な事業を行っている子会社が拒否権付種類株式又は取締役選任付種類株式を当該上場会社以外のものに発行する場合で、その種類株式の発行が当該上場会社に対する買収の実現を困難にする方策であると認められる場合」を上場会社における拒否権付種類株式発行と同等に扱う可能性があることと、「既上場会社が新たに拒否権付種類株式を発行する場合については、既存の一般株主の利益が侵害されるおそれが大きいため、上場廃止基準の例外の適用は慎重に行」うことを述べている[72]。

政策の流れとしては、2013年6月に新規ビジネス創出を促すためのリスクマネーの供給促進を掲げる「日本再興戦略-JAPAN is BACK-」が閣議決定され、また同年12月に出された金融審議会「新規・成長企業へのリスクマネーの供給のあり方等に関するワーキング・グループ」の報告書でも、新規・成長企業の出口戦略を多様化するためのIPO活性化策等がうたわれており、証券取引所としてもこうした株式の審査基準の明確化により利用を促す方針と考えられる[73]。

確かに、機関投資家側がIPOによる利益の短期的分配に高い関心を持つこともあるし、また国内のIT企業の創業者に上場によって有利に資金にアクセスできる機会を与えるべきだとの議論も考えられる。国内市場への上場という条件を捨象して考えると、そのような

および同年3月7日「買収防衛策の導入に係る上場制度の整備等に伴う株券上場審査基準等の一部改正について」6頁参照。

[72] 東証の有価証券上場規程207条及び214条では、本則市場及びマザーズへの新規上場申請が行われた株券等の上場審査項目が列挙されており、各条の「(5)その他公益又は投資者保護の観点から当取引所が必要と認める事項」の一内容として、新規上場申請に係る内国株券等が無議決権株式又は議決権の少ない株式である場合において適合する必要のある要件(a～f)が、東証の「上場審査等に関するガイドライン」に列挙されている。
要件a「極めて小さい出資割合で会社を支配する状況が生じた場合に無議決権株式又は議決権の少ない株式のスキームが解消できる見込みのあること」、要件d「当該新規上場申請に係る内国株券等が議決権の少ない株式である場合には、議決権の多い株式について、その譲渡等が行われるときに議決権の少ない株式に転換される旨が定められていること」など。

[73] 東京証券取引所は、2014年2月に「IPOの活性化等に向けた上場制度の見直しについて」と題するリリースにおいて、(1)新規上場時の株主数基準の引き下げや、(2)議決権種類株式に係る上場審査の観点の明確化等の所要の制度整備を、本年3月を目途に実施すると公表した。その後、3月24日に、「IPOの活性化等に向けた上場制度の見直しに係る有価証券上場規程等の一部改正について」という書面で新規上場時の株主数基準の引き下げを発表した。現行上場審査における議決権種類株式の取り扱いについては、7月2日に「議決権種類株式に係る上場審査の観点の明確化のための上場審査等に関するガイドラインの一部改正について」が発表されており、ガイドラインⅡ 6.(4)を改正している。

場合もその場合も、機関投資家側からの実効的な圧力が期待できる環境は維持されるべきだろう。日本では株主提案権が広く認められているという事情があるが、ガバナンス是正を求めるような代表訴訟の利用が活発とはいえない。こうした事情や日本の株主の分布、性格などを考えれば、個別のスキームによるものの、株主による監督・是正権を最初から奪うような種類株式や、支配株主に付される議決権の割合を高く維持しすぎるスキームなどには問題がありうる。そうした問題を指摘しつつ、その規制を証券市場に委ねることに対しては、最初から非常に健全な種類株式しか上場させないことで証券取引所の機会を奪っているとの批判もありえよう[74]。ただし、法令で解決しようとすれば、「環境次第で不当になりうる条項」や「一律に最適な期限を決めることのできないサンセット条項」を会社法の規定に書き込むことの限界に直面する。また、市場間の競争があるとはいっても、他の市場もこうした議決権種類株式を積極的に取り入れているとはいえない。2018年4月に香港、同年6月にはシンガポール証券取引所が議決権種類株式の上場を許可する方針を発表したが、シンガポールの場合、2017年7月にプライマリーリスティングが先行していることを条件に議決権種類株式のセカンダリーリスティングを認めており、独立取締役や監査役の選解任、定款変更、リバーステイクオーバー、清算および上場廃止において1株1議決権の原則を復活させること、セーフガードとして取締役会の委員会構造、サンセット条項の挿入が求められている。また新たなルールとして、複数議決権発行先の明示、複数議決権株式の許された対象以外への譲渡や責任のある理事の退任の際の複数株式の強制転換、資本増加の際の複数議決権株式増加は特別決議によるべきこと、複数議決権株式の割合を普通株式と比較で増加させることの禁止、総会開催や議決権行使の要件などについてのルールも定められた[75]。

4−2　上場会社による種類株式の発行と長期的保有

　上場会社と株主との間の長期的関係構築を促進しようとする場合、法によって種類株式制度導入のハードルを下げると、会社の株主分布次第で、望ましくない利益移転が伴う可能性があるように思われる。しかし、逆に分散が進んだ会社では、会社による自主的な種類株式の導入に期待することは難しい。十分に議決権の分散した上場会社においては、極端な議決権種類株式を発行しない限り、発行による支配権プレミアムは発生しがたい。だが、支配株主の持株割合が、経営に批判的な長期的投資家とあまり差がない場合、そうし

---

[74] ただし、証券取引所は種類株式発行会社の上場の機会自体は与えつつ、上場される市場等を区別し、何らかの情報を市場に発信するなど会社法に比べて柔軟な制度作りが可能である。シンガポール市場が行ったコンサルテーションにもそのような提言は見られたし、投資会社側で議決権種類株式発行会社を排除したIndexと含むものとを併設する対応もそうした考慮に基づくものと思われる。

[75] Jeff Jackson, June 28, 2018 "Dual Class Share Structures Get the Green Light in Singapore"
https://www.glasslewis.com/dual-class-share-structures-get-the-green-light-in-singapore/

た投資家の持ち分が同時に強くなるような仕組みは、支配株主にとって副作用が大きい。また、経営陣が会社支配を強めるためにこの制度を導入することには投資家は反対するだろう。

　会社法は株主権の相対的な地位関係を維持することに細心の注意を払ってきた。一定の事項に対する議決権の制限や拒否権を付した種類株式を導入するに際しては、定款変更（466条・309条2項11号）、株主総会による有利発行承認決議を経る手続（201条1項・199条）が存在し、株主の意見が事前に反映される仕組みになっているうえ、322条1項により、種類株主が受ける不利益について一定の拒否権が設定されている（ただし、定款で排除が可能）。また、実務においても、企業価値研究会における提言を反映して、上場審査において既上場会社による種類株式発行は慎重に審査するとされている[76]。こうしたなかで、企業側は配当等による種類株の創出を工夫することになるが、トヨタが長期保有志向で譲渡制限および段階的に累増する配当を付したAA種類株式を導入した際でさえ、その目的（外国投資家などからイノベーションに興味がある固定的な株主への株主層の入れ替え）が経営陣の保身のためであるかどうかが明らかでなくとも、その導入は他の議案に比べれば顕著に賛成割合が低かったと指摘される[77]。長期的な関係の構築については、望ましさの判定や導入手法をすべて企業の自助努力に任せてよいか、なお注視が必要といえる。

以上

---

[76] 研究会報告の提言は、種類株式の利用に伴う弊害として、理論的に、以下の3点が考えられるとしていた。
①種類株主間の利害調整が適切に行われない結果として、一方の種類株主が他方の利益を害するような措置が行われてしまうおそれ。
②効率的な支配権の移転が行われない、又は、非効率な支配権の移転が行われるおそれ。
③既上場会社が新たに種類株式を発行する場合には、既存株主が（上記①・②を含め）不測の損害を被るおそれ。
[77] 加藤　前掲注4　17頁。

資料　資料1

VIRGINIA LAW REVIEW

VOLUME 103   JUNE 2017   NUMBER 4

ARTICLES

THE UNTENABLE CASE FOR PERPETUAL DUAL-CLASS STOCK

Lucian A. Bebchuk* and Kobi Kastiel**

The desirability of a dual-class structure, which enables founders of public companies to retain a lock on control while holding a minority of the company's equity capital, has long been the subject of a heated debate. This debate has focused on whether dual-class stock is an efficient capital structure that should be permitted at the time of initial public offering ("IPO"). By contrast, we focus on how the passage of time since the IPO can be expected to affect the efficiency of such a structure.

Our analysis demonstrates that the potential advantages of dual-class structures (such as those resulting from founders' superior leadership skills) tend to recede, and the potential costs tend to rise, as time passes from the IPO. Furthermore, we show that controllers have perverse incentives to retain dual-class structures even when those structures become inefficient over time. Accordingly, even those who believe that dual-class structures are in many cases efficient at the time

---

* James Barr Ames Professor of Law, Economics, and Finance and Director of the Program on Corporate Governance, Harvard Law School.
** Research Director of the Project on Controlling Shareholders, Harvard Law School Program on Corporate Governance.
This Article is part of the research undertaken by the Project on Controlling Shareholders. For valuable comments, we are grateful to seminar and conference participants at Harvard Law School, the Fall 2015 Meeting of the International Corporate Governance Network, and the 2016 Annual Meeting of the American Law and Economics Association, as well as Aaron Bernstein, John Coates, Jesse Fried, Assaf Hamdani, Oliver Hart, Howell Jackson, Reinier Kraakman, Gregory Shill, Holger Spamann, and Yishay Yafeh. Eric Goodwin and David Mao provided valuable research assistance. For disclosure of outside activities of the authors, see their curricula vitae available on their respective websites.

of the IPO should recognize the substantial risk that their efficiency may decline and disappear over time. Going forward, the debate should focus on the permissibility of finite-term dual-class structures—that is, structures that sunset after a fixed period of time (such as ten or fifteen years) unless their extension is approved by shareholders unaffiliated with the controller.

We provide a framework for designing dual-class sunsets and address potential objections to their use. We also discuss the significant implications of our analysis for public officials, institutional investors, and researchers.

Keywords: corporations, dual-class, controlling shareholders, corporate governance, agency costs, sunset.
JEL Classification: G32, G34, K22

INTRODUCTION 587
I. THE STAKES 594
   A. The Importance of Dual-Class Companies 594
   B. The Policy Debate 596
      1. In the United States 596
      2. Around the World 599
   C. Reframing the Debate 601
II. POTENTIAL COSTS AND THE TIME DIMENSION 602
   A. Costs 602
   B. The Time Dimension 604
      1. Erosion of the Controllers' Superiority 604
      2. Decrease in the Controller's Equity Capital 607
III. POTENTIAL BENEFITS AND THE TIME DIMENSION 609
   A. Superior Leadership Skills 610
   B. Long Termism 611
   C. Oversight Benefits 612
IV. THE PERSISTENCE OF INEFFICIENT STRUCTURES 613
   A. Resistance to a Sale 614
   B. Resistance to a Unification 616
V. SUNSETTING DUAL-CLASS STRUCTURES 618
   A. Designing Sunset Clauses 619
      1. Fixed-Time Sunset 619
      2. Triggering-Event Sunset 620
      3. Ownership-Percentage Sunset 621
      4. Addressing Circumvention 622
   B. Objections 623
      1. The Panglossian Objection 623
      2. One Size Does Not Fit All 624
      3. Discouraging IPOs 625
      4. The End-Period Problem 626
VI. GOING FORWARD 627
   A. Public Officials 627
   B. Investors and Advisors 629
   C. Researchers 630
CONCLUSION 631

INTRODUCTION

IN 1990, Viacom Inc., a prominent media company, adopted a dual-class capital structure, consisting of two classes of shares with differential voting rights. This structure enabled Viacom's controlling shareholder, Sumner Redstone, to maintain full control over the company while holding only a small fraction of its equity capital.[1] At the time, Redstone was already one of the most powerful and successful figures in Hollywood.[2] Indeed, three years earlier, he had purchased Viacom in a hostile takeover, exhibiting the array of savvy and daring business maneuvers that subsequently helped him transform Viacom into a $40 billion entertainment empire that encompasses the Paramount movie studio and the CBS, MTV, and Showtime television networks.[3] Investors during the 1990s could have reasonably been expected to be content with having Redstone safely at the helm.

---

[1] Sumner Redstone indirectly controls Viacom through National Amusements, Inc. ("NAI"), while holding only 8% of Viacom's equity capital. See Viacom Inc. Proxy Statement (Form DEF 14A) 22 (Dec. 16, 2016) (explaining that NAI owns approximately 79.8% of the voting interest and 10% of the equity interest in Viacom, and that NAI is controlled by Redstone through the Sumner M. Redstone National Amusements Trust, which owns shares in NAI representing 80% of the voting interest of NAI).
[2] Michael J. de la Merced, How Sumner Redstone Went from Army Cryptographer to Media Mogul, N.Y. Times (May 5, 2016), https://www.nytimes.com/2016/02/07/business/media/how-sumner-redstone-went-from-army-cryptographer-to-media-mogul.html.
[3] Id.; Sydney Ember, "He Can't Speak," Lawyer Says as Redstone Word War Rages, N.Y. Times, July 1, 2016, at B3.

Fast-forward twenty-six years to 2016: Ninety-three-year-old Redstone faced a lawsuit, brought by Viacom's former CEO and a long-time company director, alleging that Redstone suffered from "profound physical and mental illness[,]" "has not been seen publicly for nearly a year[,]" can no longer stand, walk, read, write or speak coherently[,] . . . cannot swallow[,] and requires a feeding tube to eat and drink."[4] Indeed, in a deposition, Redstone did not respond when asked his original family birth name.[5] Some observers expressed concerns that "the company has been operating in limbo since the controversy erupted."[6] However, public investors, who own approximately 90% of Viacom's equity capital, remained powerless and without influence over the company or the battle for its control.

Eventually, in August 2016, the parties reached a settlement agreement that ended their messy legal battles, providing Viacom's former CEO with significant private benefits and leaving control in the hands of Redstone.[7] Notably, despite the allegation and the evidence that surfaced, the settlement prevented a court ruling on whether Redstone was legally competent.[8] Note that even a finding of legal competency would have hardly reassured public investors: Legal competence does not by itself qualify a person to make key decisions for a major company.[9] Moreover, once Redstone passes away or is declared to be legally in-

competent, legal arrangements in place would require the control stake to remain in an irrevocable trust that would be managed by a group of trustees, most of whom have no proven business experience in leading large public companies.[10] Thus, even assuming that Viacom's governance structure was fully acceptable to public investors two decades ago, this structure has clearly become highly problematic for them.

Let us now turn from Viacom to Snap Inc. The company responsible for the popular disappearing-message application has recently gone public with a multiple-class structure that would enable the company's co-founders, Evan Spiegel and Robert Murphy, to have lifetime control over Snap.[11] Given that they are now only twenty-six and twenty-eight years old, respectively, the co-founders can be expected to remain in control for a period that may last fifty or more years.[12]

Public investors may be content with having Spiegel and Murphy securely at the helm in the years following Snap's initial public offering ("IPO"). After all, Spiegel and Murphy might be viewed by investors as responsible for the creation and success of a company that went public at a valuation of nearly $24 billion.[13] However, even if the Snap co-founders have unique talents and vision that make them by far the best individuals to lead the company in 2017 and the subsequent several years, it is hardly certain that they would continue to be fitting leaders down the road. The tech environment is highly dynamic, with disruptive innovations and a quick pace of change, and once-successful founders could well lose their golden touch after many years of leading their companies. Thus, an individual who is an excellent leader in 2017 might become an ill-fitting or even disastrous choice for making key decisions in 2037, 2047, or 2057. Accordingly, as the time since Snap's IPO grows, so does the risk that Snap's capital structure, and the co-founders' resulting lock on control, will generate costly governance problems.

---

[4] Emily Steel, Viacom Chiefs Take Trust Battle to Court, N.Y. Times, May 24, 2016, at B1; see also Ember, supra note 3, at B3 (noting that lawyers for Viacom's CEO stated that Redstone "was mentally incapacitated and had been unduly influenced by Shari Redstone").

[5] Peter Elkind, Did Summer Redstone's Testimony Help Him?, Fortune (May 6, 2016, 4:09 PM), http://fortune.com/2016/05/06/did-sumner-redstones-testimony-help-him/ [https://perma.cc/GM38-KGQV] ("Midway through the short deposition, the interpreter shifted to asking Redstone to spell out his answers by pointing to individual letters shown to him. He seemed unable to do this.").

[6] Emily Steel, Redstone's Busy October: 3 Cases in 3 Courts in 3 States, N.Y. Times, July 30, 2016, at B2; see also James B. Stewart, How Dauman Lost the Battle for Viacom, N.Y. Times, Aug. 26, 2016, at B1 ("Given the uncertainty, companies didn't want to make deals with Viacom, and key employees threatened to leave. Viacom shares have been battered, dropping 46 percent over the last two years.").

[7] See Viacom Inc., Current Report (Form 8-K) 2–5 (Aug. 18, 2016).

[8] The issue of Redstone's competency was the subject of court battles in both Massachusetts and California. See Ember, supra note 3, at B3; Emily Steel, Redstone Removes Viacom Chief from Trust and Parent Board, N.Y. Times, May 21, 2016, at B1.

[9] Steven Davidoff Solomon, Hearing Shows Little Is Known on Who Controls Viacom, N.Y. Times: DealBook (June 24, 2016), http://www.nytimes.com/2016/06/25/business/dealbook/hearing-shows-little-is-known-on-who-controls-viacom.html ("Even if he is competent,' it does not appear that Mr. Redstone is in good shape.").

[10] See Steel, supra note 8, at B1.

[11] Steven Davidoff Solomon, Snap's Plan Is Most Unfriendly to Outsiders, N.Y. Times: DealBook (Feb. 3, 2017), https://www.nytimes.com/2017/02/03/business/dealbook/snap-ipo-plan-evan-spiegel.html?_r=0 ("[T]he founders' control goes away only if they die.").

[12] Snap Inc., Amendment No. 2 to Form S-1 Registration Statement 130 (Feb. 16, 2017) [hereinafter Snap Registration Statement].

[13] Michael J. de la Merced, Snap Prices I.P.O. at $17 per Share, Valuing Company at $24 Billion, N.Y. Times, Mar. 2, 2017, at B1.

The examples of Viacom and Snap highlight an important dimension that has thus far received insufficient attention—the passage of time since a company's IPO. This Article seeks to provide a comprehensive, systematic analysis of how the potential costs and benefits of a dual-class structure—and thus the overall efficiency of such a structure—change over time.

Our analysis demonstrates that, as time passes, the potential costs of a dual-class structure tend to increase while the potential benefits tend to erode. As a result, even if the structure were efficient at the time of the IPO, there would be a substantial risk that it would not remain so many years later, and this risk would keep increasing as time passes. Furthermore, we show that controllers have strong incentives to retain a dual-class structure even when that structure becomes inefficient over time. Thus, even those who believe that a dual-class structure is often efficient at the time of the IPO should recognize the perils of providing founders with perpetual or even lifetime control.

In the debate over dual-class structures, which has focused on whether and when it is desirable for companies to go public with a dual-class structure, we side with those opposed to dual-class IPOs.[14] Our analysis of the midstream perils of dual-class structures highlights a significant cost of such structures. This cost weighs against dual-class IPOs and should be taken into account in any assessment of their value.[15]

The key contribution of this Article, however, is to demonstrate that even supporters of dual-class IPOs should agree to take one option—that of a perpetual dual-class structure—off the table. Going forward, the debate should be limited to the choice between (1) precluding dual-class structures altogether and (2) permitting dual-class structures that sunset after a fixed period of time (such as ten or fifteen years) unless their ex-

---

[14] For a recent article by one of us that expresses concerns about the use of a dual-class structure at the IPO of a prominent company, see Lucian Bebchuk, Alibaba's Governance Leaves Investors at a Disadvantage, N.Y. Times: DealBook (Sept. 16, 2014, 2:00 PM), http://dealbook.nytimes.com/2014/09/16/alibabas-governance-leaves-investors-at-a-disadvantage/ [https://perma.cc/BFN9-8CNP].

[15] The costs and benefits of dual-class structures have long been the subject of academic study. See, e.g., the well-known surveys of theoretical and empirical work by Mike Burkart & Samuel Lee, One Share - One Vote: The Theory, 12 Rev. Fin. 1 (2008), and Renée Adams & Daniel Ferreira, One Share-One Vote: The Empirical Evidence, 12 Rev. Fin. 51 (2008). However, the large literature on the subject has not focused on the time dimension, which is the central focus of this Article.

---

tension is approved by shareholders unaffiliated with the controller. The case for a perpetual dual-class structure, we show, is untenable.[16]

Our analysis is organized as follows. Part I explains the substantial stakes in the policy debate that we seek to reframe. We begin by discussing the importance of dual-class companies in the United States and around the world. A significant number of U.S. public companies—including such well-known companies as CBS, Comcast, Facebook, Ford, Google, News Corp., and Nike—have dual-class structures.[17] Furthermore, since Google decided to use a dual-class structure for its 2004 IPO, a significant number of "hot" tech companies have followed its lead.[18]

Part I also discusses the long-standing debate over the desirability of dual-class structures. The New York Stock Exchange ("NYSE") prohibited dual-class structures for approximately sixty years, until the mid-1980s, and they are still prohibited or rare in some jurisdictions, such as the United Kingdom and Hong Kong.[19] However, the rules now prevailing in the United States, as well as in some other jurisdictions around the world, permit the use of dual-class stock.[20] Moreover, the debate on the

---

[16] Although some investors have expressed support for sunset provisions in dual-class companies, see, e.g., Canadian Coal. for Good Governance, Dual Class Share Policy 10–12 (Sept. 2013) [hereinafter The CCGG Policy], http://www.ccgg.ca/site/ccgg/assets/pdf/dual_class_share_policy.pdf [https://perma.cc/9AZE-3PCS], our work provides the first comprehensive analysis of sunset provisions and the untenable case for dual-class structures that do not use them. For earlier work that expresses support for sunsets in other corporate-law contexts, see Lucian Arye Bebchuk, Why Firms Adopt Antitakeover Arrangements, 152 U. Pa. L. Rev. 713, 751–52 (2003), and John C. Coates IV, Ownership, Takeovers and EU Law: How Contestable Should EU Corporations Be?, in Reforming Company and Takeover Law in Europe 677, 704 (Guido Ferrarini et al. eds., 2004).

[17] See Edward Kamonjoh, Investor Responsibility Research Ctr. Inst., Controlled Companies in the Standard & Poor's 1500: A Follow-up Review of Performance & Risk 84–87 (Mar. 2016). https://irrcinstitute.org/wp-content/uploads/2016/03/Controlled-Companies-IRRCI-2015-FINAL-3-16-16.pdf [https://perma.cc/M5LU-Y64M]. In 2015, Google announced a corporate reorganization that created a holding company, Alphabet Inc., with Google as a subsidiary. Julia D'Onfro, Google is Now Alphabet, Bus. Insider: Tech Insider (Oct. 2, 2015, 10:56 AM), http://www.businessinsider.com/google-officially-becomes-alphabet-today-2015-10 [https://perma.cc/NB2J-DU6Y]. Because the enterprise is largely still known as Google, however, that name will be used in this paper.

[18] See infra notes 23–24.

[19] For a discussion on the past prohibition of dual-class stock in the United States, see infra notes 28–35 and accompanying text. For a review of the restrictions on dual-class stock in other jurisdictions, see infra notes 46–55 and accompanying text.

[20] See infra notes 26–27, 35 and accompanying text.

subject is still ongoing—both in jurisdictions that prohibit dual-class structures and those that permit them.

Part II analyzes how the potential costs of dual-class structures change over time. These costs tend to increase for two major reasons. To begin, in a dynamic business environment, even a founder who was the fittest leader at the time of the IPO might eventually become an inferior leader due to aging or changes in the business environment, and this risk increases the expected costs of providing the founder with a lifetime lock on control. Indeed, the expected costs of a lifetime lock on control are likely to be especially large when the founder is young or even middle-aged at the time of the IPO.

Concerns about the emergence of inferior leadership over time are further aggravated when the dual-class structure enables a transfer of the founder's lock on control to an heir who might be unfit to lead the company. Furthermore, many dual-class structures enable controllers to substantially reduce their fraction of equity capital over time without relinquishing control, and controllers often do so to diversify their holdings or finance other investments or assets. When the wedge between the interests of the controller and those of the public investors grows over time, the agency costs of a dual-class structure can also be expected to increase.

Part III then analyzes how the potential benefits of a dual-class structure can be expected to change over time. Dual-class structures are often justified on the grounds that the founder of a company going public has skills, abilities, or vision that makes her uniquely fit to be at the helm. Many years later, however, the founder's superiority as the company's leader, and with it the expected value of having the founder retain a lock on control, could erode or disappear altogether. Another potential benefit often ascribed to dual-class structures is that they insulate management from short-term market pressures. However, the expected benefit from such insulation is likely to be larger when the controller is a fitting leader for the company and likely to decline when the passage of time makes the controller ill fitting for the leadership role. Finally, it might be suggested that insulation from market forces might be beneficial to companies that are new to the public market, but any such potential benefit is again expected to decline and eventually disappear as time passes from the IPO.

Part IV explains why public officials and investors cannot rely on private ordering to eliminate dual-class structures that become inefficient with time. We show that controlling shareholders, especially those who hold a small fraction of equity capital, have significant perverse incentives to retain a dual-class structure that has become inefficient, even when dismantling it—via a conversion to a one-share, one-vote structure or a sale of the company—would produce substantial efficiency gains. The reason is that the controller would capture only a fraction of the efficiency gains, which would be shared by all shareholders, but would fully bear the cost of forgoing the private benefits of control associated with the dual-class structure.[21]

To address the distorted incentives of controllers to retain dual-class structures even when those structures become substantially inefficient, an IPO dual-class structure can include a sunset provision stipulating the structure's expiration after a fixed period of time, such as ten or fifteen years. Part V discusses the merits and design of such sunset provisions. To enable the retention of structures that remain efficient, we explain that the initially specified duration of the dual-class structure could be extended if such extension is approved by a majority of the shareholders unaffiliated with the controller. We also address potential objections to arrangements that preclude or discourage perpetual dual-class structures. In particular, we respond to objections that (1) perpetual dual-class structures should be presumed efficient if they are chosen by market participants and (2) allowing perpetual structures is necessary to induce founders to go public.

Finally, Part VI discusses the implications of our analysis for policy-making, investors, and corporate-governance research. Public officials and institutional investors should consider precluding or discouraging IPOs that set a perpetual dual-class structure. They should also be attentive to the aggravated agency problems that are posed by companies that went public with perpetual dual-class structures a long time ago. Researchers should take the time dimension into account in their analyses of dual-class structure and should test several empirical predictions that

---

[21] For earlier work by one of us that analyzes how controllers' private interests may lead them to make inefficient decisions midstream, see Lucian Arye Bebchuk, Efficient and Inefficient Sales of Corporate Control, 109 Q.J. Econ. 957, 964–68, 974–80 (1994), and Lucian Arye Bebchuk & Mark J. Roe, A Theory of Path Dependence in Corporate Ownership and Governance, 52 Stan. L. Rev. 127, 142–49 (1999).

Part VI puts forward. We hope that future assessments of dual-class structures will be informed by the problems that we identify in this Article and the framework of analysis that we put forth.

I. THE STAKES

This Part lays out the institutional and policy background to our discussion. Section A explains the importance of dual-class companies in the United States and around the world. Section B describes the longstanding and ongoing debate over whether issuers should be permitted to go public with dual-class structures. Finally, Section C explains how this debate could be advanced by recognizing the significance of a key dimension to the assessment of dual-class structures—the time that has passed since the IPO.

A. *The Importance of Dual-Class Companies*

Dual-class companies play an important role in the U.S. economy. As indicated in Table 1, these companies are significantly represented in the leading stock indices and have an aggregate market capitalization exceeding $3 trillion as of July 2016.[22]

Table 1: Dual-Class Companies in Major Indices (2016)

	S&P 100	S&P 500	Russell 1000	Russell 3000
Number	9	32	83	245
Percentage of Index	9%	6.4%	8.4%	8.2%
Total Market Cap (in Trillions)	$2.26	$2.79	$3.18	$3.35

Furthermore, there has been an upward trend in the adoption of dual-class stock since Google went public with a dual-class structure in 2004

---

[22] The data was collected from the Bloomberg database and is current as of July 11, 2016. Consistent with previous studies, we excluded REITs from the list of dual-class companies.

and was followed by well-known tech companies, such as Facebook, Groupon, LinkedIn, Snap, Trip Advisor, and Zynga.[23] Indeed, according to data-provider Dealogic, "[m]ore than 13.5 percent of the 133 companies listing shares on United States exchanges in 2015 have set up a dual-class structure . . . compare[d] with . . . just 1 percent in 2005."[24]

The use of dual-class stock is not limited to the tech industry. Major companies with dual-class structures operating in other sectors include AMC, Berkshire Hathaway, Cablevision, CBS, Comcast, Estée Lauder, Ford, Hershey, News Corp, Nike, Ralph Lauren, Tyson Foods, and Viacom.[25]

Dual-class companies are also quite common in many other jurisdictions around the world.[26] A well-known survey of 464 companies in sixteen European countries conducted by Institutional Shareholder Services ("ISS") in 2007 revealed that 24% of sampled companies had dual-class shares.[27] Prominent examples of large foreign companies with dual-class stock include Alibaba, the Chinese e-commerce giant, and Ericsson, the Swedish telecommunications company. The global prevalence of this

---

[23] Maureen Farrell, In Snap IPO, New Investors to Get Zero Votes, While Founders Keep Control, Wall St. J. (Jan. 16, 2017, 8:24 PM), http://www.wsj.com/articles/in-snap-ipo-new-investors-to-get-zero-votes-while-founders-keep-control-1484568034 (presenting evidence that "[b]etween 2012 and 2016, roughly 19% of U.S. tech firms that went public did so with dual-class structures—more than double the share over the prior five-year period"). Our research using Compustat to identify dual-class IPOs in recent years indicates that Facebook, Groupon, LinkedIn, Trip Advisor, and Zynga adopted this structure when they went public. For information on Snap's dual-class structure, see supra notes 11–13.

[24] See Steven Davidoff Solomon, Shareholders Vote with Their Dollars to Have Less of a Say, N.Y. Times: DealBook (Nov. 4, 2015), http://www.nytimes.com/2015/11/05/business/dealbook/shareholders-vote-with-their-dollars-to-have-less-of-a-say.html [https://perma.cc/T86Z-CHAY].

[25] See Kamonjoh, supra note 17, at 84–90.

[26] For data on the global use of dual-class structures, see Hong Kong Exchs. & Clearing Ltd., Concept Paper, Weighted Voting Rights, at III-1 to III-17 (Aug. 2014) [hereinafter HKEX Report] and Shearman & Sterling LLP, Institutional S'holder Servs. & European Corp. Governance Inst., Report on the Proportionality Principle in the European Union 15, 26–27 (May 18, 2007) [hereinafter Report on the Proportionality Principle], http://www.ecgi.org/osov/documents/final_report_en.pdf [https://perma.cc/4HDK-APPU].

[27] See Report on the Proportionality Principle, supra note 26, at 23, 25. Bennedsen and Nielsen report similar results using a much larger sample of more than 4,000 companies in fourteen Western European countries. See Morten Bennedsen & Kasper Meisner Nielsen, Incentive and Entrenchment Effects in European Ownership, 34 J. Banking & Fin. 2212, 2214 (2010).

structure, therefore, makes the topic and findings of this Article important to policymakers both in the United States and around the world.

B. The Policy Debate

This Section describes the heated policy debate that has been waged, both in the United States and in other jurisdictions, between supporters and opponents on the use of dual-class structures by companies going public. This debate is ongoing and quite alive, both in jurisdictions that currently place such limitations and those that do not.

1. In the United States

The era of prohibition. In 1926, the NYSE decided not to list the stocks of companies with either nonvoting common stock or unequal voting rights.[28] This decision came in response to a public outcry, initially inspired by Harvard economist William Ripley, against the issuance of nonvoting common stock by several prominent companies, including Dodge Brothers.[29] The NYSE explained that its "one share, one vote" policy was grounded in the NYSE's "long-standing commitment to encourage high standards of corporate democracy . . . and accountability to shareholders."[30] For six decades, the NYSE insisted on preserving its one-share, one-vote rule.

The move to permissibility. In 1985, facing increasing competition from other U.S. exchanges that offered to list companies with dual-class share structures, and after General Motors threatened to leave for NASDAQ, the NYSE proposed amendments to its listing requirements that would permit listed companies to use dual-class structures.[31] In response, the Securities and Exchange Commission ("SEC") adopted Rule 19c-4 in 1988 to limit the ability of existing companies with one-share, one-vote structures to move to dual-class structures.[32] Although the District of Columbia Court of Appeals invalidated this Rule on grounds that the SEC lacked authority to adopt it,[33] the SEC persuaded the main stock exchanges to prohibit dual-class recapitalizations under their listing standards.[34] As such, while U.S. companies still face constraints on introducing a dual-class structure midstream, they have been largely free to go public with a dual-class structure for about three decades.[35]

The continuing opposition. The decision of U.S. regulators and stock exchanges to permit the use of dual-class structures by IPO companies did not end the battle over the desirability of the practice. A wave of dual-class IPOs, intensifying after Google employed the structure when it went public in 2004, rekindled the public and academic discourse about it. Institutional investors, their advisors, and prominent thought leaders have all expressed strong opposition to the use of dual-class structures.

The Council of Institutional Investors ("CII")—an organization of more than 140 public, union, and corporate pension funds—petitioned the stock exchanges to adopt a one-share, one-vote policy.[36] In June

---

[28] For detailed accounts of the history of dual-class structures in the United States, see NYSE's Proposed Rule Changes on Disparate Voting Rights, 18 Sec. Reg. & L. Rep. (BNA) No. 37, at 1389 (Sept. 19, 1986) [hereinafter NYSE's Proposed Rule Changes]; Louis Lowenstein, Shareholder Voting Rights: A Response to SEC Rule 19c-4 and to Professor Gilson, 89 Colum. L. Rev. 979, 979–85 (1989); and Joel Seligman, Equal Protection in Shareholder Voting Rights: The One Common Share, One Vote Controversy, 54 Geo. Wash. L. Rev. 687, 693–707 (1986).
[29] See Seligman, supra note 28, at 694.
[30] Id. at 699.
[31] See NYSE's Proposed Rule Changes, supra note 28, at 1389–92. The proposed amendment permitted both new issuances of dual-class stock and recapitalizations midstream but required that the latter be approved by a majority of independent directors and public shareholders unaffiliated with the controller. Id. at 1392; see also Ronald J. Gilson, Evaluating Dual Class Common Stock: The Relevance of Substitutes, 73 Va. L. Rev. 807, 807 n.1 (1987) (discussing the pressures that prompted the NYSE to alter its policy); Alison Smith et al., Exchanges Divided by Dual-Class Shares, Fin. Times (Oct. 3, 2013), https://www.ft.com/content/e18a6138-2b49-11e3-a1b7-00144feab7de.
[32] Voting Rights Listing Standards; Disenfranchisement Rule, 53 Fed. Reg. 26,376 (July 12, 1988) (codified as amended at 17 C.F.R. § 240.19c-4 (2009)), invalidated by Bus. Roundtable v. SEC, 905 F.2d 406, 417 (D.C. Cir. 1990).
[33] Bus. Roundtable, 905 F.2d at 417.
[34] Order Granting Approval to Rule Changes Relating to the Exchanges' and Association's Rules Regarding Shareholder Voting Rights, 59 Fed. Reg. 66,570 (Dec. 27, 1994).
[35] See, for example, NYSE Listed Company Manual § 313.00 (1992), which prohibits dual-class recapitalizations for listed companies but provides several exceptions for the listing of multiple classes of shares, including the issuance of multiple classes prior to the IPO that are maintained after the company has gone public. See also NASDAQ Stock Market Rules, at r. 5640 (restricting the reduction of voting rights of common-stock shareholders but permitting companies to issue additional shares of already "existing super voting stock"), http://nasdaq.cchwallstreet.com/NASDAQTools/PlatformViewer.asp?selectednode=chp%5F1%5F1%5F4%5F3&manual=%2Fnasdaq%2Fmain%2Fnasdaq%2Dequityrules%2F [https://perma.cc/Y5V3-LMCT].
[36] Letter from the Council of Institutional Investors to Edward S. Knight, Executive Vice President and General Counsel, NASDAQ OMX Group (Mar. 27, 2014), http://www.cii.org/files/issues_and_advocacy/correspondence/2014/03_27_14_CII_letter_to_nasdaq_one_share

2013, Senator Elizabeth Warren joined CII in urging U.S. exchanges to limit the use of dual-class stock.[37] Leading mutual funds, such as Vanguard, Fidelity, and T. Rowe Price, have expressed general opposition to dual-class structures.[38] Prominent pension funds, including the California State Teachers' Retirement System ("CalSTRS"), the California Public Employees' Retirement System ("CalPERS"), and the Florida State Board of Administration ("Florida SBA"), have expressed similar opposition.[39] A recent survey indicates that this view is shared among many institutional investors.[40]

Leading shareholder advisory groups have also expressed strong opposition to dual-class structures. For example, ISS denounced them as "an autocratic model of governance."[41] Similarly, GMI Ratings warned that using a dual-class share structure "can pose a serious risk to a company's public shareholders."[42]

The opposition to dual-class structures has become so widely accepted that it was incorporated in recent documents attempting to identify minimum and consensus standards of acceptable corporate-governance practices. Such opposition was included in a set of corporate-governance principles that were put forward by a group of leading executives that included not only CEOs of asset managers but also those of major public companies.[43] Such opposition was also subsequently incorporated in the set of consensus governance principles adopted by a coalition of institutional investors managing in the aggregate more than $17 trillion.[44]

2. Around the World

Variation in regulation. Dual-class companies are permitted and common in many jurisdictions around the world. Such jurisdictions include Canada, Denmark, Finland, the Netherlands, Sweden, and Switzerland.[45] At the same time, the rules or conventions of other important jurisdictions prohibit or discourage companies from going public with dual-class structures. The Hong Kong Stock Exchange ("HKSE") has prohibited this practice since 1987.[46] In the United Kingdom, the general

---

[37] Letter from Elizabeth Warren, U.S. Senator, to John Carey, Vice President–Legal, NYSE Regulation, Inc. and NYSE Euronext & Edward Knight, Executive Vice President and General Counsel, NASDAQ OMX (June 5, 2013), http://www.warren.senate.gov/files/documents/Senator%20Warren%20letter%20to%20NYSE,%20Nasdaq%20-%206-5-2013.pdf [https://perma.cc/SH7H-56MM].

[38] For statements reflecting the opposition of these mutual funds to dual-class structures, see Fid. Invs., Corporate Governance and Proxy Guidelines § VI.C, https://www.fidelity.com/about-fidelity/fidelity-by-numbers/fmr/proxy-guidelines [https://perma.cc/C9JE-39M2]; T. Rowe Price, Proxy Voting Policies, https://www3.troweprice.com/usis/content/troweorp/en/utility/policies/_jcr_content/maincontent/polices_row_1/para-mid/thiscontent/pdf_link/pdffile [https://perma.cc/24TQ-V2NL]; and Vanguard, Vanguard's Proxy Voting Guidelines, at pt. IV.G https://about.vanguard.com/vanguard-proxy-voting/voting-guidelines [https://perma.cc/93TH-XNVW].

[39] For statements in opposition to dual-class structures in the proxy voting guidelines or annual reports of these public pension funds, see Cal. Pub. Emps.' Ret. Sys., Statement of Investment Policy for Global Governance 12 (Mar. 16, 2015), https://www.calpers.ca.gov/docs/policy-global-governance.pdf [https://perma.cc/48GZ-8K64]; Cal. State Teachers' Ret. Sys., Corporate Government Principles 15 (July 14, 2016), http://www.calstrs.com/sites/main/files/file-attachments/corporate_governance_principles_1.pdf [https://perma.cc/W3QV-74GA]; and Fla. State Bd. of Admin., Corporate Governance & Proxy Voting Guidelines 37–38 (2016), https://www.sbafla.com/fsb/Portals/FSB/Content/CorporateGovernance/ProxyVoting/2016_SBACorpGovPrinciplesProxyVotingGuidelines.pdf?ver=2016-08-08-144634-157 [https://perma.cc/58ZS-WPHL].

[40] The ISS survey included 120 responses from institutional investors. Fifty-seven percent supported negative recommendations against directors at companies that go public with dual-class stock. Marc Goldstein, 2016–2017 Annual Benchmark Voting Policy Survey, Harv. L. Sch. F. on Corp. Governance & Fin. Reg. (Oct. 5, 2016), https://corpgov.law.harvard.edu/2016/10/05/2016-2017-annual-benchmark-voting-policy-survey/ [https://perma.cc/3SEC-YCZ3].

[41] Institutional S'holder Servs., The Tragedy of the Dual Class Commons 1, 3 (Feb. 13, 2012), http://online.wsj.com/public/resources/documents/facebook0214.pdf [https://perma.cc/RUG8-RN23] (also noting that "[t]he adverse implications of Balkanized ownership interests can linger for years, producing unintended consequences").

[42] Kimberly Gladman, The Dangers of Dual Share Classes, Harv. L. Sch. F. on Corp. Governance & Fin. Reg. (May 21, 2012), https://corpgov.law.harvard.edu/2012/05/21/the-dangers-of-dual-share-classes/ [https://perma.cc/6USD-A9ZV].

[43] Margaret Popper et al., Commonsense Principles of Corporate Governance, Harv. L. Sch. F. on Corp. Governance & Fin. Reg. (July 22, 2016), https://corpgov.law.harvard.edu/2016/07/22/commonsense-principles-of-corporate-governance/ [https://perma.cc/P713-824V].

[44] Inv'r Stewardship Grp., Corporate Governance and Stewardship Principles, Harv. L. Sch. F. on Corp. Governance & Fin. Reg. (Feb. 7, 2017), https://corpgov.law.harvard.edu/2017/02/07/corporate-governance-and-stewardship-principles/ [https://perma.cc/GHV4-5WRN].

[45] See supra notes 26–27.

[46] The HKSE listing rules do not permit the listing of companies with shares that have a voting power that does not bear a reasonable relationship to the equity interest of those shares. Such listing is permitted only in "exceptional circumstances," but the HKSE has thus far not listed a company using this exception. See HKEX Report, supra note 26, at 25–28.

hostility of institutional investors has practically precluded the use of dual-class structures.[47] In 2012, Manchester United, the well-known English soccer club, went public on the NYSE rather than the London stock exchanges in order to use a dual-class structure.[48] In Brazil, the Novo Mercado (New Market), an important segment within the Sao Paulo Stock Exchange, imposes a mandatory one-share, one-vote requirement.[49] In addition, some other countries in Continental Europe, including Belgium, Germany, Luxembourg, Poland, and Spain, currently limit the use of dual-class structures.[50]

The continuing debate. The heated debate over the use of dual-class stock still continues. In some jurisdictions that limit the dual-class structure, there has been a push to relax them. For instance, in Hong Kong, the securities exchange faced tremendous pressure to deviate from its one-share, one-vote principle to prevent Alibaba from listing else-

---

[47] Id., at III-12 to III-13 (noting that institutional shareholders are generally hostile to these structures); Fabio Braggion & Mariassunta Giannetti, At the Origins of the Non-Voting Shares' Discount: Investor Preferences vs. Fundamentals 1 (Dec. 2012) (unpublished manuscript) http://cn.ckgsb.com/Userfiles/doc/bg%20At%20the%20Origins%20of%20the%20Non-Voting%20Shares%E2%80%99%20Discount%20december%202012.pdf [https://perma.cc/N3U7-KP37] (describing the history of dual-class in the UK); see also Smith et al., supra note 31 (quoting Julian Franks, a professor of finance at London Business School, stating that "[t]he UK market believes in the principle of 'one share, one vote' even if that trumps efficiency").
[48] Steven Davidoff Solomon, In Manchester United's I.P.O., a Preference for American Rules, N.Y. Times: DealBook (July 10, 2012, 2:32 PM), http://dealbook.nytimes.com/2012/07/10/in-manchester-uniteds-i-p-o-a-preference-for-u-s-rules [https://perma.cc/FK2A-72TW].
[49] Ronald J. Gilson et al., Regulatory Dualism as a Development Strategy: Corporate Reform in Brazil, the United States, and the European Union, 63 Stan. L. Rev. 475, 488–91 (2011).
[50] OECD Steering Grp. on Corp. Governance, Lack of Proportionality Between Ownership and Control: Overview and Issues for Discussion 14–17 (2007), http://www.oecd.org/daf/ca/corporategovernanceprinciples/40038351.pdf [https://perma.cc/P5ZX-2GY7] (listing the countries that prohibit this practice). Note, however, that in some of those countries, such as Germany, the issuance of nonvoting shares with preferential rights to dividends (to compensate for the absence of voting rights) is permitted and is sometimes even prevalent. Report on the Proportionality Principle, supra note 26, at 7. The European Union also attempted to curb the unilateral use of high-voting shares to block takeovers, enacting a breakthrough rule in 2004. Directive 2004/25/EC of the European Parliament and of the Council of 21 April 2004 on Takeover Bids, Official J. Eur. Union L142/12 (Apr. 30, 2004). In practice, however, this directive has had little effect because it only sets the breakthrough rule as a default and member countries are allowed to opt out of it. See Guido Ferrarini, "One Share-One Vote: A European Rule?," 3 Eur. Company Fin. L. Rev. 147, 166–68 (2006).

---

where.[51] In response, the exchange conducted comprehensive research and a public consultation on potential changes to listing rules that would permit dual-class stock.[52] The city's market regulators and large institutional investors objected to such changes and, as this Article went to print, the exchange still preserved its policy.[53] In the United Kingdom, the Financial Conduct Authority recently issued a discussion paper seeking feedback on possible changes to enhance the attractiveness of U.K. capital markets, including making it easier for companies to list with dual-class structures.[54]

At the same time, in some jurisdictions that permit dual-class structures, institutional investors have advocated for limits on such structures. For example, in Canada, a broad coalition of large institutional shareholders called for placing limits on the use of dual-class structures.[55]

C. Reframing the Debate

The preceding Sections have described the long-standing and ongoing debate, both in the United States and around the world, over the use of

---

[51] See Neil Gough, Hong Kong I.P.O. Structure Is Fine as Is, Investor Survey Finds, N.Y. Times: DealBook (Apr. 15, 2014, 4:51 AM), http://dealbook.nytimes.com/2014/04/15/hong-kong-i-p-o-structure-is-fine-as-is-investor-survey-finds/ [https://perma.cc/9CFT-2S77] (citing Alibaba's executives and regulators who expressed concerns that "Hong Kong could lose a huge franchise for good" and that "the rest of the world [will] pass[] it by"). For articles examining the desirability of pressures produced by regulatory competition, see, for example, William L. Cary, Federalism and Corporate Law: Reflections upon Delaware, 83 Yale L.J. 663 (1974); Lucian Arye Bebchuk, Federalism and the Corporation: The Desirable Limits on State Competition in Corporate Law, 105 Harv. L. Rev. 1435 (1992); Roberta Romano, Empowering Investors: A Market Approach to Securities Regulation, 107 Yale L.J. 2359 (1998); Oren Bar-Gill et al., The Market for Corporate Law, 162 J. Institutional & Theoretical Econ. 134 (2006).
[52] See HKEX Report, supra note 26, at 5; see also Gough, supra note 51 (noting that HKEX was "widely expected to introduce a public consultation on potential changes to the city's listing rules . . . to get formal feedback on allowing nontraditional shareholding structures").
[53] See Jacky Wong, Hong Kong Stock Exchange Kills Dual-Class Share Plan, Wall St. J. (Oct. 5, 2015, 6:52 AM), http://www.wsj.com/articles/hong-kong-stock-exchange-kills-dual-class-share-plan-1444042360 (noting that "Hong Kong's stock exchange said it has terminated a plan to allow dual-class shares" and describing regulators' opposition to that plan). Also, a survey conducted in 2014 among seventy institutional investors in Hong Kong shows that "nearly all respondents were opposed to dual-class shareholding." Gough, supra note 51.
[54] Fin. Conduct Auth. Discussion Paper, Review of the Effectiveness of Primary Markets: The UK Primary Markets Landscape 7–8, 20–23 (Feb. 2017).
[55] See The CCGG Policy, supra note 16, at 5–6.

dual-class stock. This debate has focused on whether public companies should be permitted to adopt dual-class structures when they go public. Accordingly, participants in this debate have focused on whether a dual-class structure is likely to be efficient at the time of the company's IPO.

In this Article, however, we seek to reorient the debate by highlighting a key dimension for the assessment of dual-class structures: the time that has passed since the IPO. We focus on the ways in which the efficiency of a dual-class structure is likely to change as time passes from the IPO. Our analysis shows that, even if a dual-class structure were to be efficient at the time of the IPO, it would likely become inefficient many years down the road. Accordingly, we wish to reframe the debate by taking one option—a perpetual dual-class structure—off the table. Going forward, the debate should be only over whether companies would be allowed to go public with finite-life dual-class structures—that is, structures that sunset after a fixed period of time (such as ten or fifteen years) unless their extension is approved by shareholders unaffiliated with the controller.[56]

II. POTENTIAL COSTS AND THE TIME DIMENSION

This Part analyzes how the potential costs of using a dual-class capital structure can be expected to change over time. Section A discusses the potential costs of dual-class structures, and Section B introduces the time dimension and considers its effect on these costs.

A. Costs

Two fundamental problems arise from the use of dual-class stock: entrenchment and low equity holdings. Entrenchment insulates controllers from the disciplinary force of the market for corporate control that otherwise might limit the ability of a poorly performing controller to continue leading the company. At the same time, controllers with low equity holdings bear only a small fraction of the negative effects of their actions on the company value while capturing the full private benefits. Thus, controllers' incentives regarding certain issues may become distorted and misaligned with the preferences of public investors.[56]

[56] See Lucian Arye Bebchuk et al., Stock Pyramids, Cross-Ownership, and Dual Class Equity: The Mechanisms and Agency Costs of Separating Control from Cash-Flow Rights, in

The combination of entrenchment and limited equity holdings produces serious problems. For a widely held company with low equity holdings but no entrenchment, the market for corporate control imposes certain limits on managers' ability to underperform or act in ways contrary to the interests of public investors. Conversely, while the market for corporate control could not replace and thus discipline a majority owner of a controlled company, her large equity stake in the controlled company provides powerful financial incentives to maximize the company's value. She bears most of the costs of her actions and captures most of their benefits. Without both market discipline and strong financial incentives, a controller with a minority equity stake may favor choices that increase the private benefits of control even if those choices substantially diverge from those of other public shareholders, and no threat of removal exists to prevent her from pursuing those interests. This distortion of incentives becomes more severe when the controller of a dual-class company holds a smaller percentage of the company's equity capital.[57]

A wide range of distorted choices may result from entrenchment and low incentives. Such distorted choices may include the appointment or retention of the controller or a family member as an executive rather than a better outside candidate, engagement in inefficient self-dealing transactions with an entity that is affiliated with the controller, the usurpation of an opportunity that would be more valuable in the hands of the company rather than the controller, or other choices aimed at increasing private benefits of control at the expense of the value received by other shareholders.

More generally, the empirical evidence indicates that the combination of entrenchment and low equity holdings reduces company value, distorts controller incentives, and increases extraction of private benefits of control. Paul Gompers, Joy Ishii, and Andrew Metrick, studying U.S. dual-class companies over 1995–2002, found evidence that these companies exhibited increased agency costs and reduced value.[58] The study also showed that the larger the "wedge"—the gap between the control-

Concentrated Corporate Ownership 295, 298–301 (Randall K. Morck ed., 2000) (presenting a detailed description of the dual-class mechanism and the distortions it creates).
[57] For an analysis demonstrating this point, see id.
[58] See Paul A. Gompers et al., Extreme Governance: An Analysis of Dual-Class Firms in the United States, 23 Rev. Fin. Stud. 1051, 1051–54 (2010).

ler's fraction of voting rights and her fraction of equity capital—the more severe the resulting reductions in the company's value.[59]

Using the same sample as Gompers et al., Ronald Masulis, Cong Wang, and Fei Xie examined how the divergence between insider voting rights and equity capital at dual-class companies affects the extraction of private benefits of control. They reported that, as that divergence widens, corporate cash reserves are worth less to outside shareholders, CEOs receive higher levels of compensation, managers are more likely to make value-destroying acquisitions, and capital expenditures contribute less to shareholder value.[60]

B. The Time Dimension

The costs of a dual-class structure are likely to increase over time for two main reasons: the likely erosion of any superior skills that the controller might have had at the time of the IPO and the likely decrease in the controller's fraction of equity capital.

1. Erosion of the Controller's Superiority

At any given time, the costs of providing a founder with a lock on control depend on the likelihood that the controller is no longer the most suitable person for this role. At the time of the IPO, the founder of a company may have the special skills and deep knowledge of a specific industry and business to make her uniquely fit to be at the helm.[61] Therefore, supporters of dual class often argue that it is preferable to let such a talented controller remain in control long after the IPO.[62]

However, this superior-controller argument does not provide a good basis for the use of a *perpetual* dual-class structure. While such an argument might justify the use of dual-class stock at the IPO stage, it loses most of its power with the passage of time. Consider, for instance, talented and successful entrepreneurs such as the co-founders of Snap. Even if they can currently lead their company better than anyone else, will they still be the best fit for their company, say, thirty years down the road?

Rather, many years after the IPO, there is a real possibility that the founder's superiority as the company leader will erode or even disappear. Over time, a once-successful founder may face natural limitations in a fast-evolving technological or business environment. She could also simply lose her golden touch.[63] If the founder stops being the most fitting (or even a fitting) leader, the expected costs from her lock on control could become significant. These expected costs are especially high in the case of a young founder: The longer her lock on control, the greater the risk that she would become an ill-fitting leader.

---

[59] Id. at 1084–85.

[60] Ronald W. Masulis et al., Agency Problems at Dual-Class Companies, 64 J. Fin. 1697, 1722 (2009). For a survey of the empirical evidence, see Adams & Ferreira, supra note 15. We note that, although there is significant empirical evidence on the negative effects of dual-class structures, some empirical studies suggest that such structures might also have positive effects. See, e.g., Scott W. Bauguess et al., Large Shareholder Diversification, Corporate Risk Taking, and the Benefits of Changing to Differential Voting Rights, 36 J. Banking & Fin. 1244, 1244–46 (2012); Valentin Dimitrov & Prem C. Jain, Recapitalization of One Class of Common Stock into Dual-Class: Growth and Long-Run Stock Returns, 12 J. Corp. Fin. 342, 346–47 (2006). We have questions about the findings of these papers. However, even assuming that these findings are accepted, they would not be inconsistent with the key points we develop below: that whatever the costs of a dual-class structure at the time of adoption, these costs can be expected to increase over time; and that whatever the benefits of such a structure at the time of adoption, these benefits are expected to decline over time.

[61] See, e.g., Ronald J. Gilson & Alan Schwartz, Constraints on Private Benefits of Control: Ex Ante Control Mechanisms Versus Ex Post Transaction Review, 169 J. Institutional & Theoretical Econ. 160, 168–69 (2013) (suggesting that founders can serve as a "high-powered performance monitor").

[62] When Google went public in 2004, the founders expressed their confidence that "everyone associated with Google—including new investors—will benefit from this structure." James Kristie, Dual-Class Stock: Governance at the Edge, 36 Directors & Boards 37, 37 (Sept. 2012), http://sites.udel.edu/wccg/files/2012/10/Dual-Shares-Q3-2012].pdf [https://perma.cc/J2AK-NLNZ]; see also Scott Kupor, Sorry CalPERS, Dual Class Shares Are a Founder's Best Friend, Forbes (May 14, 2013, 10:01 AM), http://www.forbes.com/sites/ciocentral/2013/05/14/sorry-calpers-dual-class-shares-are-a-founders-best-friend/#48931b3d7016 [https://perma.cc/E5R2-T94Q] ("Now imagine that, instead of Steve Jobs, Larry Page and Mark Zuckerberg at the helms of their respective companies innovating through these product cycles, the California Public Employees' Retirement System (CalPERS) was calling the shots.... In this brave new world, founder-led technology companies ... will fail to reach their full potential.").

[63] See Steven M. Davidoff, Thorny Side Effects in Silicon Valley Tactic to Keep Control, N.Y. Times, Sept. 4, 2013, at B8 ("Even when the founders stay, there hasn't always been a happy outcome."); Jeffrey Goldfarb, Monster Truck, Bus. Standard: The Smart Investor (May 9, 2015, 1:22 AM), http://smartinvestor.business-standard.com/market/Marketnews-310863-Marketnewsdet-Monster_truck.htm#.V5td3vkrfJU ("Some young leaders ... may deserve to operate unrestrained for a while. Inevitably, however, their choices increasingly tend to be at odds with the greater good."); see also supra notes 1–9 and accompanying text (discussing Viacom example).

Furthermore, dual-stock structures may enable the transfer of a lock on control to an heir of the founder, who might not be as able, talented, skilled, or driven as her predecessor. This problem is known in the economic literature as the problem of the "idiot heir."[64] Indeed, there is evidence that companies run by descendants often underperform other family companies that are managed by their founders or by hired external managers.[65] A structure that provides the founder's family with a perpetual lock on control forgoes the benefits of optimal succession of leadership upon the founder's departure.

Relatedly, the standard design of private equity partnerships reflects an implicit understanding that the advantages of superior leadership skills tend to fade over time. In such funds, the general partner has full control over the management of the fund's assets—but only for a *finite* period, commonly on the order of ten years.[66] This structure sets a default that counteracts the natural tendency towards inertia: If the track record of the general partner (or other information) suggests that she no longer remains the best choice to manage the fund, the fund's investors are not stuck with her.[67] Certainly, the general partner often persuades investors to keep their assets under her management by simply rolling them into a new fund. But requiring investor consent as an intermediate step for the continued management of assets addresses the risk that the comparative advantages of a particular general partner may erode over time.

In sum, in assessing a dual-class structure, it is important to focus not only on the merits of the founder's leadership at the time of the IPO. Regulators and investors should also consider the risk that, many years hence, the founder (or her heirs) might not have superior leadership skills and might even have inferior leadership skills. As a result, the costs of a perpetual dual-class structure can be expected to increase over time.

2. Decrease in the Controller's Equity Capital

In addition to the concern that a controller's superiority might eventually erode or even disappear, a decrease in the controller's equity capital also increases over time the agency costs generated by the controller's power. Many dual-class structures enable controllers to unload their holdings without losing control, and controllers often do so to diversify their portfolios and reduce their idiosyncratic risk.[68] At (or shortly after) the IPO stage, controllers often maintain more than a majority of the votes, either by allocating extensive voting power to the shares they hold or by holding an initial large stake in the controlled company. If, for instance, a controller initially holds 80% of the voting rights, she can sell a significant percentage of her shares without going below the 50% threshold and losing her lock on control.

In addition, some dual-class companies go public with structures that enhance the ability of controllers to unload holdings without relinquishing control. For instance, the governance documents of a dual-class

---

[64] See, e.g., Antoin E. Murphy, Corporate Ownership in France: The Importance of History, *in* A History of Corporate Governance Around the World: Family Business Groups to Professional Managers 185, 187 (Randall K. Morck ed. 2005).

[65] For empirical studies supporting this view, see Ronald C. Anderson & David M. Reeb, Founding-Family Ownership and Firm Performance: Evidence from the S&P 500, 58 J. Fin. 1301, 1316–17, 1321 (2003); Morten Bennedsen et al., Inside the Family Firm: The Role of Families in Succession Decisions and Performance, 122 Q.J. Econ. 647, 669–70 (2007); Nicholas Bloom & John Van Reenen, Why Do Management Practices Differ Across Firms and Countries?, 24 J. Econ. Persp. 203, 205, 217–18 (2010); Francisco Pérez-González, Inherited Control and Firm Performance, 96 Am. Econ. Rev. 1559, 1574–78 (2006); and Belen Villalonga & Raphael Amit, How Do Family Ownership, Control and Management Affect Firm Value?, 80 J. Fin. Econ. 385, 402–03 (2006).

[66] See Andrew Metrick & Ayako Yasuda, The Economics of Private Equity Funds, 23 Rev. Fin. Stud. 2303, 2309 (2010) ("The typical fund has a lifetime of ten years."); Jennifer Bollen, Average Private Equity Fund Life Span Exceeds 13 Years, Wall St. J. (Mar. 31, 2015, 6:45 AM), http://blogs.wsj.com/privateequity/2015/03/31/average-private-equity-fund-life-span-exceeds-13-years/ (quoting an industry expert saying that "[PE] funds have common 10-year life spans and up to a three-year extension").

[67] Addison D. Braendel & Seth Chertok, Closed-End Private Equity Funds: A Detailed Overview of Fund Business Terms, Part II, 13 J. Priv. Equity 57, 68 (2010) (discussing the dissolution of a private equity fund). Certain evergreen funds have started to emerge in recent years, but they are still "a niche part of the private equity eco-system." See Sonja Cheung, Should Asian Private Equity Think About Evergreen Funds?, Wall St. J. (Jan. 30, 2014, 1:45 PM), http://blogs.wsj.com/privateequity/2014/01/30/should-asian-private-equity-think-about-evergreen-funds/. Also, while evergreen funds formally have indefinite lives, "[e]very couple of years—typically four—[their investors] have the ability to exit or to change their investment[s]." Billy Fink, What Is an Evergreen Fund Structure?, Axial F. (Feb. 25, 2014), http://www.axial.net/forum/evergreen-fund-structure/ [https://perma.cc/L4J7-NBTT] (internal quotation marks omitted).

[68] See the data provided in Table 2. For discussions of the role of dual-class stock in reducing controllers' lack of diversification risk, see George W. Dent, Jr., Dual Class Capitalization: A Reply to Professor Seligman, 54 Geo. Wash. L. Rev. 725, 749 (1986), and Gilson, supra note 31, at 812.

company may include a provision that allocates a fixed percentage of voting rights to the controlling shareholder, without regard to the controller's equity stake.[69] Such a hardwiring provision enables a controlling shareholder to sell as many shares as she wishes and still retain control over the dual-class company.

To illustrate the tendency of controllers to reduce their holdings over the years, we examined the changes in ownership interests in the ten largest dual-class companies (based on market capitalization) as of 2015. Table 2 below documents changes in controllers' equity capital since each company's IPO (or, if the figures at the IPO are not publicly available, since the company's first public filing on the SEC's Electronic Data Gathering, Analysis, and Retrieval ("EDGAR")).[70] As we expected, the controller's equity holdings in each of these ten dual-class companies declined substantially during the examined period, averaging 11.6% as of 2015 compared to 30% initially.

This data is consistent with our claim that controllers of dual-class companies tend to reduce their fraction of equity capital over time without losing control. As a result, the gap between their interests and those of the companies' public investors grows, as do the agency costs of the dual-class structure.

Table 2: Controller's Equity Interest in Ten Largest Dual-Class Companies

Company Name	Date of First Available Filing	Initial Holdings	Holdings as of 2015
Berkshire Hathaway Inc.	1999	32%	20%
Facebook, Inc.	2012	28%	15%
Google Inc.	2004	28%	12%
Comcast Corporation	1978	42%	0.4%
NIKE, Inc.	1984	68%	31%
Ford Motor Company	1969	7.1%	1.8%
Regeneron Pharmaceuticals, Inc.	1991	7%	5%
Twenty-First Century Fox, Inc.	2005	16%	15%
CBS Corporation	1995	26%	8%
Broadcom Corporation	1999	45%	8%
Average:		**30%**	**11.6%**

Indeed, as one of us analyzes in greater detail elsewhere, the decline in the controller's equity capital usually results in a disproportionate increase in associated agency costs.[71] For instance, when one compares two dual-class companies that are identical except that one controller owns 20% of her company's equity capital and the other controller owns only 15%, the agency costs in the latter company are expected to be more than twice those in the former.[72]

This concern is significant. As Section II.A discussed, the empirical evidence indicates that the combination of entrenchment and low equity holdings reduces firm value and generates significant agency costs. Furthermore, the analysis presented in Part IV below shows that when the stake of a controlling shareholder declines over time, making the dual-class structure especially inefficient, the controller's incentives to maintain a lock on control are strengthened.

III. POTENTIAL BENEFITS AND THE TIME DIMENSION

This Part analyzes the potential benefits of a dual-class structure and how they can be expected to change over time. In particular, a dual-class structure is often justified by the superior leadership skills of the founder

---

[69] Ford has a hardwiring provision that provides the controlling family with 40% of the company's voting power, without regards to the family's equity holding. Ford Motor Co., Proxy Statement for the 2016 Annual Meeting (Schedule 14A) 72, 76 (Apr. 1, 2016).
[70] The data was hand collected from Forms S-1 and Proxy Statements of the relevant companies, filed on the SEC's EDGAR.
[71] See Bebchuk et al., supra note 56, at 301–05.
[72] See id. at 298–301.

at the time of the IPO or by the need to insulate management from short-term market pressures. However, as this Part shows, none of these arguments can support the use of dual-class stock with infinite life.

A. Superior Leadership Skills

As noted earlier, supporters of dual-class stock often argue that it could be value enhancing to provide a talented founder with a lock on control because of her superior business skills.[73] According to this view, a lock on control enables a talented founder to freely implement her strategy and "utilize" her skills to produce superior returns. These superior returns could in turn benefit not just the founder but also all other investors.[74]

This potential benefit, however, greatly depends on the controller being a superior, or at least a fitting, leader of the company. Even assuming this to be the case at the IPO stage, changes in the superior skills of a controller may occur over time due to the factors discussed in Section II.B. First, in a dynamic business environment, as time passes, even a founder who was a superior leader at the time of the IPO might become ill fitting due to aging or changes in circumstances.[75] Second, over time, a founder who had superior leadership skills might transfer the control to her heirs who lack such skills. Third, over time, the controller might reduce the fraction of equity capital she holds, and this reduction might in turn worsen the controller's incentives. When the controller turns out to be an ill-fitting leader for the company due to one or more of these factors, the "superior controller" argument for maintaining a lock on control weakens and might even reverse. Letting an ill-fitting controller determine business decisions and outcomes might be counterproductive.

Whereas private equity funds are sometimes praised as structures that enable long-term focus, they generally provide their general partners with control only for a fixed period of time, usually on the order of ten years, rather than permanently.[76] This structure might well reflect recognition that, many years down the road, a general partner's skills might

---

[73] See supra Subsection II.B.1.
[74] See, e.g., Zohar Goshen & Assaf Hamdani, Corporate Control and Idiosyncratic Vision, 125 Yale L.J. 560, 567 (2016).
[75] See supra note 63.
[76] See supra notes 66–67.

---

no longer be superior or even adequate. Similarly, any "superior controller" benefits that a dual-class structure might offer at the time of the IPO are likely, on an expected-value basis, to decline or even disappear many years after the IPO.

B. Long Termism

Another benefit that supporters ascribe to dual-class structures is that they insulate corporate decision makers from short-term market pressures and enable them to focus on the long term.[77] For instance, Snap's IPO documents state that the company's structure is intended to "permit us to continue to prioritize our long-term goals rather than short-term results."[78] According to this view, without a lock on control, founders might be concerned that they might be ousted if their short-term performance is poor and might, therefore, seek to enhance short-term prices at the expense of long-term value. With a long-term lock on control that a dual-class structure provides, so the argument goes, founders can focus on the long term and make decisions that enhance long-term value free from short-term pressures and the constant risk of being ousted.[79]

We note that this "long-termism" argument for dual-class structures lacks substantial empirical support. For example, a recent academic study finds that, compared with single-class companies, dual-class companies do not invest more either in general or in research and development.[80] Regardless, even if a dual-class structure were to offer some long-term benefits at the time of the IPO, these benefits can be expected to recede or even reverse over time.

---

[77] For early work raising the claim that dual-class stock facilitates long-term planning and reduces the distraction caused by the threat of takeovers, see Dent, supra note 68, at 748, and Daniel R. Fischel, Organized Exchanges and the Regulation of Dual Class Common Stock, 54 U. Chi. L. Rev. 119, 137–38 (1987). See also Solomon, supra note 24 ("Many defend dual-class stock because it may insulate a company from pressure to take short-term actions at the behest of shareholders."); The CCGG Policy, supra note 16, at 3 (presenting the long-term advantages of dual-class stock).
[78] See Snap Registration Statement, supra note 12, at 167.
[79] Id. (noting that the company's triple-class structure also intends to discourage transactions that may involve an actual or threatened acquisition of Snap). For a review and examination of the literature on long termism, see Lucian A. Bebchuk, The Myth that Insulating Boards Serves Long-Term Value, 113 Colum. L. Rev. 1637 (2013).
[80] Onur Arugaslan et al., On the Decision to Go Public with Dual Class Stock, 16 J. Corp. Fin. 170, 171, 174 (2010).

The expected benefits from long-term insulation are likely to be large or even positive only when the controller is a fitting leader for the company. The long-termism argument loses its force when the controller is ill fitting. An ill-fitting controller might make poor decisions not just for the short term but also for the long term.[81] When the controller becomes ill fitting, insulating her from market discipline could be counterproductive. Since the passage of time makes the controller less likely to be the fittest leader of the company, as discussed in the preceding Section, the expected benefit from long-term insulation is also likely to decline over time.

Finally, it might be argued that insulation from market forces is especially valuable for young companies with volatile value in the years following their IPOs. Whereas this view supports permitting companies to go public with a dual-class structure, it does not provide a basis for having such a structure indefinitely.[82] This view can support having a dual-class structure for only the years following the IPO and is fully consistent with sunsetting the dual-class structure when the company matures.

C. Oversight Benefits

Another potential benefit often ascribed to having a controlling shareholder is oversight benefits.[83] A controlling-shareholder structure moves power from professional managers to a controller, who has both the ability and incentives to police managers and limit their agency problems. By doing so, controllers "may better help the controlled company to re-

---

[81] Thomas J. Chemmanur & Yawen Jiao, Dual Class IPOs: A Theoretical Analysis, 36 J. Banking & Fin. 305, 305–06 (2012) (developing a model suggesting that dual-class stock may increase firm value in the hands of high-ability managers but may increase agency costs and reduce value in the hands of low-ability managers).

[82] See, e.g., Bebchuk, supra note 16, at 751–52 (noting that "the optimal arrangements for a publicly traded company that just went public . . . might well be different from those optimal for a large, mature publicly traded company"); William C. Johnson et al., The Lifecycle of Firm Takeover Defenses 1, 6 (Mar. 3, 2017) (unpublished manuscript) https://ssrn.com/abstract=2808208 [https://perma.cc/76GT-GCBW] (reporting that "the relation between firm value and the use of takeover defenses is positive for firms at their IPOs, and declines steadily as the firm matures, becoming negative approximately five years after the IPO").

[83] Gilson & Schwartz, supra note 61, at 168 (arguing that monitoring by controlling shareholders, including those relying on dual-class common stock, can be superior to market discipline).

---

alize the gains from professional management at lower agency costs than do markets."[84] When holding a majority of the equity capital would not be feasible or impose large risk-bearing costs on the controller, a dual-class structure would facilitate retaining a controlling-shareholder structure and thereby enable the controller to oversee and limit the power of the managers.

The size of any oversight benefits, however, likely depends on the extent to which the controller is a fitting leader for the company and has appropriate incentives. When this is no longer the case, the benefits of shifting power from managers to controllers might decline or even reverse. As discussed in Section II.B, the quality of both the controller's leadership skills and incentives can be expected to decline as time passes from the IPO due to the likely erosion of the controller's superior skills and the likely decrease in the controller's fraction of equity capital. As a result, there is a risk, growing over time, that the controller's ability and incentives to provide oversight will also diminish.[85] At the same time, monitoring by activist investors that focus on widely held firms might be discouraged by the presence of a controlling shareholder. Overall, any oversight benefits that a dual-class structure might provide at the time of the IPO can be expected to decline or even reverse over time.

IV. THE PERSISTENCE OF INEFFICIENT STRUCTURES

We have demonstrated that dual-class structures tend to become less efficient over time and that this reduced efficiency favors the choice of a dual-class structure with finite duration at the IPO stage. One can argue, however, that if a dual-class structure becomes inefficient over time, it can be expected to be eliminated by an ex-post private action. This Part analyzes the merits of this argument and explains why public officials and investors cannot rely on private ordering to eliminate dual-class structures that become inefficient with time.

Below we describe two main routes that can lead to the elimination of a dual-class structure: (1) a sale of the entire dual-class firm to an outside buyer and (2) a voluntary unification of the dual-class structure by

---

[84] Id.

[85] Recall the example of Sumner Redstone, see supra notes 4–5, who, at the age of ninety-three and with a deteriorating health condition, seems unlikely to be an effective monitor of managerial performance.

the existing controller. As we show, in both scenarios, the controller would forgo the private benefits of control associated with the dual-class structure while capturing only a fraction of the efficiency benefits generated by its elimination. As a result, controllers' structural incentives may lead them to retain a dual-class structure that becomes inefficient.

A. Resistance to a Sale

A dual-class structure could be eliminated through the sale of the entire company or all of its assets to a third party. When a dual-class company is managed inefficiently, the company's stock price is likely to be below its full potential value. In this case, it might be argued, an outside buyer could emerge and offer to purchase the whole company for a price that is at a significant premium to its market capitalization. On this view, a sale would be expected to end the inefficient dual-class structure that depressed the market value of the company.

As we explain below, however, the controlling shareholder might be unwilling to accept such a value-enhancing sale. Controlling shareholders, especially those who hold a small fraction of equity capital, have significant perverse incentives to retain a dual-class structure even when eliminating it through a sale of the company would produce significant efficiency gains for the company's shareholders. Whereas the sale would eliminate the controller's private benefits of control, the controller would capture only a minority (or even a small minority) of the produced efficiency gains, which would be shared pro rata by all shareholders.

To illustrate this distortion in controllers' incentives, consider the following simple example. Suppose that a dual-class structure enables a controller who holds 10% of the equity capital to have a lock on control. Suppose that the market value of the company is $1 billion, that the company is now managed inefficiently due to the dual-class structure, and that an outside buyer, say a given widely held company, would be willing to offer for the company a price P substantially exceeding $1 billion. Would such a sale take place?

Not necessarily. The controller would take into account not only the premium offered but also that the sale would bring to an end her control and the private benefits associated with it. Suppose that the controller derives private benefits worth 5% of the company's current value ($50 million). In this case, the controller currently holds 10% of the $1 billion

market capitalization and private benefits of $50 million, or a total value of $150 million. In the event of a sale, the controller would receive 10% of the sale price P but would lose all of her private benefits of control.[86]

Therefore, as long as 10% of P does not exceed $150 million—that is, as long as P does not exceed $1.5 billion—a sale would not be in the private interest of the controller. If the outside buyer would be willing to offer less than $1.5 billion (because it estimates the potential value gains by up to $500 million), then a value-enhancing sale will not occur. Thus, there is a wide range of situations in which a sale that would produce gains from eliminating an inefficient dual-class structure would not take place.[87]

Let us now consider the problem in a more general formulation. Suppose that a controller owns α of the company's equity capital and derives B as private benefits of control and that the market capitalization of the controlled company is V. Suppose also that the current structure is inefficient, that an outside buyer would therefore be able to increase the value by a large amount of ΔV, and that the sale would eliminate the controller's private benefits of B.[88] Since the highest price the outside buyer would be willing to pay (P) is $V + \Delta V$, the transaction would not be in the private interest of the controller and could not be expected to take place as long as:

---

[86] Our analysis assumes that the acquisition price will be distributed pro rata. Of course, the controller might be willing to sell the whole company if she could get a much larger per-share price than other public investors. But, the Delaware court has placed limits on the ability of a controller to sell the controlled company to a third party in exchange for a benefit not shared by other shareholders by subjecting the transaction to the entire fairness review. See, e.g., In re John Q. Hammons Hotels Inc. S'holder Litig., No. CIV. A. 758-CC, 2009 WL 3165613, at *12 (Del. Ch. Oct. 2, 2009); In re Tele-Commc'ns, Inc. S'holders Litig., No. CIV. A. 16470, 2005 WL 3642727, at *7 (Del. Ch. Dec. 21, 2005); In re LNR Prop. Corp. S'holders Litig., 896 A.2d 169, 178 (Del. Ch. Nov. 4, 2005). Differential consideration in the event that there is a change of control is also prohibited by certain exchanges, such as the Toronto Stock Exchange. See The CCGG Policy, supra note 16, at 9–10. While such limits might well be justified, their unintended consequence is that the controller might often prefer to retain the dual-class structure even if it becomes inefficient.

[87] When considering the case of unification, we assume that existing rules against self-dealing protect public shareholders of a dual-class company from having the controller appropriate to herself a bigger fraction of the company value by, for instance, freezing out minority shareholders at a depressed price.

[88] We assume that ΔV exceeds B and that the sale would thus clearly be efficient.

$$aV + B > a[(V + \Delta V)]$$

which would be the case as long as

$$\Delta V < B/\alpha.$$

Thus, when the controller enjoys significant private benefits of control, the controller has a structural incentive to retain a dual-class structure in a range of situations in which a sale would be efficient. Note that this range expands, and the controller's perverse incentives strengthen, when the controller's fraction of equity capital (α) is smaller. Therefore, when α declines over time, the decline tends to increase the inefficiencies of a dual-class structure and strengthens the controller's incentive to retain the dual-class structure.

We should emphasize that the above distortion does not imply that such a sale would never take place. As the analysis shows, the sale would take place if the expected gain (ΔV) is sufficiently large. The key point, however, is that a sale ending in an inefficient dual-class structure would not be expected to take place for a substantial range of inefficient situations.

B. Resistance to a Unification

Another route for eliminating an inefficient dual-class structure is a voluntary conversion to a single-class structure by the controller. Yet, a controller has structural incentives to avoid such unification even if it would produce substantial efficiency gains. The distortion afflicting the controller's choice whether to have a value-enhancing unification is similar to the distortion afflicting her choice regarding a value-enhancing sale: In both cases, the controller would capture only a fraction of the efficiency gains that the transaction would produce while fully bearing the loss of the private benefits of control.

Let us again consider a controller who owns a fraction α of the company's equity capital and derives B as private benefits of control, and suppose that the market capitalization of the controlled company is V. Further suppose that the current structure is inefficient and that the unification would increase the market capitalization by a large amount of

ΔV and would eliminate the controller's private benefits of B.[89] If the conversion takes place, the controller will have her fraction α of the enhanced value $V + \Delta V$. Still, the transaction would not serve the controller's private interest under the same condition identified in the preceding section—that is, as long as $\alpha V + B > \alpha[(V + \Delta V)]$. Thus, as long as $\Delta V < B/\alpha$, the controller would retain the dual-class structure. As before, the smaller the fraction of equity capital (α) and the larger the private benefits of control (B), then the wider the range of efficient unifications that the controller would have an incentive not to effect.[90]

Here, again, our analysis does not suggest that efficient voluntary dual-class unifications will never occur. Despite the structural incentives that the controller has to retain the dual-class structure, the controller would have an incentive to unify the dual-class structure when ΔV is large enough. Our point is only that a unification that could bring an inefficient dual-class structure to an end also might not take place for a substantial range of inefficient situations.

This theoretical analysis is supported by evidence presented in a recent empirical study on dual-class unifications in Europe.[91] This study shows that controllers with low equity interest and high levels of private-benefit extraction possibilities are less likely to effect a dual-class unification. Likewise, evidence on precatory shareholder proposals to dismantle the dual-class stock of U.S. companies show that controllers tend to disregard the results even when the overwhelming majority of

---

[89] We assume that ΔV exceeds B and that the sale would thus clearly be efficient.

[90] Controllers might agree to unify the dual-class shares if they get a substantially large side payment from public investors to compensate them for the loss of their private benefits of control. The Delaware court, however, has placed limits on the ability of a controller to engage in dual-class restructuring with side payments by subjecting this type of transaction to an entire fairness review. See, e.g., Levco Alt. Fund Ltd. v. Reader's Digest Ass'n, 803 A.2d 428 (Table), 2002 WL 1859064, at *2 (Del. Aug. 13, 2002). Indeed, we were unable to identify any significant number of voluntary unifications in exchange for significant side payments either in the United States or Europe. See also Benjamin Maury & Anete Pajuste, Private Benefits of Control and Dual-Class Share Unifications, 32 Managerial & Decision Econ. 355, 365 (2011) (researching dual-class unifications in seven Western European countries and finding that only nine companies (out of 493 companies) compensate the controller for the loss of voting rights with additional stock or cash).

[91] See, e.g., Maury & Pajuste, supra note 90, at 356 (finding that "firms with lower levels of private benefit extraction possibilities, that is, the ones with a lower wedge between the voting rights and equity rights held by the controlling shareholders, the ones with a financial investor, and the ones cross-listed in the USA, are more likely to unify their share classes").

shareholders unaffiliated with the controllers vote in favor of these proposals.[92]

In sum, the theory presented in this Part suggests that controlling shareholders have substantial private incentives to retain a dual-class structure even if it becomes inefficient. This analysis of the persistence of inefficient dual-class structures is consistent with patterns documented in a recent study by ISS. The study found that dual-class companies have longer life spans than companies without such a structure.[93] The average age of these dual-class companies (31 years) was "more than double the [average] age (15 years) of firms with a single class of shares and a controlling party."[94]

V. SUNSETTING DUAL-CLASS STRUCTURES

Part III showed that as time elapses following the IPO, the costs of a dual-class structure can be expected to increase while the benefits decline. Over time, therefore, there is a growing risk that a dual-class structure will stop being an efficient capital structure, even if it were so at the outset. Furthermore, as demonstrated in Part IV, controllers have considerable private incentives to retain a dual-class structure regardless of its efficiency from the standpoint of shareholder wealth.

As noted in the Introduction, we disfavor the use of dual-class structures altogether. However, to the extent that companies are permitted to go public with a dual-class structure, our analysis calls for including an adequate sunset provision. Absent a sunset provision, the lifecycle of a dual-class structure is perpetual, and this infinite duration is likely to create growing risks and costs over time. Section A of this Part discusses the optimal design of a sunset clause. Section B addresses potential objections to such a clause.

A. Designing Sunset Clauses

Below we discuss several possible designs of a sunset clause and, in particular, the trigger for sunsetting the dual-class structure: (1) a fixed-time sunset, (2) a triggering-event sunset, and (3) an ownership-percentage sunset. We explain why we favor the use of fixed-time sunsets, address situations in which it is efficient to extend the duration of the dual-class structure, and conclude with an additional design issue—addressing attempts at circumventing the sunset clause.

1. Fixed-Time Sunset

A sunset provision with a time limitation is triggered at a predetermined date—say, ten years after the IPO. When the clause is activated, the shares with the superior voting rights automatically convert into ordinary shares, and the company's second class is eliminated. To enable the retention of structures that remain efficient, the provision may stipulate that the conversion could be delayed by additional periods of not more than ten years each, provided that the majority of shareholders unaffiliated with the controller approve such extensions. This type of sunset clause ensures that controlling shareholders would be able to retain only efficient dual-class structures. With unaffiliated shareholders determining the structure's future, the controlling shareholder is unlikely to prolong an inefficient structure that serves her private benefits at the expense of enterprise value.

We have identified several companies—including Fitbit, Groupon, Kayak, and Yelp—that recently adopted a fixed-time sunset clause at the IPO stage.[95] The duration of the dual-class structures in these cases ranged from five years to twenty years. Groupon, for example, adopted a five-year sunset clause at its IPO in 2011, and, as a result, it converted to a single-class company in 2016.[96] However, the companies adopting this type of provision still constitute a minority of dual-class IPOs.[97]

---

[92] We examined data from SharkRepellent on fifty-three shareholder proposals to dismantle dual-class structures submitted to twenty-five Russell 3000 companies between 2005 and 2014. When a proposal to eliminate dual-class structures was submitted to the same company more than once, we used the proposal that received the highest support rate. On average, these proposals obtained a support rate of 71% among shareholders unaffiliated with the controllers. Nonetheless, in all these cases, the controller chose not to implement the proposal.
[93] See Kamonjoh, supra note 17, at 22.
[94] Id.

[95] We reviewed the Forms S-1 of the fifty largest dual-class companies that went public between 2009 and 2015. Of these companies, we identified twelve that went public with a fixed-time sunset.
[96] Groupon, Inc., Amendment No. 7 to Registration Statement (Form S-1) 6, 98 (Nov. 1, 2011); Groupon, Inc., Current Report (Form 8-K) (Oct. 31, 2016).
[97] See supra note 95. Also, a review of the organizational documents of all controlled dual-class companies in the S&P 1500 shows that none of them has a sunset provision with a fixed-time limitation.

2. Triggering-Event Sunset

A second type of sunset, adopted by some dual-class companies, is a triggering-event sunset requiring a conversion to a single-class structure upon the occurrence of a specified event, such as the founder's disability, death, or reaching of retirement age.[98] This type of a sunset arrangement prevents the founder from retaining control when reaching old age or disability and from transferring control to heirs. However, such a sunset provides the founder with control for the remainder of her working life.[99]

For a founder who is young or middle-aged, such a sunset allows a lock on control that has an excessively long duration. Consider a founder who is forty years old and goes public with a sunset providing for expiration of the dual-class structure upon her reaching the age of seventy. This triggering-event sunset would likely keep the founder in power for thirty years. Considering the analysis in Parts II and III regarding the eroding efficiencies of dual-class structures over time, a three-decade duration creates substantial risks and expected costs. A founder who has decades of working life ahead of her poses substantial risks that she would not remain a fitting leader of the company throughout her entire working life. Thus, a standard triggering-event sunset that provides the founder with power over the company for the remainder of her working life is substantially inferior to a ten- or fifteen-year time limitation.

3. Ownership-Percentage Sunset

Some companies, including LinkedIn and Zynga, have recently adopted a sunset clause triggered by crossing a certain ownership percentage.[100] An ownership-percentage sunset converts the high-vote shares held by the founders into common stock when they represent less than a certain predetermined percentage of the total number of all common shares outstanding. The rationale for such a trigger is that a large equity stake provides an alignment of interest between the controller and public investors and might thus mitigate concerns associated with allowing the founder to retain control. However, although such a sunset provision may induce the controller to retain at least the specified stake during the period of control, it is unlikely to effectively address the problem of control lasting for an excessively long period.

We note that the ownership-percentage sunsets recently adopted in dual-class IPOs tend to feature low ownership thresholds. Indeed, the data that we hand-collected on U.S. dual-class companies suggest that most of them use an ownership threshold that does not exceed 10%, meaning that the controller can retain a lock on control despite a significant wedge between her voting rights and cash-flow rights.[101] When the controller owns one-tenth (or less) of the company's equity capital, the wedge between voting power and economic stake is large and the risks and potential costs of distortions are substantial.

Most importantly, sunsets with ownership-percentage triggers are unlikely to lead to an expiration of the dual-class structure. The controller can and is likely to avoid such expiration by keeping her fraction of equity ownership above the specified floor. When the private benefits associated with control are significant, the controller can be expected to stay above the ownership trigger to retain these private benefits.

---

[98] Google, Groupon, LinkedIn, and Zynga adopted such a triggering-event sunset when they went public. See HKEX Report, supra note 26, at 47.

[99] See the example of Couche-Tard, a Canadian company that operates a large chain of convenience stores. Couche-Tard had a sunset provision that was to be triggered when the youngest of the founders turned sixty-five or passed away. Although the controllers were interested in prolonging the dual-class structure, shareholders rejected a management proposal to that end in 2015, and the company had to unify its dual-class structure. See Press Release, Alimentation Couche-Tard Inc., Alimentation Couche-Tard Inc. Files Management Proxy Circular (July 24, 2015), http://www.prnewswire.com/news-releases/alimentation-couche-tard-inc-files-management-proxy-circular-518408281.html [https://perma.cc/4CGA-FKBN]; Nicolas Van Praet & Bertrand Marotte, Couche-Tard Chairman Says Bay Street Investors Blocking Founders' Control, Globe & Mail (Apr. 20, 2016), http://www.theglobeandmail.com/report-on-business/couche-tard-chairman-says-bay-street-investors-blocking-founders-control/article29699072/.

[100] See HKEX Report, supra note 26, at 46, 48. We reviewed the organizational documents of all seventy-eight controlled dual-class companies in the S&P 1500 as of 2015. Twenty-five of them adopted a sunset provision with a beneficial ownership threshold. We also reviewed the fifty largest dual-class IPOs during the period 2009–2015; 54% of these adopted a sunset with ownership threshold.

[101] Eighty percent of the dual-class companies in the S&P 1500 that adopted a sunset provision with a beneficial ownership threshold have an ownership threshold that does not exceed 10%. Similarly, 63% of the recent largest dual-class IPOs that adopted this type of sunset set a minimum ownership threshold of 10% or less.

B. Objections

This Section considers and responds to several possible objections to requiring sunsets. In particular, we examine the Panglossian objection, the "one-size-does-not-fit-all" objection, the concern that such a requirement would discourage IPOs, and the end-period problem. We conclude that these objections do not, either individually or collectively, provide a good basis for opposing sunset provisions.

1. The Panglossian Objection

We begin with an objection that we refer to as the Panglossian objection.[105] According to this objection, market forces ensure that the best governance arrangements are always adopted. Because founders taking their companies public have strong incentives to adopt a value-maximizing set of arrangements, Panglossians argue that these founders can be expected to adopt sunset clauses whenever they are value enhancing.[106] Thus, on this view, whenever controllers go public without a sunset provision, the provision is bound to be value reducing.

There are several reasons for questioning this objection. To begin, to accept the Panglossian argument, one must believe not only (1) that the market accurately prices the difference between a dual-class structure and a single-class structure, but also (2) that the market prices accurately the difference between a dual-class structure with and without a sunset clause. Belief (2) assumes a very high degree of market efficiency. Whereas IPO buyers might pay attention to and price a salient feature like a dual-class structure, they might not similarly price more subtle features, such as the presence and specifics of a sunset provision.[107]

Second, to accept the Panglossian argument, one must accept that it is commonly value maximizing for dual-class structures to have a perpetu-

---

[105] We use this term in the sense that it was used in Lucian Arye Bebchuk, The Case for Increasing Shareholder Power, 118 Harv. L. Rev. 833, 888 (2005), and Lucian A. Bebchuk, Reply, Letting Shareholders Set the Rules, 119 Harv. L. Rev. 1784, 1805–06 (2006). The term is named after Voltaire's protagonist, Dr. Pangloss, who believed that our world is "the best of all possible worlds." See Voltaire, Candide, or Optimism 17 (Burton Raffel trans., Yale Univ. Press 2005) (1759).
[106] For a general formulation of the argument that IPO pricing reflects the quality of offered governance, see Fischel, supra note 77, at 123–25, and Romano, supra note 51, at 2361–64.
[107] Bebchuk, supra note 16, at 740–42 (discussing the pricing of governance terms).

To be clear, compared with a perpetual dual-class structure that has no restrictions on reducing the controller's equity stake, an ownership-threshold sunset introducing such restrictions may provide *some* benefits. Such a provision may induce the controller to retain a larger fraction of the equity capital than she otherwise would, and thereby limit the wedge between her voting rights and cash rights as well as the potential distortions resulting from this wedge.[102] Such a sunset provision, however, inadequately addresses the problem of indefinite retention of power even when the dual-class structure becomes inefficient. By contrast, a fixed-time sunset addresses this concern directly and effectively.

4. Addressing Circumvention

Of course, as with every regulatory arrangement, policymakers who consider requiring dual-class IPOs to include a sunset should examine whether founders would be able to circumvent such a requirement. For example, founders might try to bypass such a requirement by going public with nonvoting preferred shares rather than common shares with inferior voting rights.

Such circumvention issues arise in the case of any rule that limits the use of dual-class structures. Indeed, a number of jurisdictions that prohibit dual-class IPOs, including Belgium, Estonia, Germany, Greece, Luxembourg, and Spain, have already dealt with such issues. In these jurisdictions, nonvoting-preference shares may not represent more than a certain percentage (usually up to 50%) of the company's outstanding shares.[103] Moreover, these jurisdictions usually require preferred shares to have preferential rights for dividends, which discourages their use as a circumvention device around a dual-class prohibition.[104] Finally, more generally, controllers' incentives to circumvent mandated sunset provisions are considerably weaker than their incentives to circumvent outright prohibitions on dual-class structures.

---

[102] See supra Subsection II.B.2.
[103] The size of the cap varies from jurisdiction to jurisdiction. It is 33% of the company equity capital in Belgium and Estonia; 40% in Greece; and 50% in Germany, Luxembourg, and Spain. See Report on the Proportionality Principle, supra note 26, at 19.
[104] Id.

al duration. Because founders going public with a dual-class structure have commonly not included any sunset provision, Panglossians must believe that in all these cases any time limitation whatsoever would have been value decreasing on the whole.[108] As our analysis has shown, however, the potential benefits of a dual-class structure tend to decline over time, its potential costs tend to increase over time, and controllers have private incentives that might lead them to retain a dual-class structure even if it becomes inefficient. Therefore, while there might be room for reasonable disagreement about the optimal *duration* of dual-class structures, it is in our opinion implausible to believe that perpetual duration is commonly optimal.

Of course, some Panglossians might take the view that, as a matter of principle, they oppose any mandatory limitation on the terms that controllers may choose to offer when going public. The main audience of our analysis, however, are readers who are interested in identifying which arrangements are likely to be value reducing because they are open to restricting or discouraging terms likely to be value reducing. Such readers should find of interest our demonstration that perpetual dual-class structures are unlikely to be value enhancing.

2. One Size Does Not Fit All

A related objection is the "one-size-does-not-fit-all" objection. A governance arrangement that might be optimal for some companies might not be optimal for others. Therefore, it might be argued, some dual-class structures might remain desirable several or even many decades after the IPO.

A sunset provision, however, would not necessarily result in the removal of an optimal dual-class structure after a certain period of time. Rather, such a provision merely prevents the controller from unilaterally prolonging the use of a dual-class structure that investors oppose as value reducing. If a controlling shareholder performs well and extending her control seems to be value enhancing, shareholders would be able to vote to prolong the controller's power for an additional period.

Consider the example of Fairfax, a major Canadian company that has a dual-class structure. In the summer of 2015, the controller of Fairfax brought to a shareholder vote governance changes extending his out-

---

[108] See supra notes 95 & 97 and accompanying text.

sized voting power, and these changes were approved by 68.4% of the votes cast by shareholders unaffiliated with the controller.[109] This example illustrates that investors whose money is on the line — including, critically, institutional investors — can be persuaded to extend a dual-class structure if they view such extension to be value enhancing.

3. Discouraging IPOs

Another possible objection to any proposed limitation on the use of dual-class structures is that the limitation would discourage founders from taking their company public. As a result, it might be argued, such a restriction would deprive public investors of beneficial investment opportunities. In our view, however, this concern does not justify support for perpetual dual-class structures.

Several developed-market jurisdictions, including Hong Kong and the United Kingdom, prohibit or strongly discourage the use of dual-class stock but still have well-developed capital markets with a large number of publicly traded companies.[110] The experience of these jurisdictions, as well as the history of the United States capital markets during the decades in which the leading American stock exchange prohibited dual-class structures, suggests that founder willingness to go public is robust even when dual-class structures are completely prohibited.[111] And requiring such structures to include a sunset can be expected to have less of an effect on the willingness to go public than their outright prohibition. For founders with limited personal wealth, accessing the public market at some point is commonly critical to scaling up their companies and creating liquidity for themselves and early investors.

---

[109] Press Release, Fairfax Fin. Holdings Ltd., Fairfax Calls Special Shareholders' Meeting to Consider Amendment to Terms of Multiple Voting Shares (June 12, 2015, 6:16 PM), http://www.marketwired.com/press-release/fairfax-calls-special-shareholders-meeting-consider-amendment-terms-multiple-voting-tsx-ffh-2029345.htm [https://perma.cc/GSN4-C43F]; Press Release, Fairfax Fin. Holdings Ltd., Fairfax Announces Approval of Amendments to Multiple Voting Share Terms (Aug. 24, 2015, 10:05 AM), http://www.marketwired.com/press-release/fairfax-announces-approval-of-amendments-to-multiple-voting-share-terms-tsx-ffh-2049809.htm [https://perma.cc/6E29-TP7J].

[110] See supra notes 46–50 and accompanying text.

[111] See supra notes 28–35 and accompanying text. True, founders can still choose to list their companies outside the United States, but there are heavy regulatory costs associated with foreign listings. Also, as noted earlier, the major competitors of the United States as international financial centers do not permit the use of dual-class stock, and, therefore, U.S. founders are unlikely to take their companies public elsewhere.

Some may argue that, in the current environment, founders can obtain outside equity capital from venture capital funds and other investors and thereby avoid going public. However, such outside equity investors often provide financing based on their expectation that the company will eventually provide them with an "exit" through an IPO or sale. Such investors are unlikely to be willing to become investors in a company that will permanently remain private and under the founder's control.[112]

4. *The End-Period Problem*

Another possible concern is that the adoption of a sunset clause would lead a controlling shareholder to act opportunistically in the period just before the dual-class structure is set to expire. According to this view, a controller on the precipice of losing her outsized influence might choose to act aggressively in the end period to take advantage of her power over the company while it lasts. This concern, however, does not justify perpetual dual-class structures.

First, existing corporate-law rules governing controlling shareholders would place some limits on the extent to which a controller can divert value during the end period.[113] Furthermore, to the extent that controllers are able to engage in significant value diversion in the end period, allowing perpetual control is a counterproductive response to it. Shareholders would likely be worse off having to bear the costs of such diversion indefinitely than to bear the costs of a somewhat increased diversion in the end period.

Finally, enabling shareholders unaffiliated with the controller to extend the duration of a dual-class structure that is scheduled to sunset would discourage end-period opportunism. As long as there is a chance of obtaining such an extension, its prospect would provide the controller

---

[112] Even if a founder could hypothetically find alternative private funding sources, going public would still have certain advantages. In particular, going public would tap the resources of a vast number of potential investors, enable trading in very liquid markets, and provide a convenient currency for compensating employees and making acquisitions.

[113] Delaware law, for example, places limits on the extent to which a controlling shareholder can obtain private benefits of control through related-party transactions by subjecting these transactions to judicial scrutiny. See, e.g., In re Ezcorp Inc. Consulting Agreement Derivative Litig., No. CV 9962-VCL, 2016 WL 301245, at *29–30 (Del. Ch. Jan. 25, 2016) (reviewing Delaware cases that have subjected such transactions to judicial scrutiny).

an incentive to perform well and to avoid opportunism that could discourage shareholders from voting against an extension.[114]

VI. GOING FORWARD

This Part discusses the significant implications of our analysis. In particular, we review the implications that this analysis has for public officials (Section A), institutional investors and their advisors (Section B), and researchers (Section C).

A. *Public Officials*

Our analysis has considerable implications for public officials in jurisdictions that permit the use of dual-class stock. In discussing these implications, it is useful to distinguish and consider separately (1) future dual-class IPOs and (2) existing companies that have already gone public with a perpetual dual-class structure.

Future Dual-class IPOs. Public officials should consider requiring companies that go public with a dual-class structure to include a sunset provision. In particular, we recommend a ten- or fifteen-year sunset with an option to extend that period by an affirmative vote of shareholders unaffiliated with the controller. As explained in Part IV, there are reasons to expect that the private interests of controllers might lead them to retain a dual-class structure even if it becomes inefficient and other public shareholders oppose its continued use.[115] These reasons, in turn, make it desirable to have a sunset with an extension option built into the dual-class structure.

Requiring sunsets would still enable controllers to go public with a dual-class structure and have secure control for a substantial period of time after the IPO. Furthermore, the extension option embedded into sunsets would enable a dual-class structure to remain in place if it continues to be efficient when the time for its expiration arrives. If a controlling shareholder performs well during the first ten- or fifteen-year pe-

---

[114] To the extent that one is concerned about having a sharp endpoint, one could consider using a "gradual" sunset. Under such a gradual sunset, after a period of, say, ten or fifteen years, the high-vote shares will convert to low-vote shares gradually over a period of several years. Certain issuers may prefer a gradual conversion along these lines to a one-time dropoff in voting power.

[115] See supra Section IV.A.

riod and retaining the dual-class structure appears to serve shareholder value, other shareholders can be expected to vote in favor of an extension.

Existing Dual-class Companies. The policy implications for companies that have already gone public without a sunset provision raise additional issues deserving attention that we would like to flag briefly. Our analysis indicates that leaving perpetual dual-class structures in place indefinitely can be expected to produce governance problems and efficiency losses. This analysis also indicates that, without government intervention, such companies might get "stuck" in an inefficient dual-class structure for a long time.

On the other hand, requiring companies that already went public with a dual-class structure to add ex post a sunset provision could be viewed as transferring value from controllers to public investors. To the extent that public officials are reluctant to act in a way that raises a distributive concern, they might consider coupling the introduction of sunset provisions with compensation to controllers for the loss of their superior voting rights. During the 1990s, Israeli public officials adopted rules that encouraged controllers to accept dual-class stock unifications while enabling controllers to receive compensation in the form of additional common shares for giving up their superior voting status.[116] Joining sunset provisions with compensation to the controller can benefit both public investors and controllers, especially where companies remain stuck for a long time in an inefficient dual-class structure.

Finally, to the extent that public officials enable some existing companies to retain dual-class structures without a sunset provision, they should recognize that such companies are especially prone to governance problems and agency costs. Thus, such companies would be appropriate candidates for stricter scrutiny of controller choices or other enhanced protections of public investors.[117] For example, a recent article co-authored by Assaf Hamdani and one of us puts forward the possibility of strengthening the protection of public investors in controlled com-

---

[116] Shmuel Hauser & Beni Lauterbach, The Value of Voting Rights to Majority Shareholders: Evidence from Dual-Class Stock Unifications, 17 Rev. Fin. Stud. 1167, 1169 (2004).
[117] For a review and analysis of the types of arrangements that are and are not effective for protecting public investors from controller opportunism, see Lucian A. Bebchuk & Assaf Hamdani, The Elusive Quest For Global Governance Standards, 157 U. Pa. L. Rev. 1263 (2009).

---

panies by enabling these shareholders to influence the choices of independent directors.[118] Indeed, such enhanced protections could be especially valuable and appropriate for controlled companies with an enhanced risk of governance problems.

B. Investors and Advisors

Leading institutional investors have expressed their opposition to the use of dual-class stock and have sought to end its use.[119] Both of us are skeptical of dual-class structures and would welcome a general return to single-class structures. However, in jurisdictions where institutional investors conclude that ending the use of dual-class structures is not feasible, they should at least consider pressing for the use of appropriate sunset provisions in all dual-class companies. General adoption of such sunsets would address a major concern posed by dual-class structures: the problem of long-standing structures that become increasingly costly and inefficient over time.

The leading proxy advisor, ISS, recently moved in the direction we advocate, amending its voting policies to indicate its intention to issue negative recommendations for director nominees at companies with a dual-class structure that does not include a "reasonable sunset provision."[120] We are pleased by this change and believe that our analysis provides a useful framework for any future assessment of the reasonableness of a sunset provision. This analysis suggests (1) that acceptable sunset provisions should have a fixed-time trigger rather than only a triggering-event or ownership-percentage trigger; (2) that a fixed-time duration of ten or fifteen years is reasonable; and (3) that reasonable sunset provisions should include an option to extend the dual-class structure upon the affirmative majority approval of shareholders unaffiliated with the controller.

---

[118] Lucian A. Bebchuk & Assaf Hamdani, Making Independent Directors Work, 165 U. Pa. L. Rev. (forthcoming May 2017).
[119] See supra notes 36–43 and accompanying text.
[120] See Institutional S'holder Servs., Americas: U.S., Canada, and Latin America Proxy Voting Guidelines Updates: 2017 Benchmark Policy Recommendations 4–5 (Nov. 21, 2016), https://www.issgovernance.com/file/policy/2017-americas-iss-policy-updates.pdf [https://perma.cc/QE4W-YGTH]; Institutional S'holder Servs., US Policy – Unilateral Board Actions – Multi Class Capital Structure at IPO (2016), https://www.issgovernance.com/file/policy/unilateral-board-actions-multi-class-capital-structure-at-ipo.pdf [https://perma.cc/SH9F-JX5F].

Finally, we note that "withhold" campaigns—investors withholding support from directors of companies that went public with a perpetual dual-class structure—are by themselves unlikely to be effective in discouraging such structures. As we explained, once a company goes public with a perpetual dual-class structure, the controller will be reluctant to give up her control. Because the controller has the power to elect directors, a symbolic withholding of support by institutional investors would be unlikely to apply sufficient pressure to induce controllers of existing dual-class companies to adopt sunset provisions. Institutional investors can most effectively discourage the use of perpetual dual-class structures by abstaining from participation in dual-class IPOs that do not contain appropriate sunset provisions. Whether institutional investors are capable of acting in such a way is a question that is beyond the scope of this Article. For our purposes, what is important is that such actions by institutional investors could not be expected without widespread recognition among such investors that the case for perpetual dual-class stock is untenable. We hope that this Article will contribute to such widespread recognition.

C. Researchers

Our analysis has identified and analyzed problems that would be worthwhile examining further in future research. Among other things, our analysis yields predictions that would be valuable to test empirically.

To begin, our analysis indicates that the agency costs associated with the use of dual-class stock can be expected to increase over time. Thus, the analysis implies that, controlling for relevant characteristics, the performance and valuation of dual-class companies will decline and agency costs will become more severe as the time from the IPO passes. These are empirical predictions that future research can and should examine.

In addition, our analysis suggests that dual-class structures can be expected to persist over time. We have shown that controllers have substantial private incentives to avoid a sale of a company with a dual-class structure even if such a sale would be value enhancing. Thus, our analysis implies that, controlling for relevant characteristics, companies with a dual-class structure are likely to have substantial persistence power.

More generally, future research should take the time dimension into account in any empirical or policy analysis of dual-class structures. Our work shows that the time dimension is critical. Future work should recognize that the valuation and agency consequences of a dual-class structure are expected to evolve over time in ways that have substantial implications for company performance and shareholder wealth.

Conclusion

This Article has aimed to contribute to the long-standing debate regarding the desirability of dual-class structures. We have sought to highlight the significance of a key dimension—the time that has passed since the IPO of a dual-class company—for the assessment of dual-class structures.

Our analysis has demonstrated that, over time, the potential benefits of dual-class structures can be expected to decline and the potential costs to increase. We have also shown that controllers have perverse incentives to retain dual-class structures even when those structures become substantially inefficient. Thus, as time passes from the IPO, there is a growing risk that a dual-class structure will become value decreasing and that public investors will find themselves subject to an inefficient structure with significant governance risks and costs.

Our analysis identifies a significant midstream cost of dual-class structures that should be taken into account in any overall assessment of such structures. Our key contribution, however, is to demonstrate that even those who believe that dual-class structures are often efficient at the time of the IPO, and the period following it, should have substantial concerns about dual-class structures that provide perpetual or lifetime control. All participants in the debate should accept taking such structures off the table.

Going forward, the debate should focus on the choice between (1) precluding dual-class IPOs altogether, and (2) permitting IPOs with a dual-class structure that sunsets after a fixed period of time (such as ten or fifteen years) unless its extension is approved by shareholders unaffiliated with the controller. The case for indefinite dual-class structures is untenable. Our analysis has significant implications for public officials, institutional investors, and researchers. We hope that it will prove useful and inform the future examination of dual-class structures.

資料2

【フランス】閉鎖する工場等の売却先を探す義務づける法律

海外立法情報課　服部 有希

* 2014年3月29日に、実体経済の回復を目的とする法律が制定された。同法は、閉鎖する工場等の売却先を探すよう企業に義務づけるほか、金融制度の改正を規定するものである。

1 立法の背景

近年、フランスでは、工場の閉鎖が相次いでいる。フランソワ・オランド（François Hollande）大統領は、大統領選挙運動中の2012年2月24日に、フランス北東部のフロランジュ（Florange）において、工場等の売却を検討する雇用主に売却先の探索を義務づける法案を約束した。しかし、2013年5月15日に実際に提出された法案のおおむねそれあるを見越し、工場等の売却先ではなく、売却先を探す義務づけることにとまった。議会では、この方針変更に対する批判もあったが（注1）、実体経済の回復のための2014年3月29日の法律2014-384号（注2）として成立した。この通称フロランジュ法は、金融経済の発達による短期的な経済政策の一端である実体経済を回復することを目的とする。商法典、通貨金融法典、労働法典の金融制度に関する規定を改正し、同時に、株式公開買付に関する規定を一つの柱としている。

2 閉鎖する事業所の売却先を探す義務（フロランジュ法第1条）

従業員数1,000人以上の企業（合計従業員数1,000人以上のグループ企業に属する企業を含む。）の雇用主は、集団解雇を伴う事業所（工場等を指すが、事業所の代表機関である企業委員会（comité d'entreprise）を招集し、閉鎖計画を通知しなければならない（労働法典 L.第1233-57-9条）。当該雇用主は、予定解雇者数が100人未満の場合には3か月間、250人以上の場合には4か月間、100人以上250人未満の場合には3か月間、売却先を探さなければならない（以下、「検討期間」）。
雇用主は、その際に、次のことを行う（同法典 L.第1233-57-14条）。

・売却する意思を指示し、売却先の候補への紹介書類を作成する。
・必要に応じ、事業所の環境負荷とその解決策を示す社会環境報告書を作成する。
・売却候補が事業所の再建・買収提案を通知し解決策を策定する際には企業委員会に2か月間、100人以上250人未満の場合は3か月間、250人以上の場合は企業委員会の招集から4か月間、閉鎖する事業所の売却先を探さなければならない（同法典 L.第1233-57-14条、「検討期間」）。
・同委員会に参加し、意見を述べることができる（同法典 L.第1233-57-15条）。
・売却先の検討について、企業委員会の意見を聴き、受入れを望む買収提案について、

企業委員会の意見を聴き、検討期間内の回答を求める（同法典 L.第1233-57-19条）。
雇用主は、検討期間内に買収提案がない場合又は全ての買収提案を拒否した場合、企業委員会に、売却先を探す活動を総括する報告書を提出する（L.第1233-57-20条）。
企業委員会は、雇用主が売却先を探す義務を怠り、又は妥当な買収提案を拒否したとみなす場合には、上述の報告書の提出から7日以内に、商事裁判所に提訴することができる（商法典 L.第771-1条）。この訴訟に、裁判所は雇用主に補助金等を給付した公的機関に対し、判決前2年間に企業に補助金等を給付したとの返金を求めることができる。判決が下る前に雇用主が探索を怠ったとの判決が下ったとの場合、又は不当に買収提案を拒否した場合、雇用主は補助金等を給付した公的機関に、判決前2年間に企業に補助金等を給付したとの返金を求める義務を負う。しかし、同規定は、公布前に削られた。これは、同法の実効性を担保する重要な規定が失われたことを意味する（注4）。

3 株式公開買付における企業及び従業員の保護並びに長期株主の保護強化

(1) 株式公開買付の制度改正（offre publique d'achat: OPA）（注5）は、買収者が、対象企業の株式の50%を保有することができなかった場合、不成立となる（通貨金融法典 L.第433-1-2条）。また、従来、株式又は議決権の30%以上50%以下を保有する者がその保有比率を1年で2%以上引き上げた場合には、株式公開買付を行う必要があったが、この2%の比率が1%に引き下げられた（同法典 L.第433-3条）。
(2) 株式公開買付における企業委員会の役割強化（フロランジュ法第8条）
従来、株式公開買付の申込みがあった場合、今後は、自社の企業委員会に情報提供しなければならないが、今後は、定款に別段の定めがあるものであった1株に2票の議決権から1か月以内に意見書を提出することとなった（労働法典 L.第2323-23条）。
(3) 中立原則の廃止（フロランジュ法第10条）
株式公開買付期間中、対象企業の取締役会又は監査役会は、ホワイトナイト（自らに友好的な第三者による買収）以外の対抗策を禁止していた中立原則が廃止された（商法典 L.第233-32条 III を制限する）。
(4) 2倍議決権の法制化（フロランジュ法第7条）
長期株主を認めるため、定款で任意に定めるものであった1株に2票の議決権を認める2倍議決権を、今後、株主名簿に2年以上登録されている株主に当然に付与することとした（商法典 L.第225-123条）。

注（インターネット情報は2014年7月15日現在である。）

(1) Marie Visot, "La loi Florange irrite les entreprises," Le Figaro, 2014.2.25, p.19.
(2) Loi n° 2014-384 du 29 mars 2014 visant à reconquérir l'économie réelle.
(3) Decision n° 2014-692 DC du 27 mars 2014.
(4) Luc Peillon, "La loi Florange trouve censure à son pied," Libération, 2014.3.28, pp.14-15.
(5) 『ヨーロッパM&A制度研究会報告書』日本証券経済研究所, 2010, pp.15-28.

資料3

ECGI Working Paper Series in Law

Loyalty Shares with Tenure Voting - A Coasian Bargain? Evidence from the Loi Florange Experiment

Working Paper N° 398/2018
April 2018

Marco Becht
Yuliya Kamisarenka
Anete Pajuste

We are grateful to Patrick Bolton, Benjamin Maury, Yishay Yafeh and seminar participants at SSE Riga for helpful comments. Žans Cvetkovs, Diana Karhu, Lasha Michedlishvili, Konstantins Šelegs, Artyom Semianchuk, Violeta Toncu, Davit Ubilava provided excellent research assistance. We acknowledge support from the Goldschmidt Chair at the Solvay Brussels School of Economics and Management, Université libre de Bruxelles.

© Marco Becht, Yuliya Kamisarenka and Anete Pajuste 2018. All rights reserved. Short sections of text, not to exceed two paragraphs, may be quoted without explicit permission provided that full credit, including © notice, is given to the source.

Law Working Paper N° 398/2018
April 2018

Loyalty Shares with Tenure Voting - A Coasian Bargain? Evidence from the Loi Florange Experiment

Marco Becht
Université libre de Bruxelles, CEPR and ECGI

Yuliya Kamisarenka
Stockholm School of Economics in Riga

Anete Pajuste
Stockholm School of Economics in Riga and ECGI

© Marco Becht, Yuliya Kamisarenka and Anete Pajuste 2018. All rights reserved. Short sections of text, not to exceed two paragraphs, may be quoted without explicit permission provided that full credit, including © notice, is given to the source.

This paper can be downloaded without charge from:
http://ssrn.com/abstract_id=3166494

www.ecgi.org/wp

Loyalty Shares with Tenure Voting - a Coasian bargain? Evidence from the *Loi Florange* Experiment

Marco Becht[1]
Solvay Brussels School of Economics and Management, Université libre de Bruxelles, CEPR and ECGI

Yuliya Kamisarenka[2]
Stockholm School of Economics in Riga

Anete Pajuste[3]
Stockholm School of Economics in Riga

16 April 2018[4]

Abstract

French listed companies can issue shares that confer two votes per share after a holding period of at least two years (loyalty shares with tenure voting rights). In 2014 the default rule changed from one-share-one-vote to loyalty shares. The Coase theorem predicts that *ceteris paribus* shareholders rewrite the corporate charter to preserve the pre-reform structure. The theorem also predicts that the proportion of loyalty shares in initial public offerings is unchanged. The paper shows that most one-share-one-vote companies reverted to the pre-reform contract. The exception were firms with a stake held by the French state. In initial public offerings, the new default rule had an impact; the proportion of loyalty share statutes increased from about forty to fifty percent after the passage of the law. Companies that kept the same statutes have a significantly higher market to book ratio than companies forced into a different regime. The evidence is broadly consistent with the predictions of the Coase theorem, but only in the absence of conflicted parties with veto power.

Keywords: Loyalty shares, tenure voting, time-phased voting, dual-class shares, one-share-one-vote, Coase theorem

JEL Classification: D23, K22, G32, G34

---

[1] ECARES, Solvay Brussels School of Economics and Management, Université libre de Bruxelles, 42 Avenue F. D. Roosevelt, 1050 Brussels, Belgium, e-mail: marco.becht@ulb.ac.be
[2] Stockholm School of Economics Riga, Strelnieku iela 4a, Riga, LV 1010, Latvia, e-mail:: y.kamisarenka@gmail.com
[3] Stockholm School of Economics Riga, Strelnieku iela 4a, Riga, LV 1010, Latvia, e-mail: anete.pajuste@sseriga.edu
[4] We are grateful to Patrick Bolton, Benjamin Maury, Yishay Yafeh and seminar participants at SSE Riga for helpful comments. Žans Cvetkovs, Diana Karhu, Lasha Mtchedlishvili, Konstantins Šeļegs, Artyom Semianchuk, Violeta Toncu, Davit Ubilava provided excellent research assistance. We acknowledge support from the Goldschmidt Chair at the Solvay Brussels School of Economics and Management, Université libre de Bruxelles.

Introduction

One implication of the Coase theorem (Coase, 1960) is that the initial allocation of property rights has no impact on the use of resources when transaction costs are small. Parties will privately re-contract when it is mutually beneficial. In the context of corporate law many countries allow companies to put in place alternatives to "one-share-one-vote" (OSOV). Legislators and issuers typically rely on the Coase theorem and freedom of contracting to motivate this choice. In these cases one-share-one-vote is often a "default rule" that parties can change by mutual agreement (Ayres & Gertner, 1989). In contrast, some jurisdictions see one-share-one-vote as an "immutable" rule that parties should be unable to change. For example, "immutable" listing rules prevented Alibaba, a Chinese e-commerce company, from listing shares with differential voting rights on the Hong Kong Stock Exchange. Alibaba listed on the New York Stock Exchange instead, that allows issuers to propose a range of voting right structures to potential investors.

The freedom to list on U.S. markets with charters that protect companies from unsolicited takeovers or proxy contests is controversial. To some these arrangements are the outcome of an efficient bargain that allows managers to invest in long-term projects (Chemmanur & Jiao, 2012) or to bond with suppliers (W. C. Johnson, Karpoff, & Yi, 2015); to others they represent a market failure that shuts down the market for corporate control and fosters managerial entrenchment (L.A. Bebchuk, 2013; Easterbrook & Fischel, 1996). Institutional shareholders are generally opposed to deviations from one-share-one-vote, the use of dual-class or non-voting shares is discouraged by U.S. stock index providers and there have been suggestions that dual-class IPOs should be banned or time-limited (Lucian A. Bebchuk & Kastiel, 2017).

Loyalty shares that confer multiple voting rights as a function of the holding period could be a less controversial alternative to classic dual-class shares because they treat all shareholders equally (Berger, Davidoff Solomon, & Benjamin, 2017).[5] Loyalty share charters already exist in the United States, but their operation is fraught with difficulties (Berger et al., 2017).[6] Technological solutions are available and a group of technology entrepreneurs has applied for regulatory approval to set up the Long-Term Stock Exchange (LTSE), that would only list loyalty shares with tenure voting (Osipovich & Berman, 2017). Consequently, tenure voting structures are receiving increased attention in the United States (Edelman, Jiang, & Thomas, 2018).

In contrast, France has a long tradition of loyalty shares with tenure voting that are used by more than half of French listed companies (Belot, 2005; Chene, 2008). Traditionally one-share-one-vote was the default rule, but shareholders were allowed to *opt-out* by adopting statutes that give double voting rights to "loyal" shareholders, typically after a holding period of two years, or longer. Companies that came to the stock market for the first time with a default statute provision went public with one-share-one-vote. Companies that wanted to *opt-out* could adopt loyalty shares by adding an article to their IPO statues.[7] Shareholders could always opt-in or out of a loyalty share statute later through a shareholder resolution and a 2/3 majority binding vote. Italy adopted a similar system in 2014 (Santoro, Di Palma, Guarneri, & Capogrosso, 2015).

---

[5] Loyalty shares more generally can provide long-term holders additional cash-flow and/or control rights (Bolton & Samama, 2013). The analysis in this paper is confined to loyalty shares that confer additional voting rights.
[6] In the United States, loyalty shares that involve "tenure voting" or "time-phased voting" (TPV) have been issued by at least twelve companies, including household names like the J.M. Smucker Company (Dallas & Barry, 2015). TPV statutes typically grant shareholders holding shares for at least 36 or 48 months three, five or ten votes per share.
[7] There were two variants: (1) retroactive loyalty shares: pre-IPO shareholders with a certain holding period acquired double voting rights immediately while new shareholders had to wait for at least two years, (2) new loyalty shares: all holding periods were set to zero at the IPO and all shareholders had to wait for loyalty shares. The former is close to a dual-class IPO, the latter is a genuine loyalty share offering.

In early 2014, 57% of the largest 104 French companies by market capitalization had adopted the loyalty double vote system, while the remainder had not.[8] Similarly, among initial public offerings three years prior to the passage of the law, 37% opted out by adopting loyalty shares.[9] The "Coasian" explanation is that the companies and their shareholders chose the system that is most beneficial for them as a group (Coase, 1960); shareholders opted out of the one-share-one-vote default system when it was more efficient. This could occur, for example, because loyalty shares with tenure voting are attractive for founders or families that want to retain control while offering institutional investors high degrees of secondary market liquidity (Becht, 1999; Bolton & Von Thadden, 2002). In widely held companies with one-share-one-vote investors reveal to prefer liquidity over control (Bhide, 1993).[10]

On 29 March 2014, the French government introduced a new law, known as *Loi Florange*, that changed the default voting system from one-share-one-vote to loyalty shares. The *Loi Florange* stipulated that as of 3 April 2016 shares held in registered form by the same shareholder for at least two years are automatically granted double voting rights, unless the company *opts out* of this system through a statute amendment (with a 2/3 majority in a shareholder vote). Listed companies that wanted to keep one-share-one-vote had just over two years to opt out via a shareholder vote. Equally, the default rule for public offerings became 2-year loyalty shares so IPO firms now had to deliberately *opt out* by writing one-share-one-vote into their statutes. The possibility of giving pre-IPO shareholders double voting rights immediately or starting them with single voting rights by setting the tenure voting clock to zero remained unchanged.

---

[8] In 1998, 2000 and 2002 loyalty shares were found in 68.3% of firms at the end of the year when pooling observations; pyramids were much less frequent (18.6%) and the use of voting caps (2.3%), dual class shares (1.2%) or partnerships limited by shares (1.8%) was rare (Ginglinger & Hamon, 2012).
[9] Only one company set the tenure voting clock to zero for all shareholders; the remainder was quasi-dual class and gave pre-IPO shareholders double voting rights immediately.
[10] There is empirical evidence of a tradeoff between ownership, control and liquidity in France for the period 1998-2002 involving loyalty shares (Ginglinger & Hamon, 2012)

The Coase theorem predicts that one-share-one-vote companies pre-*Florange* preserve the status quo by opting out of the loyalty share system post-*Florange*. In this paper, we use the actual behaviour of companies affected by the *Loi Florange* to test the Coasian proposition. The working hypothesis is that the listed companies affected by the law revert to their previous one-share-one-vote status, provided the transaction costs of re-contracting are sufficiently low, there are no information problems and contracts are enforceable (Bolton & Dewatripont, 2005). Among the flow of IPO firms, the proportion of one-share-one-vote companies should stay constant, *ceteris paribus*. In particular, accepting this empirical hypothesis would show that the French government's new choice of default option came at no real cost. The original endowment is irrelevant for the adoption of loyalty shares (or not) when parties can contract freely (Coase, 1960).

The empirical evidence on the stock of loyalty share firms is consistent with characterising French loyalty shares as a Coasian bargain. Our sample consists of 104 companies included in the SBF120 index comprising the most frequently traded stocks listed on the Paris Stock Exchange. Before the introduction of the *Loi Florange* in 29 March 2014, there were 59 companies with a double voting system and 45 companies adhering to the one-share-one-vote. The *Loi Florange* had a direct effect on the latter. To continue as one-share-one-vote companies after 3 April 2016 they had to pass a shareholder resolution. We find that 70% of the affected firms (31 out of 45) opted out of the new (double voting) default rule. The direct cost of opting out was negligible as the relevant decision was typically a resolution at an Extraordinary General Meeting (EGM) that took place at the time of the Annual General Meeting (AGM). On average, there were 97.4% votes *for* maintaining the one-share-one-vote system, 2.2% *against*, and 0.4 *abstain*.

The empirical evidence on the flow of charters in initial public offerings is consistent with "libertarian paternalism" (Thaler & Sunstein, 2003). The French state revised its view of what voting right structure is beneficial for the average French listed company, but companies and shareholders remained free to adopt a different arrangement. The Coase theorem predicts that the proportion of loyalty shares in IPOs remains unchanged after switching the default rule. In practice, the fraction of firms that went public with loyalty shares increased from 37% to 54% when comparing the period before and after the introduction of the law (28 March 2011 to 28 March 2014 and 29 March 2014 to 28 March 2017). The changed view of the French state had a marginal but significant effect on the adoption of loyalty shares in IPO statutes.[11]

The experiment also sheds light on further predictions of the Coase theorem. The theorem assumes that property rights are well defined and the contract parties do not free ride by not taking part in costly contract negotiations, for example by not voting at the AGM or by not reading the IPO prospectus. It also assumes that contracting parties are not conflicted (Ellingsen & Paltseva, 2016). The *Loi Florange* experiment allows us to test these assumptions because it changed the power of certain blockholders. Empirically we should see reversion to the old regime when property rights were *de facto* unaltered, but not necessarily when control rights were changed.

The de facto control rights of shareholders that collectively commanded more than two thirds of the votes did not change. A supermajority could pass a loyalty share resolution before the *Loi Florange* and equally block its adoption after the reform. The same was true for minority shareholders commanding less than one third of the votes. They could not block the adoption of loyalty shares before the *Loi Florange* and could not force their removal after the law came into effect. As a result, the law did not affect decision making in these cases. Decision rights did change for shareholders commanding between one third and two third of the votes.

Before the *Loi Florange* these levels of voting support were not sufficient to introduce the double vote system, but afterwards they were sufficient to block a return to one-share-one-vote. This qualification does not apply to IPO companies that could choose their charter without shareholder approval before and after the passage of the *Loi Florange*.

The evidence is consistent with the notion that the Coase theorem fails in the presence of a conflicted trading partner. Empirically a subsample of 14 companies failed to switch back to one-share-one-vote. In half of these cases the issue was not put to a vote because the outcome was clear; there was a large shareholder with the power to block the reversal. The other cases were voted but the OSOV resolution failed to get the necessary two-thirds supermajority. In five cases the resolution did attract a simple majority. Most of the companies that did not revert had the French state as a shareholder, often with a minority position that was boosted to a permanent blocking minority by the introduction of loyalty shares.

We also investigate the impact of loyalty shares on firm values. There is evidence that firms with voting rights that are proportional to cash flow rights have higher stock valuations (L. Bebchuk, Cohen, & Ferrell, 2009; Bennedsen & Nielsen, 2010; Gompers, Ishii, & Metrick, 2010), an observation that is often attributed to anticipated takeover premia (Adams & Ferreira, 2008; Becht, Bolton, & Röell, 2003). Loyalty shares make hostile takeovers more difficult, but the effect is more moderate than for dual-class shares. Any shareholder can benefit from double voting rights and the superior voting power is not transferrable.

The Coase theorem predicts that the valuation of firms that keep the same voting structure is unchanged, whereas the valuation of firms that had one-share-one-vote but are forced to adopt loyalty shares should have lower valuation. Our empirical evidence shows a positive (but insignificant) value premium (Tobin's Q) in firms offering loyalty shares both before

---

[11] It is also possible that the type of company that went public changed; we control for this separately.

and after the *Loi Florange*.[12] We also find the lowest valuations among firms that switched from OSOV into the loyalty (double vote) system after the *Loi Florange*. However, this holds for both before and after the law, i.e. in March 28, 2014 and April 4, 2016, respectively.[13] This finding suggests that the presence of the state is more important for valuation than the voting structure. The state already had a strong presence in the "switchers", but post-Florange it became possible to exercise the same degree of influence with a smaller capital stake.

Behavioural economics has cast doubts on the Coase theorem and offers theoretical explanations why default rules might matter. Inconsistent with Coase, experimental evidence points to an endowment effect: individual are less willing to sell a good than they are willing to buy it (Kahneman, Knetsch, & Thaler, 1990). In the context of voting rights, the endowment effect would imply that investors require more compensation to give up loyalty shares than they would be willing to pay for receiving them, and the same if they were endowed with one-share-one-vote.

Theoretical explanations for the "status quo" bias include an aversion towards cognitive or physical effort (Tversky & Kahneman, 1975) or the belief that the default rules reflect socially desirable behaviour so there is a rationale for inaction (E. J. Johnson, Bellman, & Lohse, 2002; McKenzie, Liersch, & Finkelstein, 2006). Inaction might also reflect incidental moods or emotions (Shevchenko, Von Helversen, & Scheibehenne, 2014). In contrast, when agents have well-defined preferences they will opt out of default rules that do not maximize their utility, regardless of the nature of the default (Beshears, Choi, Laibson, & Madrian, 2009). In the case of loyalty shares the decision makers should have well defined preferences because they are usually professional asset managers.

The *Loi Florange* experiment is also related to the "short termism" literature. French loyalty shares are mostly about control, but presumably they also have a positive effect on holding periods. One justification for the introduction of loyalty shares in Italy, the United States and soon in Belgium is that they reward long-term capital. The *Loi Florange* allows us to test this proposition and we do so by comparing holding periods between companies with and without loyalty shares before and after the reform. Although the average holding period decreases at a slower speed in loyalty share firms than in OSOV firms, there is no significant difference in the average holding periods between the two groups before and after the *Loi Florange*. This finding is consistent with scepticism about loyalty shares with tenure voting as a solution to a perceived short termism problem in widely held companies (Fried, 2014; Roe, 2013). The finding is also consistent with previous evidence on ownership and liquidity in the French markets; loyalty shares enhance liquidity by allowing controlling shareholders to hold smaller blocks than would be the case with one-share-one-vote (Ginglinger & Hamon, 2012).

The remainder of the paper is organized as follows. Section 1 provides an overview of the 2014 law reform (the *Loi Florange*) we use for identification, Section 2 describes the sample design and data, Section 3 reports the results and Section 4 concludes.

1. The Loi Florange

Law 2014-384 of 29 March 2014 is a "law aiming to take back control of the real economy"[14] by strengthening long-term investors at the expense of short-term speculators and is similar in spirit to the *LTSE Listing* initiative in the U.S. It is better known as *Loi Florange*, named after the city of Florange in the North East of France, a region that has been dominated by mining and steel. It was motivated by events that took place in 2012. ArcelorMittal—the steel group

---

[12] The positive valuation for French loyalty share structures adopted before the Loi Florange contrasts with the valuation discount observed in dual-class share companies worldwide (Bennedsen & Nielsen, 2010; Gompers et al., 2010).

[13] As of March 2014, the average Tobin's Q of future "switchers" is 1.11, compared to 1.41 of single class firms that did not switch, and an average of 1.65 for loyalty share firms.

[14] LOI n° 2014-384 du 29 mars 2014 visant à reconquérir l'économie réelle (https://www.legifrance.gouv.fr/affichTexte.do?cidTexte=JORFTEXT000028811102)

created in 2006 by the merger of Arcelor and Mittal Steel—took the decision to close a set of profitable blast furnaces in Florange. The Mittal group was built and is controlled by the entrepreneur Lakshmi Mittal through the serial acquisitions of underperforming steel assets. Once the assets were brought under Mittal Steel control they were restructured, often involving plant closures and layoffs. The operations were often debt financed. In 2005 Forbes Magazine listed London based Mr Mittal as the third wealthiest individual in the World, with an estimated net worth of 25 US$ billion. The announced closure coincided with the re-election campaign of socialist President François Hollande, who promised reforms.

The *Loi Florange* contains three chapters. Chapters 1 and 2 are directly related to plant closures. Chapter 1 forces companies to look for a buyer before allowing the permanent closure of a plant. Chapter 2 gives workers the possibility to purchase the assets. Chapter 3 contains "measures to promote long term shareholding" in listed companies.

To achieve the latter, *inter alia*, Article 7 modified French company law (the *Code de commerce*). Article L225-123 of the Commercial Code allowed listed companies to adopt a loyalty share provision in their statues that gave shareholders two votes per share after a certain holding period. It was modified by Article 7 (V) of the Act that set loyalty shares as the default rule. The new Article states that "in all companies admitted for trading on a regulated market, the double voting rights set out in the first paragraph [of this Article], unless there is a statutory provision to the contrary before the Act comes into force, [...] will apply by law to all shares [...] which have been held by the same shareholder for two years".[15]

---

[15] "Dans les sociétés dont les actions sont admises aux négociations sur un marché réglementé, les droits de vote double prévus au premier alinéa sont de droit, sauf clause contraire des statuts adoptée postérieurement à la promulgation de la loi n° 2014-384 du 29 mars 2014 visant à reconquérir l'économie réelle, pour toutes les actions entièrement libérées pour lesquelles il est justifié d'une inscription nominative depuis deux ans au nom du même actionnaire."

The Act came into force on 3 April 2016 so companies had just over two years to opt out. For an amendment to come into force, two-thirds of the company's shareholders had to vote for the resolution *not to* grant the double voting rights, i.e. to *opt out* of the *Loi Florange*. The companies willing to stay with the one-share-one-vote structure had to submit their bylaw amendments by 31 March 2016.

The substance of the law has traits of "libertarian paternalism" (Thaler & Sunstein, 2003). The state clearly expressed a preference for loyalty shares yet it preserved the freedom of IPO companies to go public with a one-share-one-vote charter. It also allows existing companies to adopt one-share-one-vote via a shareholder vote with a two-thirds majority. However, the *Loi Florange* is not a pure form of "libertarian paternalism" because it did intervene in existing property rights. The actions of the French state as a regulator benefitted the French state as a shareholder. The law allowed the state to lock in existing loyalty share arrangements by giving itself a blocking minority. It also allowed the state to sell larger amounts of equity without having to fear losing the loyalty share privilege. These advantages were shared by employee shareholders and private block holders in one-share-one-vote companies that were previously unable to muster the two thirds majority necessary to pass a loyalty share resolution. A neutral law would have grandfathered all existing loyalty share arrangements and merely changed the default rule for new public offerings.

The implementation of the long-term shareholder policy was entrusted to Emmanuel Macron, the Economy Minister at the time. Mr Macron gave a series of speeches where he expressed the view that the *Loi Florange* gives the state a more dynamic and powerful role as a shareholder. The willingness of France to use the new rules strategically became evident in a number of headline cases. At car manufacturer Renault, the state acquired €1.23bn worth of additional shares to block the return to one-share-one-vote proposed by Renault's board and supported by institutional investors. In the case of Air

France the state raised its stake to 17.6% to successfully block a one-share-one-vote management proposal (Chassany, 2015; Stothard, 2015). The state also defeated one-share-one-vote management proposals at Alstom and Engie; and a shareholder proposal at Orange, the latter with support from the board (Table 6).

2. Methodology and Data

The paper uses the identifying variation provided by the *Loi Florange* to test two main hypotheses. One, if the distribution of French loyalty shares before Florange resulted from a Coasian bargain, firms that used one-share-one-vote prior to the Act, should have opted out of the new (double voting) system. The exception should be cases where the bargaining power of shareholders with special interests changed, in particular in the case of the French state. In addition, the valuation of companies that could successfully retain their preferred control structure should be higher, ceteris paribus, than of companies that were forced into a different control regime by the *Loi Florange*. Two, if the use of loyalty shares in initial public offerings resulted from a Coasian bargain, the proportion of loyalty shares in initial public offerings should be unchanged.

Table 1 reports the list of companies used in our empirical work. We use companies included in the SBF 120 index, a French stock market index with the 120 most frequently traded stocks listed on the Paris Stock Exchange (Euronext Paris), as of January 1, 2016. We exclude ten firms incorporated outside of France, since the changes in French corporate law did not affect them. We also exclude six companies that went public after the introduction of the Act on 29 March 2014. The final sample includes 104 companies.

We group the companies into five categories: (1) loyalty share companies that offered loyalty shares prior to the Act and kept offering them after the Act came into force (58 "*Double-Double*" companies), (2) loyalty share class companies that opted out of the Act with bylaw amendments and kept the one-share-one-vote structure (31 "*Single-Single*" company), (3) one-share-one-vote companies that did not have a shareholder vote switched to loyalty shares on 3 April 2016 by default (7 "*Single-Double (automatic)*" companies)[16], (4) one-share-one-vote companies that had a shareholders resolution to revert to one-share-one-vote but failed to obtain the necessary two-third majority also switched to loyalty shares on 3 April 2016 by default (7 "*Single-Double (after failed vote)*" companies), and (5) one company that offered loyalty shares but voted to adopt one-share-one-vote ("*Double-Single*"). The names of companies in each category are listed in Table 1.

(Insert Table 1 about here)

For companies that had loyalty shares before the Act, we investigate the date of the double voting system adoption. In 12 out of 12 most recent IPOs (from June 1999 or later), the double voting system was in place already at the IPO. It suggests that loyalty shares are the result of a Coasian bargain during the initial public offering (see, for example, the case of Edenred in Appendix 1). We do not investigate earlier IPOs due to data availability constraints. Interestingly, the 59 firms with loyalty shares as of March 2014 have gone public a significantly longer time ago than the 45 firms with one-share-one-vote. The median public age of double voting firms is 27 years compared to 19 years for single voting firms, which is a significant difference at the 1% level.

Valuation measure

Tobin's Q is the main valuation measure in this paper. It is defined as market value of assets divided by the book value of assets. Market value of assets is market value of equity plus

---

[16] This group includes one company (Sopra Steria Group) that voted in favor of adopting the double voting system in June 2014 (with 74.2% votes FOR and 25.8% votes AGAINST). The classification of this company into this "passive" group does not affect the empirical analysis because in our empirical analysis, we group all the companies that switched from one-share-one-vote into the double vote system irrespective of the "method" of switch (passive or active).

book value of assets minus book value of equity. Market value of equity is a product of the amount of shares outstanding and share price. In order to calculate Tobin's Q for March 28, 2014 (just before the Act) and April 4, 2016 (right after the enforcement of the Act), we retrieve market value of equity exactly on these dates and take the book value of assets and equity as of December 31, 2013 and December 31, 2015, respectively – the closest date for which accounting data is available. As a result, Tobin's Q for 104 companies in the sample is calculated at two time points:

$$Q_{i, 28/03/2014} = \frac{\text{MV of Equity}_{i, 28/03/2014} + \text{BV of Assets}_{i, 31/12/2013} - \text{BV of Equity}_{i, 31/12/2013}}{\text{BV Assets}_{i, 31/12/2013}}$$

$$Q_{i, 04/04/2016} = \frac{\text{MV of Equity}_{i, 04/04/2016} + \text{BV of Assets}_{i, 31/12/2015} - \text{BV of Equity}_{i, 31/12/2015}}{\text{BV Assets}_{i, 31/12/2015}}$$

for i=1…n, where BV is "book value", MV is "market value", and Q is "Tobin's Q".

All input variables for Tobin's Q are extracted from Bloomberg. In rare cases with missing financial variables in the database, we add data directly from the annual reports. Tobin's Q is winsorized at the 5% level on both ends.

The distribution of Tobin's Q according to the decision category is presented in Table 2. The total average Tobin's Q on both key dates is 1.51. This parallels the SBF120 index values on 28 March 2014 and 4 April 2016 being almost identical, 3454 and 3446, respectively. We observe that the highest Tobin's Q is for the companies that offered loyalty double vote shares before the Act and were not influenced by the Act. Tobin's Q is considerably higher for the companies that made a decision to keep the single-class shares as compared to the companies that failed to opt out of the Act or those that passively accepted the new default option.

(Insert Table 2 about here)

Control Variables

When measuring the effect of loyalty shares on firm value, we include the same control variables as Bennedsen and Nielsen (2010). Those are firm size, financial leverage, sales growth, return on assets, and asset tangibility. Most of the variables are extracted from Bloomberg as of December 31, 2013 and December 31, 2015; few missing values are added from the companies' annual reports. We estimate firm size as log of assets following the methodology of Claessens et al. (2002) and Lins (2003). The effect of the firm size on firm value is rather ambiguous. Large companies have better disclosure and face a lower risk of financial distress. However, smaller firms have better growth opportunities (Claessens et al., 2002). Leverage is calculated as book value of long-term debt over book value of assets. Higher leverage can have either a positive effect from reduced profit diversion by limiting free cash flow at hand or a negative effect from increased probability of financial distress. Sales growth is the year-on-year change in sales revenue (current year versus previous year). We expect a positive correlation between sales growth and firm value, as the sales growth approximates the company's growth opportunities (Claessens et al., 2002). Return on assets is net income divided by book value of assets. As high net income is a positive indicator of firm's accounting performance, we expect a positive relationship between return on assets and firm value. Asset tangibility is measured by net property, plant, and equipment divided by total assets. Asset tangibility presumably has a negative correlation with firm value, as the companies with lower asset tangibility will most likely have higher number of intangible assets (e.g. human capital) generating cash flows. All financial variables are winsorized at the 5% level on both ends.

In all the regressions, we control for industry effects. Eleven industry dummies are created according to the Global Industry Classification Standard: industrials, materials, information technology, financials, health care, consumer staples, energy, consumer discretionary, utilities, real estate, and telecommunication services.

Ownership Variables

Following the methodology of Bennedsen and Nielsen (2010), we include ownership variables such as dual (loyalty share) dummy, cash flow stake, and control minus ownership (wedge) in the analysis. The ownership data are taken from the annual reports. Dual dummy is set to one if the company is offering loyalty shares to its shareholders and zero otherwise. As we analyze two points in time, 28 March 2014 and 4 April 2016, the dual dummy is a time-variant variable. There are 59 dual-class companies on 28 March 2014 and 72 dual-class companies on 4 April 4 2016 (see Table 3).

(Insert Table 3 about here)

The cash flow stake is the share of the cash flow rights held by the largest controlling shareholder. The largest controlling shareholder is defined according to the amount of voting rights and is a shareholder or group of shareholders acting in concert that holds at least 10% of voting rights. Control minus ownership (wedge) is the difference between the controlling shareholder's voting rights and cash flow stake. We mark the 14 companies that switched from one-share-one-vote system into the loyalty double vote system as a result of the *Loi Florange* with a dummy variable equal to 1, called switch dummy.

We distinguish the following five controlling shareholder types: *family* including private persons with the same surname, *corporation* including private companies whose major shareholder is not one of the direct owners in the sample company, *financial* including financial institutions and insurance companies, *state* including state, cities and municipalities, and *dispersed* including companies that do not have a shareholder that holds at least 10% of voting rights. Ownership variables are recorded as of December 31, 2013 (before the Act) and December 31, 2016 (after the enforcement of the Act). Table 3 reports the frequency of firms according to the five controlling shareholder types. We also track the ownership changes from the end of 2013 to 2016 (unreported). Complete change is if the previous (in 2013) largest controlling shareholder does not hold at least 10% of the votes at the end of 2016. There are 13 complete ownership changes. A partial change is if the previous largest shareholder is not the largest shareholder any more but still holds at least 10% of the votes. There are 4 partial ownership changes. There are no ownership changes in the remaining 87 sample companies.

For one of the tests we require the aggregate cash flow stake held by institutional investors. This information is extracted from Thomson Reuters Eikon, by summing the percentage of outstanding shares owned by all the shareholders under investor type "Funds". As we require pre-*Florange* institutional ownership, we select the filing date December 31, 2013.

Descriptive Statistics

Table 4 presents descriptive statistics for variables used in this study. Panel A reports the values as of 28 March 2014 and Panel B – as of 4 April 2016. The average Tobin's Q is 1.51 in both time points. The largest shareholder has on average 32.9% (32.3%) of the voting rights and 28.6% (27.2%) of the cash flow rights in 2014 (2016).

(Insert Table 4 about here)

In Table 5, we report the distribution of votes and cash-flow rights held by the largest shareholder by different ownership types. Family is the most frequent ownership type among the largest shareholders (33.7% as of end 2013), followed by corporation (22.1%) and dispersed firms (18.3%). Family owners have the highest average voting stake (46.7%) and the highest average wedge (control minus ownership) (8.0%). The average wedge in the whole sample is 4.25% at the end of 2013 and 5.15% at the end of 2016. Interestingly, the average wedge among state owned companies has increased from 0.69% at the end of 2013 (way below average) to 5.70% at the end of 2016 (above average).

(Insert Table 5 about here)

Figure 1 plots the equity stake held by the largest owner against the resulting voting stake before the reform (31 December 2013).

(Insert Figure 1 about here)

3. Results

In this section we present the empirical results for the impact of the *Loi Florange* on the adoption of loyalty shares and their value effect.

Table 1 shows that 70% (31 out of 45) of one-share-one-vote firms that were affected by the introduction of the new (double voting) default, i.e. made statute amendments to preserve the single voting structure after 3 April 2016. For brevity, we call this group "single-single" firms. The remaining 30% (14 out of 45) OSOV firms switched into the loyalty (double voting) system either after a failed vote to maintain the OSOV structure (7 firms) or automatically without a vote (7 firms). There were 58 firms that were not affected by the *Loi Florange* because they offered loyalty shares already before the Act was introduced. We call this group "double-double". Finally, there is one company (Legrand) that had loyalty shares prior to the *Loi Florange*, i.e. would not be affected by the Act, but decided to abandon the double voting system and become an OSOV company through a shareholder vote. The Legrand case illustrates that shareholders can re-contract by voting in favour of statute amendments.

(Insert Table 6 about here)

Table 6 reports the voting results for the resolutions to maintain the one-share-one-vote system.[17] The respective resolution typically was one of many (20-30) on the AGM/EGM agenda. Panel A shows that in the "single-single" group all resolutions were sponsored by management (the board), on average 97.4% of shareholders (participating in the EGM) voted FOR maintaining the one-share-one-vote system. There were only 2.2% votes *against* and 0.4% *abstain*. The average participation rate (quorum) in the respective AGM/EGM was 69.6%. In one case, BNP Paribas, opposition from a minority block to revert to one-share-one-vote could be overcome despite a relatively low attendance rate (see Appendix 2).

Panel B of Table 6 reports the voting results for resolutions to maintain one vote per share in a sample of seven firms that rejected the respective resolution ("single-double (after failed vote)" group). To adopt the bylaw amendments that would keep one vote per share, 66.67% (2/3) FOR votes were required. If instead a simple majority 50%+1 vote had been required, only two out of seven firms (Engie and Orange) would have succeeded in abandoning the OSOV structure. The average participation rate (quorum) in these meetings was 63.0%. As a result, 49.5% of participants and only 31.1% of total votes (including the non-participating free-riders) could block the resolution to keep the OSOV structure in place.[18]

---

[17] For a sample resolution, see the meeting notice of Klepierre (11 December 2014). The proposed new Article 28 reads: "In all meetings, subject to any restrictions stipulated in the prevailing legislation, shareholders shall have one vote per share held or represented without restriction. Pursuant to the option provided for in article L.225-123 of the French Commercial Code, double voting rights will not be conferred on fully paid shares that have been registered in the name of the same shareholder for a period of at least two years."

[18] Participation rates at AGMs are endogenous and difficult to model. High participation rates are more likely when shareholders expect ex-ante to be pivotal (Cvijanovic, Groen-Xu, & Zachariadis, 2017).

Panel B of Table 6 also shows that five resolutions were sponsored by management (the board) and two by shareholders. Institutional Shareholder Services (ISS), the proxy advisory firm, recommended to vote in favour of one-share-one-vote in all cases. The recommendation of the board is more surprising. The board of Air France-KLM, Alstom SA, Engie SA and Renault SA recommended to vote for one-share-one-vote and thereby against the French state. The board of Veolia put forward a one-share-one-vote resolution but recommended to vote against it. The boards of Orange and Vivendi recommended to vote against the respective shareholder resolution.

Why did shareholders fail to file one-share-one-vote resolutions in all cases? Figure 2 plots the equity stake held by the largest owner against the resulting voting stake before the reform (31 December 2013). The strategic importance of the 33% blocking minority threshold for the "Single-Double" group is clearly visible. All seven firms without a shareholder vote had a shareholder commanding 33.33% or more of the voting rights. Even with an attendance rate of 100% the largest shareholder would have been able to block reversal from loyalty shares to one-share-one-vote. In the group that voted, in six of the seven companies the largest shareholder held a stake smaller than 33.33%. There seems to have been some residual doubt regarding the outcome, especially in the two companies with 100% free float (represented by a single marker at [0,0]). This evidence supports the notion that the *Loi Florange* changed the bargaining power of loyalty share proponents. In 11 out of 14 cases the largest owner was unable to introduce loyalty shares before the reform.

(Insert Figure 2 about here)

In Table 7, we report a probit analysis of the likelihood of switching from a single vote into a double vote system. The sample includes all the 45 single vote firms prior to the *Loi Florange* (March 2014). The results show a significant increase in the likelihood of a switch if the largest blockholder is the state; compared to any other ownership type, the probability of switching increases by 0.62 in this case. The prevalence of switchers among the state-owned firms is also documented in Table 3. Before the *Loi Florange* (March 2014), there were 12 firms where the state controlled the largest block and only 3 (25%) had loyalty shares. After the Act came into force, the number of firms where the state controlled the largest block increased to 13 and now 11 (84.6%) had loyalty shares. As expected, higher institutional ownership reduces the likelihood of switching to loyalty shares—a one standard deviation increase in the cash flow stake held by the institutional investors reduces the probability of switching by 0.12. This effect, however, is statistically insignificant.

(Insert Table 7 about here)

As mentioned earlier, the divergence between the control rights and cash flow rights (wedge) in state controlled firms increased from 0.69% before the *Loi Florange* to 5.7% after. As an example, in a one-share-one-vote firm with market capitalization of EUR 20 billion, an investor would require EUR 1 billion to increase the voting stake by 5%. The French government could effectively enhance its control rights by changing the default option from a single into a double vote system (See Appendix 3). The *Loi Florange* created a fundamental change in property rights in some cases, and the majority opinion was oppressed, as shown in Table 6.

As a result, the overall fraction of loyalty (double vote) firms increased significantly from 56.7% in March 2014 to 69.3% in April 2016 (Table 3), and the average divergence between control and cash flow rights (wedge) at the same time (insignificantly) increased from 4.25% to 5.15% (Table 5). Figures 3 and 4 plot the equity stake held by the largest owner against the resulting voting stake after the reform (31 December 2016) for the switchers from one share-one vote to loyalty shares and all the sample firms, respectively.

(Insert Figures 3 and 4 about here)

In addition to observing an increase in the stock of firms with loyalty shares, the Coase theorem also predicts that there should be no change in the flow of firms. Existing holdings of the state and other block holders should have no effect. For this reason, we study all IPOs on Euronext Paris three years prior to the Act (i.e. from March 28, 2011 to March 28, 2014) and three years after the Act (i.e. from March 29, 2014 to March 28, 2017). Table 8 reports an increase in the fraction of firms that went public with loyalty shares from 36.7% pre-*Florange* to 53.5% post-*Florange*, a difference that is significant at the 10% level. Additionally, we observe a decrease in the fraction of firms with loyalty shares that granted double voting rights retroactively, from 90.9% before to 69.6% after the *Loi Florange*. This evidence is consistent with the notion that loyalty shares became more acceptable after the reform. However, it is also possible that the IPO stream in the pre- and post-period were just different.

(Insert Table 8 about here)

In addition to giving long term shareholders disproportionate control, loyalty shares with tenure voting should also promote "loyalty" in the form of longer holding periods. Using the simplified definition from Bolton and Samama (2013), we estimate the average holding period (in years) as the ratio of the average of the total market value of the shares outstanding at the start and at the end of the year and the value of shares traded in a year, i.e. the inverse of the average annual turnover. From Figure 5 we see that there is no additional loyalty from loyalty shares and the decrease in average holding periods for French companies is unbroken by the reform.

(Insert Figure 5 about here)

Although the rise in high frequency trading contributes to decreasing holding periods globally, we are interested in the relative changes in this measure between one share-one vote firms and firms that offer loyalty shares. Table 9 reports the average holding period in each category in the years 2013 (pre-*Florange*) and 2017 (post-*Florange*). We find that the drop in average holding period is smaller among loyalty share firms ("double-double" category) than among OSOV firms ("single-single" category), this difference being significant at the 10% level. However, the average holding periods of loyalty share firms and OSOV firms are not significantly different both before and after the Act, supporting the sceptical view about the impact of short-termism on average holding periods (Roe, 2013).

(Insert Table 9 about here)

Value effect

The univariate analysis of Tobin's Q in Table 2 show that the highest valuations are in the subsample of 58 firms that had double vote system as of March 2014 and were not affected by the *Loi Florange*. In March 2014, the mean Tobin's Q in "double-double" group is 1.65 that is higher than in other groups (significant at the 1% level). The Tobin's Q remains higher in this group in April 2016 (significant at the 5% level). The lowest valuations, in turn, are observed in the subsample of 14 firms that switched from single into double vote system. The mean Tobin's Q of the switchers is 1.11 before and after the Act (significantly lower at the 1% level). The probit results in Table 7 reveal a higher probability of switches among low Q firms.

Finally, we turn to the multivariate regression results in Table 10. In this table, we replicate the main cross-sectional value regressions of Bennedsen and Nielsen (BN) (2010) in two time points – March 28, 2014 (models (1) to (4)), and April 4, 2016 (models (5) to (9)). The variable of interest is the dual dummy, which takes the value of one if a firm uses loyalty (double voting) shares. We also report a specification with the control minus ownership (wedge). The respective variables in BN (2010) are called the disproportionality dummy (DP) and the degree of disproportionality (DPP). Unlike BN, we do not find a negative valuation effect from the disproportional ownership structure (models (1) and (2)). In fact, firms with loyalty shares have higher (but insignificant) valuations when we introduce the standard controls, which supports our hypothesis that loyalty shares are *better* than the classical differential voting shares because any shareholder can gain double votes after certain time period and, moreover, the double votes are not transferrable. We find some weak support to the BN result that market dislikes the use disproportional ownership structures by families (model (3)). Model (4) adds an interaction between the dual dummy and the state ownership. We find weak evidence that market also dislikes the use of disproportional ownership structures by the state.

(Insert Table 10 about here)

In further models of Table 10, we estimate the cross-sectional value regressions on April 4, 2016, when the default loyalty double voting system became effective. We observe a decrease in the loyalty share "premium" from 0.15 to a discount of -0.051 (models (1) and (5). The reason behind this drop becomes apparent in model (6). The sample of double vote firms in 2016 is "contaminated" by the switchers, the firms that used to be single vote and became double vote either automatically or after a failed vote on preserving the one vote per share. As observed in the univariate analysis, the switchers are the firms with the lowest Qs in both 2014 and 2016. The regression models (6) to (8) confirm the negative and significant value effect among these switching firms.

The main results hold in the difference-in-difference regression models (1) and (2) in panel B of Table 10. We find no significant difference in Tobin's Q before and after the treatment, i.e.

the *Loi Florange*. In model (1) we define all OSOV companies to be treated by the *Loi Florange*. The Tobin's Q in OSOV companies is (insignificantly) lower than in double voting companies, and there is no treatment effect. In model (2) the treated group includes only those 14 companies that switched from single vote to double vote. Once again, we find significantly lower Tobin's Q among the switchers, both before and after the treatment.[19]

There can be several reasons behind the negative valuations among firms that switched from single into double vote system. First, in many of these firms there is a state controlled block, and they are likely to have important social or political goals instead of pure shareholder value maximization (see the regression model (9)). Second, loyalty shares have been suggested as good takeover defences (Moschetto & Teulon, 2015). In this context, the *Loi Florange* with its focus on shareholder long-termism could have served as a "camouflage" for the true intention of preventing a takeover. However, this is also true for companies that had loyalty shares throughout the period. It is more likely that the lower valuation is due to the strong presence of the state as the main shareholder in the one-share-one-vote to loyalty share "switcher" group.

4. Conclusions

One-share-one-vote was the default rule in French company law before 2014. Shareholders could opt-out by adopting a regime that grants double voting rights after the shares are held for a number of years. Companies could also go public with a loyalty share provision in their statutes. In almost all cases the pre-IPO shareholders retained double voting rights. The new post-IPO shareholders started off with one-share-one-vote and only acquired double voting

---
[19] One could alternatively study the value effect with an event study methodology. The main obstacle in implementing this methodology is the precise definition of the event date. We perceive the multivariate Tobin's Q analysis to be more appropriate for our purpose. We have also implemented an event study around the general meeting in which the resolution to maintain the one-share-one-vote system was included. The (not reported) results are insignificant, which is generally in line with no change in Tobin's Q before and after the *Loi Florange*.

rights after a holding period of at least two years. In one case the pre-IPO shareholders gave up their double voting rights and all shareholders started off with one-share-one-vote. Double voting rights accrued to those shareholders that continued to hold the shares for at least two years after the IPO. On 28 March 2014, just under half of the blue chip SBF 120 index companies had adopted loyalty shares. In the previous three years 37 percent of IPOs came to the market with loyalty share statutes.

In 2014 the French state introduced the Law 2014-384 of 29 March 2014, the *Loi Florange*, that reversed the default rule as of April 4, 2016. Loyalty shares became the "new normal" and shareholders had to opt-out if they wanted to adopt one-share-one-vote. The change of default rule had aspects of "libertarian paternalism" (Thaler & Sunstein, 2003). Companies still had a chance to adopt the rule an absolute majority of shareholders prefer, but the state expressed a clear preference for loyalty shares. Previously the French state had expressed a preference for one-share-one-vote that was consistent with the voting policies of many institutional investors and proxy advisers. The change in emphasis was justified by a concern about short-termism and, implicitly, the rise of international hedge fund activism (Becht, Franks, Grant, & Wagner, 2017).

However, the law was not neutral. It did not grandfather existing control structures but changed the allocation of property rights. France the regulator introduced a law that gave favourable treatment to France the shareholder. Pre-reform the French state had found it hard to assemble a supermajority to opt out of one-share-one-vote for most of its holdings; post-reform the state had enough votes to lock in the newly granted loyalty shares. In these cases, the reform was equivalent to an "immutable" rule that imposed loyalty shares on these companies.

Loyalty switchers, companies that transited from one-share-one-vote to loyalty shares through the introduction of the *Loi Florange*, had an average Tobin's Q that was significantly lower than companies that preserved their pre-reform control structure. The finding is consistent with the French state pursuing objectives other than shareholder value maximisation. Interestingly, the switch itself did not lower Tobin's Q. It was already lower before the reform. The result suggests that the law did not change the way these companies are managed; it merely made the French state's influence over them more permanent. It also allows the French state to reduce the size of its capital stakes to generate revenue, while keeping the same degree of control.

Absent the French state, institutional shareholders generally voted to return to one-share-one-vote. They behaved exactly as the Coase theorem predicts; *ceteris paribus* shareholders want to renegotiate and return to the original efficient contract. The idea that loyalty shares and one-share-one-vote statutes were allocated efficiently before the reform is supported by the high and unchanged Tobin's Q in both cases. There is no significant change in Tobin's Q for companies that maintained the same control structure. The evidence suggests that French loyalty shares are the result of a Coasian bargain, but only in the absence of conflicted parties with veto rights.

The *Loi Florange* itself allowed the French state to permanently tighten its grip on a number of listed companies it considers "strategic" without the approval of existing shareholders. The new default rule does seem to have an effect on the proportion of initial public offerings with loyalty statutes. It is too soon to tell if this effect is permanent and if the increased use of loyalty share statutes is efficient.

References

Adams, R., & Ferreira, D. (2008). One Share-One Vote: The Empirical Evidence. *Review of Finance*, *12*(1), 51–91. https://doi.org/10.1093/rof/rfn003

Ayres, I., & Gertner, R. (1989). Filling Gaps in Incomplete Contracts: An Economic Theory of Default Rules. *The Yale Law Journal*, *99*(1), 87–130. https://doi.org/10.2307/796722

Bebchuk, L., Cohen, A., & Ferrell, A. (2009). What Matters in Corporate Governance? *The Review of Financial Studies*, *22*(2), 783–827. https://doi.org/10.1093/rfs/hhn099

Bebchuk, L.A. (2013). The myth that insulating boards serves longterm value. *Columbia Law Review*, *113*(10), 1637–1694.

Bebchuk, Lucian A., & Kastiel, K. (2017). The Untenable Case for Perpetual Dual-Class Stock. *Virginia Law Review*, *103*(4), https://doi.org/10.2139/ssrn.2954630

Becht, M. (1999). European corporate governance: Trading off liquidity against control. *European Economic Review*, *43*(4), 1071–1083. https://doi.org/10.1016/S0014-2921(98)00115-9

Becht, M., Bolton, P., & Röell, A. (2003). Corporate Governance and Control. In *Handbook of the Economics of Finance* (Vol. 1, pp. 1–109). Elsevier. https://doi.org/10.1016/S1574-0102(03)01005-7

Becht, M., Franks, J., Grant, J., & Wagner, H. F. (2017). Returns to Hedge Fund Activism: An International Study. *Review of Financial Studies*, *30*(9), 2933–2971.

Belot, F. (2005). *Droit de vote double e "voting caps": quel impact pour les entreprises francaises?* (Master Thesis). Université Paris Dauphine.

Bennedsen, M., & Nielsen, K. M. (2010). Incentive and entrenchment effects in European ownership. *Journal of Banking & Finance*, *34*(9), 2212–2229. https://doi.org/10.1016/j.jbankfin.2010.02.007

Berger, D. J., Davidoff Solomon, S., & Benjamin, A. (2017). Tenure Voting and the U.S. Public Company. *Business Lawyer*, *2*(72), 295–324.

Beshears, J., Choi, J. J., Laibson, D., & Madrian, B. C. (2009). The importance of default options for retirement saving outcomes: Evidence from the United States. In *Social security policy in a changing environment* (pp. 167–195). University of Chicago Press.

Bhide, A. (1993). The hidden costs of stock market liquidity. *Journal of Financial Economics*, *34*(1), 31–51. https://doi.org/10.1016/0304-405X(93)90039-E

Bolton, P., & Dewatripont, M. (2005). *Contract theory*. Cambridge, Mass: The MIT Press.

Bolton, P., & Samama, F. (2013). Loyalty-Shares: Rewarding Long-term Investors. *Journal of Applied Corporate Finance*, *25*(3), 86–97. https://doi.org/10.1111/jacf.12033

Bolton, P., & von Thadden, E. L. (2002). Blocks, Liquidity, and Corporate Control. *The Journal of Finance*, *53*(1), 1–25. https://doi.org/10.1111/0022-1082.15240

Chassany, A.-S. (2015, May 8). State lifts Air France stake to win vote. *Financial Times (FT.Com)*.

Chemmanur, T. J., & Jiao, Y. (2012). Dual class IPOs: A theoretical analysis. *Journal of Banking & Finance*, *36*(1), 305–319. https://doi.org/10.1016/j.jbankfin.2011.07.010

Chene, N. (2008). *Le droit de vote double en France. Panorama de son utilisation et impact en termes de valorisation des sociétés* (Master Thesis). HEC Paris.

Chow, J. (2015, November 5). Renault Independent Directors: Double-Voting Rights Upset Alliance With Nissan. *Dow Jones Institutional News*.

Claessens, S., Djankov, S., Fan, J. P. H., & Lang, L. H. P. (2002). Disentangling the Incentive and Entrenchment Effects of Large Shareholdings. *The Journal of Finance*, *57*(6), 2741–2771. https://doi.org/10.1111/1540-6261.00511

Coase, R. H. (1960). The Problem of Social Cost. *The Journal of Law & Economics*, *3*, 1–44.

Cvijanovic, D., Groen-Xu, M., & Zachariadis, K. E. (2017). *Free-Riders and Underdogs: Participation in Corporate Voting* (SSRN Scholarly Paper No. ID 2939744). Rochester, NY: Social Science Research Network. Retrieved from https://papers.ssrn.com/abstract=2939744

Dallas, L. L., & Barry, J. M. (2015). Long-Term Shareholders and Time-Phased Voting. *Delaware Journal of Corporate Law*, *40*, 541–646.

Easterbrook, F. H., & Fischel, D. R. (1996). *The Economic Structure of Corporate Law*. Harvard University Press.

Edelman, P. H., Jiang, W., & Thomas, R. S. (2018). *Will Tenure Voting Give Corporate Managers Lifetime Tenure?* (SSRN Scholarly Paper No. ID 3107225). Rochester, NY: Social Science Research Network. Retrieved from https://papers.ssrn.com/abstract=3107225

Ellingsen, T., & Paltseva, E. (2016). Confining the Coase Theorem: Contracting, Ownership, and Free-Riding. *The Review of Economic Studies*, 83(2), 547–586. https://doi.org/10.1093/restud/rdw001

Fried, J. M. (2014). The Uneasy Case for Favoring Long-Term Shareholders. *Yale Law Journal*, 124, 1554–1627.

Ginglinger, E., & Hamon, J. (2012). Ownership, control and market liquidity. *Finance*, 33(2), 61–99.

Gompers, P. A., Ishii, J., & Metrick, A. (2010). Extreme Governance: An Analysis of Dual-Class Firms in the United States. *The Review of Financial Studies*, 23(3), 1051–1088. https://doi.org/10.1093/rfs/hhp024

Johnson, E. J., Bellman, S., & Lohse, G. L. (2002). Defaults, Framing and Privacy: Why Opting In-Opting Out!. *Marketing Letters*, 13(1), 5–15. https://doi.org/10.1023/A:101504420731S

Johnson, W. C., Karpoff, J. M., & Yi, S. (2015). The bonding hypothesis of takeover defenses: Evidence from IPO firms. *Journal of Financial Economics*, 117(2), 307–332. https://doi.org/10.1016/j.jfineco.2015.03.008

Kahneman, D., Knetsch, J. L., & Thaler, R. H. (1990). Experimental Tests of the Endowment Effect and the Coase Theorem. *Journal of Political Economy*, 98(6), 1325–1348. https://doi.org/10.1086/261737

Lins, K. V. (2003). Equity Ownership and Firm Value in Emerging Markets. *Journal of Financial and Quantitative Analysis*, 38(1), 159–184. https://doi.org/10.2307/4126768

McKenzie, C. R. M., Liersch, M. J., & Finkelstein, S. R. (2006). Recommendations Implicit in Policy Defaults. *Psychological Science*, 17(5), 414–420. https://doi.org/10.1111/j.1467-9280.2006.01721.x

Moschetto, B.-L., & Teulon, F. (2015). An anti-takeover strategy by limitation of voting rights: A model and a numerical approach. *Estrategia Anti-OPA Limitando Los Derechos de Voto: Un Enfoque Teórico y Numérico.*, 20(1), 52–66.

Osipovich, A., & Berman, D. K. (2017, October 16). Silicon Valley Vs. Wall Street: Can the New Long-Term Stock Exchange Disrupt Capitalism? *Wall Street Journal*. Retrieved from https://www.wsj.com/articles/silicon-valley-vs-wall-street-can-the-new-long-term-stock-exchange-disrupt-capitalism-1508151600

Roe, M. J. (2013). Corporate Short-Termism—In the Boardroom and in the Courtroom. *The Business Lawyer*, 68(4), 977–1006.

Santoro, A., Di Palma, C., Guarneri, P., & Capogrosso, A. (2015). Deviations from the One Share - One Vote Principle in Italy: Recent Developments - Multiple Voting Rights Shares and Loyalty Shares. *Bocconi Legal Papers*, 5, 141–170.

Shevchenko, Y., Von Helversen, B., & Scheibehenne, B. (2014). Change and status quo in decisions with defaults: The effect of incidental emotions depends on the type of default. *Judgment and Decision Making*, 9(3), 287.

Stothard, M. (2015, April 16). French companies fight back against Florange double-vote law. Retrieved 22 September 2017, from https://www.ft.com/content/05314dfe-e27d-11e4-ba33-00144feab7de

Thaler, R. H., & Sunstein, C. R. (2003). Libertarian Paternalism. *The American Economic Review*, 93(2), 175–179.

Tversky, A., & Kahneman, D. (1975). Judgment under Uncertainty: Heuristics and Biases. In *Utility, Probability, and Human Decision Making* (pp. 141–162). Springer, Dordrecht. https://doi.org/10.1007/978-94-010-1834-0_8

Vidalon, D. (2010, July 2). France's Edenred shines in bourse debut. *Reuters News*.

Table 1
Sample companies
Panel A: SBF 120 companies included in the sample

№	Company	28 March 2014	4 April 2016	№	Company	28 March 2014	4 April 2016	№	Company	28 March 2014	4 April 2016
	Double - Double [1]				**Double - Double [1] (continued)**				**Single - Single [2]**		
1	Accor SA	Loyalty 2 years	Loyalty 2 years	39	Schneider Electric SE	Loyalty 2 years	Loyalty 2 years	73	Air Liquide SA	Single	Single
2	Alten SA	Loyalty 4 years	Loyalty 4 years	40	SEB SA	Loyalty 5 years	Loyalty 5 years	74	Atos SE	Single	Single
3	Altran Technologies SA	Loyalty 4 years	Loyalty 2 years	41	SFR Group SA	Loyalty 2 years	Loyalty 2 years	75	BNP Paribas SA	Single	Single
4	Arkema SA	Loyalty 2 years	Loyalty 2 years	42	Societe BIC SA	Loyalty 2 years	Loyalty 2 years	76	Capgemini SA	Single	Single
5	AXA SA	Loyalty 2 years	Loyalty 2 years	43	Societe Generale SA	Loyalty 2 years	Loyalty 2 years	77	Credit Agricole SA	Single	Single
6	BioMerieux	Loyalty 5 years	Loyalty 5 years	44	Sodexo SA	Loyalty 4 years	Loyalty 4 years	78	DBV Technologies	Single	Single
7	Bouygues SA	Loyalty 2 years	Loyalty 2 years	45	TechnipFMC PLC	Loyalty 2 years	Loyalty 2 years	79	Euler Hermes Grou	Single	Single
8	Bureau Veritas SA	Loyalty 2 years	Loyalty 2 years	46	Teleperformance	Loyalty 4 years	Loyalty 4 years	80	Eutelsat Communic	Single	Single
9	Carrefour SA	Loyalty 2 years	Loyalty 2 years	47	Thales SA	Loyalty 2 years	Loyalty 2 years	81	Fonciere Des Regio	Single	Single
10	Casino Guichard	Loyalty 4 years	Loyalty 2 years	48	TOTAL SA	Loyalty 2 years	Loyalty 2 years	82	Gaztransport Et Te	Single	Single
11	CGG SA	Loyalty 2 years	Loyalty 2 years	49	Ubisoft Entertainment SA	Loyalty 2 years	Loyalty 2 years	83	Gecina SA	Single	Single
12	Danone SA	Loyalty 2 years	Loyalty 2 years	50	Valeo SA	Loyalty 2 years	Loyalty 2 years	84	ICADE	Single	Single
13	Dassault Systemes SE	Loyalty 2 years	Loyalty 2 years	51	Vallourec SA	Loyalty 4 years	Loyalty 4 years	85	Innate Pharma SA	Single	Single
14	Edenred	Loyalty 2 years	Loyalty 2 years	52	Vicat SA	Loyalty 4 years	Loyalty 4 years	86	JCDecaux SA	Single	Single
15	Eiffage SA	Loyalty 2 years	Loyalty 2 years	53	Wendel SA	Loyalty 2 years	Loyalty 2 years	87	Klepierre	Single	Single
16	Essilor International SA	Loyalty 2 years	Loyalty 2 years	54	Zodiac Aerospace	Loyalty 4 years	Loyalty 4 years	88	Korian SA	Single	Single
17	Eurazeo SA	Loyalty 2 years	Loyalty 2 years	55	Maurel Et Prom	Loyalty 2 years	Loyalty 2 years	89	L'Oreal SA	Single	Single
18	Eurofins Scientific SE	Loyalty 3 years	Loyalty 3 years	56	Michelin	Loyalty 4 years	Loyalty 4 years	90	Mercialys SA	Single	Single
19	Faurecia	Loyalty 2 years	Loyalty 2 years	57	Plastic Omnium	Loyalty 2 years	Loyalty 2 years	91	Metropole Televisi	Single	Single
20	Genfit	Loyalty 2 years	Loyalty 2 years	58	Saint Gobain	Loyalty 2 years	Loyalty 2 years	92	Natixis SA	Single	Single
21	Groupe Eurotunnel SE	Loyalty 2 years	Loyalty 2 years					93	Neopost SA	Single	Single
22	Hermes International	Loyalty 4 years	Loyalty 4 years		**Single - Double (after a failed vote) [3]**			94	Nexans SA	Single	Single
23	Ilid SA	Loyalty 3 years	Loyalty 3 years	59	Air France-KLM	Single	Loyalty 2 years	95	Nexity SA	Single	Single
24	Imerys SA	Loyalty 2 years	Loyalty 2 years	60	Alstom SA	Single	Loyalty 2 years	96	Rexel SA	Single	Single
25	Ingenico Group SA	Loyalty 2 years	Loyalty 2 years	61	Engie SA	Single	Loyalty 2 years	97	Rubis SCA	Single	Single
26	Ipsen SA	Loyalty 2 years	Loyalty 2 years	62	Orange SA	Single	Loyalty 2 years	98	SCOR SE	Single	Single
27	IPSOS	Loyalty 2 years	Loyalty 2 years	63	Renault SA	Single	Loyalty 2 years	99	Suez	Single	Single
28	Kering	Loyalty 2 years	Loyalty 2 years	64	Veolia Environnement SA	Single	Loyalty 2 years	100	Technicolor SA	Single	Single
29	Lagardere SCA	Loyalty 4 years	Loyalty 4 years	65	Vivendi SA	Single	Loyalty 2 years	101	Television Francais	Single	Single
30	LVMH Moet Hennessy	Loyalty 3 years	Loyalty 3 years					102	Unibail-Rodamco S	Single	Single
31	Orpea	Loyalty 2 years	Loyalty 2 years		**Single - Double (automatically) [4]**			103	Vinci SA	Single	Single
32	Pernod Ricard SA	Loyalty 10 years	Loyalty 10 years	66	Aeroports de Paris	Single	Loyalty 2 years				
33	Peugeot SA	Loyalty 4 years	Loyalty 2 years	67	Bollore SA	Single	Loyalty 2 years		**Double - Single [5]**		
34	Publicis Groupe SA	Loyalty 2 years	Loyalty 2 years	68	CNP Assurances	Single	Loyalty 2 years	104	Legrand SA	Loyalty 2 years	Single
35	Remy Cointreau SA	Loyalty 4 years	Loyalty 4 years	69	Dassault Aviation SA	Single	Loyalty 2 years				
36	Safran SA	Loyalty 2 years	Loyalty 2 years	70	Electricite de France SA	Single	Loyalty 2 years				
37	Sanofi	Loyalty 2 years	Loyalty 2 years	71	Havas SA	Single	Loyalty 2 years				
38	Sartorius Stedim Biotech	Loyalty 4 years	Loyalty 4 years	72	Sopra Steria Group	Single	Loyalty 2 years				

Variable Definitions

Main Dependent Variable

Tobin's Q	(Market value of equity + Book value of total assets − Book value of equity) divided by (Book value of total assets)

Ownership Variables

Dual dummy	1 if company has a disproportional ownership structure; and 0 otherwise
Control minus Ownership (Wedge)	Controlling shareholder's votes minus the cash flow stake
Amount of voting rights	Controlling shareholder's share of the voting rights
Cash flow stake	Controlling shareholder's share of the cash flow rights
Family dummy	1 if the controlling shareholder is a family; and 0 otherwise
State dummy	1 if the controlling shareholder is the government (including public sector); and 0 otherwise
Financial dummy	1 if the controlling shareholder is a financial institution; and 0 otherwise
Company dummy	1 if the controlling shareholder is an unlisted corporation; and 0 otherwise
Dispersed	1 if there is no controlling shareholder; and 0 otherwise
Switch dummy	1 if the company switched from one-share-one-vote into loyalty share system in the sample period
Institutional ownership	Total share of cash flow rights held by institutional investors

Control Variables

Size	The natural logarithm of total assets (in million EUR)
Leverage	Long term debt divided by total assets
Sales growth	Revenue growth (a year-on-year change in sales revenue)
Return on assets	Net income divided by total assets (in %)
Asset tangibility	Net property, plant, and equipment divided by total assets
Industry dummies	Eleven sectors specified according to the Global Industry Classification Standard: industrials, materials, information technology, financials, health care, consumer staples, energy, consumer discretionary, utilities, real estate, and telecommunication services

Definitions

Controlling shareholder	The largest shareholder or group of shareholders acting in concert that hold at least 10 percent of the voting rights

113

Table 2

Tobin's Q by the decision group (before and after the *Loi Florange*)

Decision group	N	Mean (28 March 2014)	Mean (4 April 2016)
Double - Double[1]	58	1.65	1.62
Single - Single[2]	31	1.41	1.46
Single - Double (after failed vote)[3]	7	0.98	1.02
Single - Double (automatically)[4]	7	1.23	1.19
Double - Single[5]	1	2.14	2.06
Total	104	1.51	1.51

Note.
[1] Companies that offered loyalty shares before the *Loi Florange* was introduced and were not influenced by the Act
[2] Companies that managed to opt out of the *Loi Florange* before 3 April 2016
[3] Companies that failed to opt out the *Loi Florange* and had to offer loyalty shares as of 3 April 2016
[4] Companies that passively accepted the new double vote system (as stipulated by L.225-123 of the French Commercial Code)
[5] Companies that stopped offering loyalty shares and introduced single class shares

Note. Panel A shows the list of 104 companies included in the sample:
[1] Companies that offered loyalty shares before the Florange Act was introduced and were not influenced by the Act
[2] Companies that managed to opt out of the Florange Act before 3 April 2016
[3] Companies that failed to opt out the Florange Act and had to offer loyalty shares as of 3 April 2016
[4] Companies that passively accepted the new double vote system (as stipulated by L.225-123 of the French Commercial Code)
[5] Companies that stopped offering loyalty shares and introduced single class shares

Table 1 (continued)

Panel B: SBF 120 companies excluded from the sample

№	Company	28 March 2013	4 April 2016	№	Company		№	Company
		IPO after 28 March 2014			Headquartered outside France			
1	Amundi	-	OSOV	7	Aperam		12	Euronext
2	Elior Group	-	OSOV	8	Arcelor Mittal		13	Ses
3	Elis	-	Loyalty 2 years	9	Gemalto		14	Nokia
4	Europcar	-	Loyalty 2 years	10	Solvay		15	Stmicroelectronics
5	Spie	-	Loyalty 2 years	11	Airbus Group		16	Lafargeholcim Ltd
6	Worldline	-	Loyalty 2 years					

Note. Panel B shows the SBF120 companies excluded from the sample. Companies headquartered outside France are not influenced by the changes in French Law. Companies that went public after the adoption of Florange Act are also excluded from the sample.

Table 4

Descriptive statistics

Panel A. Descriptive statistics as of 28 March 2014

Variable	Observations	Mean	Median	Min	Max	Standard deviation
Tobin's Q	104	1.51	1.33	0.91	3.20	0.61
Size	104	9.26	9.05	7.05	12.89	1.57
Leverage (%)	104	18.73	16.50	0.62	46.87	13.15
Sales growth (%)	104	0.56	-0.33	-34.99	29.82	11.92
Return on assets (%)	104	1.36	1.45	-4.54	5.13	2.24
Asset tangibility (%)	104	21.58	13.49	0.89	82.77	22.08
Voting rights (%)	104	32.89	28.67	0.00	84.70	25.29
Cash flow stake (%)	104	28.64	23.78	0.00	84.56	23.19
Control minus Ownership Wedge (%)	104	4.25	0.00	0.00	16.80	5.76

Panel B. Descriptive statistics as of 4 April 2016

Variable	Observations	Mean	Median	Min	Max	Standard deviation
Tobin's Q	104	1.51	1.30	0.91	3.20	0.64
Size	104	9.48	9.27	7.05	12.89	1.49
Leverage (%)	104	19.02	17.11	0.62	46.87	13.21
Sales growth (%)	104	4.90	7.69	-34.99	29.82	16.17
Return on assets (%)	104	1.30	1.56	-4.54	5.13	2.15
Asset tangibility (%)	104	21.03	11.71	0.89	82.77	22.53
Voting rights (%)	104	32.31	26.40	0.00	90.32	27.15
Cash flow stake (%)	104	27.16	20.25	0.00	85.73	24.00
Control minus Ownership Wedge (%)	104	5.15	2.55	-1.82	18.60	5.94

Note. *Tobin's Q* is market value of equity plus book value of total assets minus book value of equity, all divided by book value of total assets. *Size* is logarithm of total assets. *Leverage* is long term debt divided by total assets. *Growth* is a year-on-year percentage change in sales revenue. *Asset tangibility* is net property, plant, and equipment divided by total assets. *Return on assets* is net income divided by total assets. *Controlling shareholder* is the largest shareholder or group of shareholders acting in concert that hold at least 10 percent of voting rights. *Amount of voting rights* is the controlling shareholder's share of voting rights. *Cash flow stake* is the controlling shareholder's share of cash flow. *Degree of disproportionality* is the controlling shareholder's votes minus cash flow stake.

Table 3

Share of companies with disproportional ownership structure and Tobin's Q by ownership type

Ownership type	28 March 2014					4 April 2016				
	Total number of firms	Mean Tobin's Q (total firms)	Number of dual-class firms	(Proportion of dual class firms in the respective ownership category)	Mean Tobin's Q (dual-class firms)	Total number of firms	Mean Tobin's Q (total firms)	Number of dual-class firms	(Proportion of dual class firms in the respective ownership category)	Mean Tobin's Q (dual-class firms)
Family	35	1.77	28	(80.00)	1.76	35	1.74	31	(88.57)	1.69
Corporation	23	1.53	9	(39.13)	1.99	19	1.56	9	(47.37)	1.75
Financial	15	1.34	8	(53.33)	1.31	16	1.31	9	(56.25)	1.23
State	12	1.20	3	(25.00)	1.40	13	1.20	11	(84.62)	1.15
Dispersed	19	1.35	11	(57.89)	1.46	21	1.41	12	(57.14)	1.46
Total	104	1.51	59	(56.73)	1.66	104	1.51	72	(69.23)	1.52

Note. Table shows the share of companies with disproportional ownership structure and the Tobin's Q before and after the adoption of the *Loi Florange* for each shareholder category. Controlling shareholder is the largest shareholder or group of shareholders acting in concert that hold at least 10 percent of voting rights. Ownership types are: *family* including private persons with the same surname, *corporation* including private companies whose major shareholder is not one of the direct owners in the sample company, *financial* including financial institutions and insurance companies, *state* including state, cities and municipalities, *dispersed* including the companies that do not have a controlling shareholder. Tobin's Q is market value of equity plus book value of total assets minus book value of equity, all divided by book value of total assets.

Table 5
Panel A: Distribution of Control and Ownership Rights as of 31 December 2013

Ownership type			Largest shareholder by owner category				
	N	(% of total)	Amount of Votes (%)		Cashflow stake (%)		Wedge (%)
			Mean	Median	Mean	Median	Mean
Family	35	(33.65)	46.74	50.55	38.72	40.91	8.02
Corporation	23	(22.12)	40.85	35.68	36.34	35.68	4.51
Financial	15	(14.42)	26.90	25.62	23.62	20.58	3.28
State	12	(11.54)	36.79	28.60	36.10	27.07	0.69
Dispersed	19	(18.27)	0.00	0.00	0.00	0.00	0.00
Total	104	(100.00)	32.89	28.67	28.64	23.78	4.25

Panel B: Distribution of Control and Ownership Rights as of 31 December 2016

Ownership type			Largest shareholder by owner category				
	N	(% of total)	Amount of Votes (%)		Cashflow stake (%)		Wedge (%)
			Mean	Median	Mean	Median	Mean
Family	35	(33.65)	47.09	55.58	37.68	40.42	9.40
Corporation	19	(18.27)	45.12	41.27	40.06	41.26	5.07
Financial	16	(15.38)	20.45	17.00	18.20	14.75	2.25
State	13	(12.50)	40.55	33.95	34.84	25.91	5.70
Dispersed	21	(20.19)	0.00	0.00	0.00	0.00	0.00
Total	104	(100.00)	32.31	26.40	27.16	20.25	5.15

Note. Table shows the types of controlling shareholders and means and medians of amount of voting rights, cashflow stake, and the difference between votes and cash flow stake for each different owner category. Controlling shareholder is the largest shareholder or group of shareholders acting in concert that hold at least 10 percent of voting rights. Ownership types are: *family* including private persons with the same surname, *corporation* including private companies whose major shareholder is not one of the direct owners in the sample company, *financial* including financial institutions and insurance companies, *state* including state, cities and municipalities, *dispersed* including the companies that do not have a controlling shareholder. *Wedge* is the amount of votes minus the cash flow stake of the controlling shareholder.

Table 6
Voting results for proposal to (re)introduce one-share-one-vote (opting out of the Loi Florange L.225-123)

	Sponsor	Votes Present (%)	For (%)	Against (%)	Abstain (%)	Margin (%)	Threshold (%)	Outcome	Mgmt	ISS
			Panel A: Single - Single							
Air Liquide SA	M	47.31	93.08	0.53	6.39	27.08	66	Pass	For	For
Atos SE	M	54.62	97.70	2.30	0.00	31.70	66	Pass	For	For
BNP Paribas SA	M	64.91	78.23	21.71	0.06	12.23	66	Pass	For	For
Capgemini SA	M	62.33	95.27	4.73	0.00	29.27	66	Pass	For	For
Euler Hermes Group	M	91.60	99.99	0.01	0.00	33.99	66	Pass	For	For
Eutelsat Communications	M	75.74	99.84	0.06	0.10	33.84	66	Pass	For	For
Foncière Des Régions	M	79.07	99.93	0.03	0.04	33.93	66	Pass	For	For
Gecina SA	M	77.51	99.58	0.35	0.07	33.58	66	Pass	For	For
ICADE	M	76.71	99.70	0.28	0.02	33.70	66	Pass	For	For
Innate Pharma SA	M	51.86	99.58	0.42	0.00	33.58	66	Pass	For	For
Klepierre	M	84.38	99.93	0.07	0.00	33.93	66	Pass	For	For
Korian SA	M	78.58	99.64	0.36	0.00	33.64	66	Pass	For	For
L'Oreal SA	M	75.93	99.80	0.07	0.13	33.80	66	Pass	For	For
Mercialys SA	M	83.97	97.90	0.16	1.94	31.90	66	Pass	For	For
Metropole Television SA	M	61.33	99.71	0.28	0.01	33.71	66	Pass	For	For
Natixis SA	M	82.88	99.13	0.86	0.01	33.13	66	Pass	For	For
Neopost SA	M	67.40	98.81	1.19	0.00	32.81	66	Pass	For	For
Nexans SA	M	77.43	99.62	0.02	0.36	33.62	66	Pass	For	For
Nexity SA	M	75.94	99.88	0.09	0.03	33.88	66	Pass	For	For
Rexel SA	M	61.20	98.33	1.66	0.01	32.33	66	Pass	For	For
SCOR SE	M	62.06	96.59	3.41	0.00	30.59	66	Pass	For	For
Suez	M	69.80	95.29	4.70	0.01	29.29	66	Pass	For	For
Technicolor SA	M	60.54	88.46	11.52	0.02	22.46	66	Pass	For	For
Unibail-Rodamco SE	M	57.08	99.99	0.01	0.00	33.99	66	Pass	For	For
Vinci SA	M	60.35	99.34	0.58	0.08	33.34	66	Pass	For	For
Average		69.62	97.41	2.22	0.37	31.41				

			Panel B: Single - Double (after failed vote)							
Air France-KLM	M	58.59	56.63	43.27	0.10	-9.37	66	Fail	For	For
Alstom SA	M	61.48	52.01	47.82	0.17	-13.99	66	Fail	For	For
Engie SA	M	65.91	39.96	60.02	0.02	-26.04	66	Fail	For	For
Orange SA	S	67.20	43.30	56.69	0.01	-22.70	66	Fail	Against	For
Renault SA	M	72.45	60.53	39.39	0.08	-5.47	66	Fail	For	For
Veolia Environnement SA	M	56.21	51.19	48.79	0.02	-14.81	66	Fail	Against	For
Vivendi SA	S	59.03	50.05	49.85	0.10	-15.95	66	Fail	Against	For
Average		62.98	50.52	49.40	0.07	-15.48				

| | | Panel C: Double - Single (Special meeting on abandoning loyalty share system) | | | | | | | | |
| Legrand | M | 86.60 | 98.51 | 1.49 | 0.00 | 32.51 | 66 | Pass | For | For |

Table 7

Probability of switching into the loyalty share system

State dummy	1.768***
	(0.683)
Tobin's Q	-1.527*
	(0.839)
Size	-0.0506
	(0.169)
Leverage	-3.042
	(2.149)
Institutional ownership	-3.455
	(2.564)
Constant	2.666
	(2.360)
Observations	45
Pseudo R2	0.348

Note. The results of a probit regression in which the dependent variable is a dummy variable that equals 1 if the company that had one share one vote on 28 March 2014 started granting double votes as of 4 April 2016 (the *Switch dummy*). The sample includes only single class companies. Tobin's Q is market value of equity plus book value of total assets minus book value of equity, all divided by book value of total assets. Size is logarithm of total assets. Leverage is long term debt divided by total assets. State dummy is 1 if the controlling shareholder is state; and 0 otherwise. Controlling shareholder is the largest shareholder or a group of shareholders acting in concert that hold at least 10 percent of voting rights. Institutional ownership is the aggregate cash flow stake held by institutional investors (e.g. mutual funds). Standard errors are reported in parentheses: *** p<0.01, ** p<0.05, * p<0.1.

Table 8

IPO Flow on Euronext Paris (March 28, 2011 - March 28, 2017)

	Number of firms			Fraction of IPO firms with loyalty shares (from Total)	Fraction of firms with retroactive double vote (from Loyalty shares)
	One-share-one-vote	Loyalty shares	Total		
Before 28 March 2014	19	11	30	36.7	90.9
After 28 March 2014	20	23	43	53.5	69.6
Total	39	34	73	46.6	76.5
p-value of Mean equality test (Before vs. After)				*0.080*	*0.090*

Note. Table shows the number of IPOs on Euronext Paris between March 28, 2011 and March 28, 2017, i.e. three years before and after the *Loi Florange*. The last column reports the fraction of firms with loyalty shares that offered double voting rights retroactively, i.e. all the shareholders that had held shares for at least X number of years prior to the IPO immediately received double voting rights; the remaining firms granted double voting rights *after* X number of years from the IPO date.

Table 10
Panel A: The effect of loyalty shares on firm value (Dependent variable = Tobin's Q)

	Results as of 28 March 2014				Results as of 4 April 2016				
	(1)	(2)	(3)	(4)	(5)	(6)	(7)	(8)	(9)
Size	-0.124***	-0.125***	-0.124***	-0.129***	-0.150***	-0.126***	-0.138***	-0.138***	-0.149***
	(-3.331)	(-3.227)	(-3.271)	(-3.297)	(-3.592)	(-2.912)	(-3.167)	(-3.150)	(-3.450)
Leverage	-0.326	-0.386	-0.280	-0.348	-1.162**	-1.260**	-1.191**	-1.206**	-1.185**
	(-0.588)	(-0.692)	(-0.497)	(-0.616)	(-2.072)	(-2.292)	(-2.141)	(-2.124)	(-2.090)
Asset tangibility	0.0244	0.0492	0.0434	-0.0175	0.109	0.0828	0.0102	0.00511	0.0773
	(0.0764)	(0.154)	(0.125)	(-0.0503)	(0.343)	(0.261)	(0.0321)	(0.0158)	(0.247)
Sales growth	0.00798	-0.0491	-0.0529	0.0109	-0.0642	-0.0892	-0.0766	-0.0673	-0.0401
	(0.0201)	(-0.117)	(-0.140)	(0.0271)	(-0.179)	(-0.250)	(-0.213)	(-0.187)	(-0.108)
Return on assets	0.0518**	0.0536**	0.0529**	0.0544**	0.0605*	0.0547	0.0578*	0.0570	0.0611*
	(2.018)	(2.101)	(2.071)	(2.073)	(1.805)	(1.601)	(1.675)	(1.624)	(1.755)
Cash flow stake	0.165	0.0631	0.119	0.135	0.121	0.248	0.238	0.237	0.125
	(0.704)	(0.278)	(0.412)	(0.540)	(0.557)	(1.082)	(1.034)	(1.027)	(0.561)
Dual dummy	0.149		0.211	0.174	-0.0507	0.00317	0.00166	0.00255	-0.0197
	(1.334)		(1.611)	(1.471)	(-0.375)	(0.0218)	(0.0114)	(0.0173)	(-0.141)
Family dummy			0.227						
			(0.873)						
Dual dummy * Family dummy			-0.258						
			(-0.908)						
Wedge		0.921							
		(0.910)							
State dummy				0.105			0.206	0.170	0.596*
				(0.622)			(1.348)	(0.691)	(1.962)
Dual dummy * State dummy				-0.303					-0.683**
				(-1.336)					(-2.084)
Switch dummy						-0.345**	-0.426***	-0.457***	
						(-2.407)	(-2.910)	(-2.657)	
Switch dummy * State dummy								0.0853	
								(0.285)	
Constant	2.513***	2.604***	2.470***	2.563***	3.051***	2.838***	2.933***	2.940***	3.029***
	(6.052)	(5.952)	(5.961)	(5.865)	(6.585)	(5.864)	(6.024)	(5.961)	(6.282)
Industry effects	YES	YES	YES	YES	YES	YES	YES	YES	YES
Observations	104	104	104	104	104	104	104	104	104
Adjusted R-squared	0.370	0.364	0.364	0.360	0.387	0.407	0.408	0.402	0.392

Table 9
Average holding period by the decision group (before and after the *Loi Florange*)

Decision group	N	Mean (2013)	Mean (2017)	Change (2017) - (2013)
Double - Double[1]	57	2.35	2.27	-0.07
Single - Single[2]	30	3.18	2.31	-0.87
Single - Double (after failed vote)[3]	7	1.02	1.20	0.18
Single - Double (automatically)[4]	7	7.87	4.53	-3.33
Double - Single[5]	1	1.63	1.90	0.28
Total	102	2.88	2.36	-0.51
p-value of the difference between (1) and (2)				0.0627

Note. Average holding period is the ratio of the average of the total market value of the shares outstanding at the start and at the end of the year and the value of shares traded in a year, as in (Bolton & Samama, 2013). The sample includes 102 French SBF index companies (all except GTT and SFR Group, for which complete trading data for years 2013 and 2014 are not available).

[1] Companies that offered loyalty shares before the *Loi Florange* was introduced and were not influenced by the Act
[2] Companies that managed to opt out of the *Loi Florange* before 3 April 2016
[3] Companies that failed to opt out the *Loi Florange* and had to offer loyalty shares as of 3 April 2016
[4] Companies that passively accepted the new double vote system (as stipulated by L.225-123 of the French Commercial Code)
[5] Companies that stopped offering loyalty shares and introduced single class shares

Figure 1

Pre-Reform Equity and Voting Stakes of Largest Owners
(31 December 2013)

Default Rule: One-Share-One-Vote

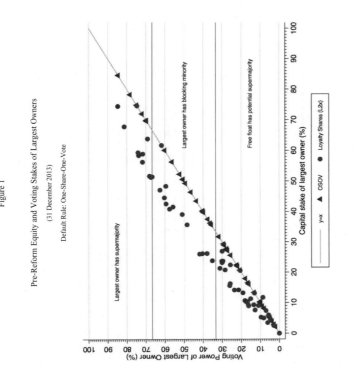

Note: The markers for 3 companies with 100% free float are plotted as a single observation.

Panel B: The difference-in-differences effect of loyalty shares on firm value (Dependent variable = Tobin's Q)

	(1)	(2)
Size	-0.139***	-0.118***
	(-4.905)	(-4.105)
Leverage	-0.764**	-0.808**
	(-2.057)	(-2.144)
Asset tangibility	0.0781	0.0742
	(0.365)	(0.347)
Sales growth	-0.123	-0.188
	(-0.495)	(-0.755)
Return on assets	0.0564***	0.0549***
	(2.714)	(2.694)
Cash flow stake	0.149	0.237
	(0.946)	(1.478)
Time dummy (1 after treatment)	0.0374	0.0483
	(0.391)	(0.635)
Treated (all OSOV companies)	-0.139	
	(-1.389)	
Time ## Treated	0.00909	
	(0.0709)	
Treated switch (OSOV companies that switched)		-0.285***
		(-3.026)
Time ## Treated switch		-0.0557
		(-0.503)
Constant	2.869***	2.637***
	(8.924)	(8.265)
Industry effects	YES	YES
Observations	208	208
Adjusted R-squared	0.420	0.434

Note. Table reports the regressions of Tobin's Q on financial, ownership and governance variables. In Panel A columns (1) to (4) report cross-sectional regression on 28 March 2014. Columns (5) to (9) report cross-sectional regressions on 4 April 2016. In panel B columns (1) and (2) report the difference-in-difference analysis (panel data). Tobin's Q is market value of equity plus book value of total assets minus book value of equity, all divided by book value of total assets. Size is logarithm of total assets. Leverage is long term debt divided by total assets. Growth is a year-on-year percentage change in sales revenues. Asset tangibility is net property, plant, and equipment divided by total assets. Return on assets is net income divided by total assets. Controlling shareholder is the largest shareholder or group of shareholders acting in concert that hold at least 10 percent of voting rights. Amount of voting rights is the controlling shareholder's share of voting rights. Cash flow stake is the controlling shareholder's share of cash flow. Wedge is the controlling shareholder's votes minus cash flow stake. Dual dummy is one for companies with a disproportional ownership structure, and zero otherwise. Family dummy is one if the controlling shareholder is a family; and zero otherwise. State dummy is one if the controlling shareholder is the government (including public sector), and zero otherwise. Switch dummy is one if the company switched from one-share-one-vote system into loyalty share system between 28 April 2014 and 4 April 2016. All regressions control for industry fixed effects. Eleven industries are specified according to the Global Industry Classification Standard.. Robust t-statistics in parentheses. *** p<0.01, ** p<0.05, * p<0.1.

Figure 2

One-Share-One-Vote to Loyalty Share "Switchers"

(31 December 2013)

Equity and Voting Stake of Largest Owner

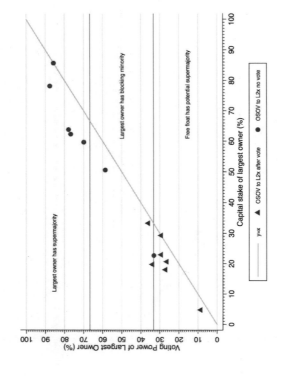

Note: The Figure shows 14 companies that switched from one-share-one-vote before the introduction of the *Loi Florange* to loyalty shares after the law came into effect. The observations marked with a triangle transited after a failed shareholder vote; for the observations marked by a circle there was no shareholder vote and loyalty shares applied by default.

Figure 3

One-Share-One-Vote to Loyalty Share "Switchers"

(31 December 2016)

Equity and Voting Stake of Largest Owner

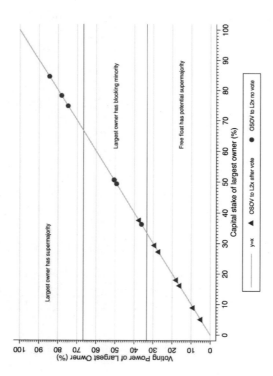

Note: The Figure shows 14 companies that switched from one-share-one-vote before the introduction of the *Loi Florange* to loyalty shares after the law came into effect. The observations marked with a triangle transited after a failed shareholder vote; for the observations marked by a circle there was no shareholder vote and loyalty shares applied by default. The *Loi Florange* was in force on 31 December 2016. Hence the voting power reported on the vertical axis includes the voting power of the largest owner obtained as a result of switching to loyalty shares.

Figure 4

Post-Reform Equity and Voting Stake of Largest Owner

(31 December 2016)

Default Rule: Loyalty Shares

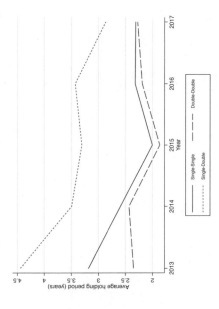

Note: The markers for 9 companies with 100% free float are plotted as a single observation at (0,0).

Figure 5

Average holding period for French companies (years) before and after the *Loi Florange*

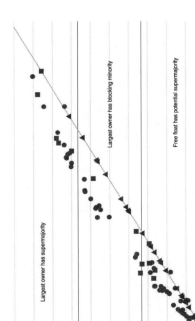

Note: Average holding period is the ratio of the average of the total market value of the shares outstanding at the start and at the end of the year and the value of shares traded in a year, as in (Bolton & Samama, 2013). The sample includes 102 French SBF index companies (all except GTT and SFR Group, for which complete trading data for years 2013 and 2014 are not available). "Single-Single" group includes companies that managed to opt out of the *Loi Florange* before 3 April 2016 and stayed OSOV (30 firms). "Double-Double" group includes companies that offered loyalty shares before the *Loi Florange* was introduced and were not influenced by the Act (57 firms). "Single-Double" group includes companies that failed to opt out the *Loi Florange* or passively accepted the new double vote system, and thus had to offer loyalty shares as of 3 April 2016 (14 firms).

Appendix 1 - Edenred — Going Public with Loyalty Shares

During the Shareholders' Meeting on June 29, 2010 Accor Group, a European leader in hotels and a global leader in corporate services approved the demerger of its two main businesses: Hospitality and Services. This decision was made with the purpose to expand the business abroad and boost its growth (Prospectus for the initial public offering of Edenred, 2010). The Services unit was named Edenred and was listed on July 2, 2010 on Euronext Paris right after the demerger (Vidalon, 2010). The spun-off company adopted loyalty shares according to which "a double voting right is attached to all fully paid-up shares that have been held in a registered share account in the name of a single shareholder for at least two years". The shares sold to another holder would lose their double voting rights, whereas transfers through inheritance or to spouse/relative do not disrupt the 2-year holding period.[20] Immediately after the IPO all shareholders had single voting rights (one-share-one-vote) for two years. On December 31, the largest shareholders were a concert party composed of the private equity fund Eurazeo and Colony Capital (27.38% ownership and votes), Morgan Stanley Investment (8.83%) and Southeastern Asset Management (6.55%). These shareholders could have voted switch from loyalty shares to one-share-one-vote with a two third majority. Equally, the concert party alone was able to block the switch.

Shareholder structure as of 31 December 2010:

	Number of shares and votes	% capital	% votes
Colony Capital/ Eurazeo (acting in concert)	61 844 245	27.38%	27.38%
Morgan Stanley Investment Management	19 944 400	8.83%	8.83%
Southeastern Asset Management	14 799 800	6.55%	6.55%
Other institutional investors	118 204 697	52.33%	52.33%
Other retail investors	11 104 254	4.91%	4.91%
TOTAL	225 897 396	100.00%	100.00%

---

[20] Prospectus for the initial public offering of Edenred (2010) Retrieved from: https://www.edenred.com/sites/default/files/pdf/documentations/information-reglementee-et-communiques/prospectus-introductionbourseedenred-juin2010-en.pdf

Appendix 2 : BNP Paribas — the importance of attendance rates (free riding)

The Combined General Meeting of BNP Paribas took place on May 13, 2015 during which the Article 18 of the Articles of Association was amended by adding the following phrase: "by exemption from the last paragraph of article L.225-13 of the French Commercial Code, each share carries one voting right, and no share has a double voting right" (www.bnpparibas.com). This amendment helped the company to opt out of the automatic granting of double voting rights. To adopt the bylaw amendment, two thirds of the present shareholders had to vote in favour of the amendment. In case of BNP Paribas the decision to keep one-share-one-vote structure was not made unanimously: 21.71% of the attending shareholders (or 14.1% of all the shareholders) voted against the opting out of the *Loi Florange* (see Table 6). If 33.33% of the attending shareholders would have voted against the amendment, the double voting rights would be granted to all shares registered in the name of the same shareholder for at least two years. The ownership structure of BNP Paribas is shown below. It is likely that SFPI, the investment company of the Belgian state, and many of the employees voted in favour of double voting rights. These two groups jointly held around 15% of the voting rights. This case illustrates the importance of the attendance rate, which was 64.9% in the case of BNP Paribas. An active minority block (~15%) together with a high free-riding rate could boost the vote AGAINST one-share-one-vote.

Shareholder structure as of 31 December 2014:

	Number of shares (in millions)	% capital	% votes
SFPI	127.75	10.3%	10.3%
Grand Duchy of Luxembourg	12.87	1.0%	1.0%
Employees	64.36	5.2%	5.2%
Corporate officers	0.33	ns	ns
Treasury shares	3.4	0.3%	-
Retail shareholders	56.35	4.5%	4.5%
Institutional investors	944.94	75.8%	76.1%
Other and unidentified	35.95	2.9%	2.9%
TOTAL	1245.96	100%	100%

Source: https://invest.bnpparibas.com/en/general-shareholders-meeting/agm-13-may-2015/documents

Appendix 3. Renault — state action to block reversion to one-share-one-vote

Despite an appeal from Renault's Board of Directors to oppose the adoption of double voting rights, on April 30, 2015, Renault felt short of two-third votes needed to opt out of the *Loi Florange*. Almost 61% of the attending shareholders voted for opting out of the automatic granting of double voting rights (see Table 6), whereas 66% were needed in order to keep one-share-one-vote structure. Shortly before the Shareholders' General Meeting, Emanuel Macron, the former French Economy Minister, increased the government's stake in Renault from 15% to almost 20% making the state the largest shareholder in Renault. This helped to ensure the adoption of the *Loi Florange*. After the automatic granting of double voting rights, the government held 33.95% of total voting rights, which destabilized the long-lasting alliance between Nissan and Renault. The capital and technological partnership between two automotive companies had been in place for almost 20 years. Nissan holds 15% of Renault's shares, but according to French cross-shareholding rules does not have any voting rights (Chow, 2015). The ownership structure of Renault is shown below.

	As of 31/12/2016			As of 31/12/2015			As of 31/12/2014		
	Number of shares (in millions)	% capital	% votes	Number of shares (in millions)	% capital	% votes	Number of shares (in millions)	% capital	% votes
French State	58,387,915	19.7%	34.0%	58,387,915	19.7%	23.6%	44,387,915	15.0%	17.8%
Nissan Finance Co.	44,358,343	15.0%	-	44,358,343	15.0%	-	44,358,343	15.0%	-
Daimler Pension Trust	9,167,391	3.1%	3.1%	9,167,391	3.1%	3.7%	9,167,391	3.1%	3.7%
Employees	6,168,600	2.1%	4.07%	6,157,300	2.1%	2.48%	7,384,900	2.5%	2.97%
Treasury shares	4,649,545	1.6%	-	3,573,737	1.2%	-	2,555,983	0.9%	-
Public	172,990,490	58.5%	59.0%	174,077,598	58.9%	70.3%	187,867,752	63.5%	75.5%
TOTAL	295,722,284	100%	100%	295,722,284	100%	100%	295,722,284	100%	100%

about ECGI

The European Corporate Governance Institute has been established to improve corporate governance through fostering independent *scientific research and related activities*.

The ECGI will produce and disseminate high quality research while remaining close to the concerns and interests of corporate, financial and public policy makers. It will draw on the expertise of scholars from numerous countries and bring together a critical mass of expertise and interest to bear on this important subject.

The views expressed in this working paper are those of the authors, not those of the ECGI or its members.

www.ecgi.org

ECGI Working Paper Series in Law

Editorial Board

Editor Luca Enriques, Allen & Overy Professor of Corporate Law, Faculty of Law, University of Oxford

Consulting Editors John Coates, John F. Cogan, Jr. Professor of Law and Economics, Harvard Law School

Paul Davies, Senior Research Fellow, Centre for Commercial Law, Harris Manchester College, University of Oxford

Horst Eidenmüller, Freshfields Professor of Commercial Law, University of Oxford

Amir Licht, Professor of Law, Radzyner Law School, Interdisciplinary Center Herzliya

Roberta Romano, Sterling Professor of Law and Director, Yale Law School Center for the Study of Corporate Law, Yale Law School

Editorial Assistants Tamas Barko, University of Mannheim
Sven Vahlpahl, University of Mannheim
Vanessa Wang, University of Mannheim

www.ecgi.org\wp

Electronic Access to the Working Paper Series

The full set of ECGI working papers can be accessed through the Institute's Web-site (www.ecgi.org/wp) or SSRN:

Finance Paper Series http://www.ssrn.com/link/ECGI-Fin.html
Law Paper Series http://www.ssrn.com/link/ECGI-Law.html

www.ecgi.org\wp

資料 4

EU「黄金株」事件・再考
EU 'GOLDEN SHARE' CASES REVISITED

九州大学大学院法学研究院　上田純子
Junko UEDA, Kyushu University
uejun@law.kyushu-u.ac.jp

Abstract

The European Court of Justice (ECJ) has handed down a number of judgments regarding 'golden shares'. The cases are brought against the background of liberalisation of the economy of the member states which results in the creation of privatised companies from formerly state-owned enterprises. In these cases, so-called 'golden shares' accompanied by special powers including the rights to limit general shareholders' voting rights, approval rights and vetoes vested with shareholders are issued to the authority, including the relevant ministers and government officials, via the articles of association of the company under the special act of the member state, which may authorise the company to adopt such company articles, or under laws and regulations of the member state. Obviously, the purpose of the issuance is to maintain State control over the company even after its privatisation. The cases are, without exception, brought by the European Commission (Commission) against the member state. The plaintiff, the Commission, argues that the issuance of 'golden shares' infringes the obligations under the Treaty Establishing the European Community (EC)/ Treaty on the Functioning of the European Union (TFEU) provisions of the defendant, the member state. The relevant provisions of the EC/TFEU are the free movement of capital or/and freedom of establishment. This article thoroughly examines the 13 relevant cases (including one joined cases) before the ECJ which have been reported or posted at the EU official website to date, the final judgments of which were made between 1999 and 2010, and reflects upon the theoretical points raised by these cases.

The article is divided into three parts. The first part overviews the facts and judgment of each case. Prior to the cases coming up, the Commission published its Communication entitled 'Communication of the Commission on certain aspects concerning intra-EU investment' in 1997, where it interprets that special shares of a discriminatory nature could violate Treaty provisions of the free movement of capital and freedom of

EUIJ-Kyushu Review
Issue 1 - 2011

EU「黄金株」事件・再考
EU 'Golden Share' Cases Revisited

上田純子
Junko UEDA

Print edition: ISSN 2186-8239
Online edition: ISSN 2186-3385

establishment. It allows the exceptions of justification under Treaty provisions (such as Articles 52 and 65 of TFEU). Also non-discriminatory/indistinctly applicable golden shares could be justified under the imperative requirements' on the condition that the minimum standards for the excise of the special powers are known in advance in a precise, objective and stable manner and at any event the principle of proportionality is respected. The leading cases of the ECJ may be those handed down on the same day, 4 June 2002; namely, the Commission against Portugal, France and Belgium. Out of the 13 cases, only in the Belgian case, the member state's defense was admitted by the ECJ. A veto in lieu of a prior approval and limitation of the exercise of special powers with clear wording may be the dividing line between the cases.

The second part classifies the 'golden shares' at issue picked up from the cases in the first part and discusses a desirable model of governance, using 'golden shares', for the industries, of which any threat to the undertaking may jeopardise a fundamental interest of society.

The concluding part of the article highlights the theoretical issues, including the definition of the free movement of capital, the relationship between the free movement and freedom of establishment, the applicability of free movement Treaty provisions to 'golden shares' as State measures and the applicability of the Keck standards, the practice of applying the principle of proportionality in the 'golden share' cases and the applicability of Article 345 of TFEU.

はじめに

「黄金株」事件は、欧州における1980年代からの官-民間／民-民間の企業再編のいわば副産物として、1990年代から欧州司法裁判所（以下、ECJ）に多く係属している[2]。「黄金株」(golden shares)とは、一般的には、拒否権等の「特権」が付与された種類株式のことを指す[3]が、ECJに係属した一連の事案は、少なくとも欧州裁判所判例集（以下、ECRという）やウェブ式データベースにおいて公表されたものを見る限り、すべて、従前の国営会社における法令や定款により、主務大臣等に黄金株を保有させ、当該会社における政府の安定的支配権を民営化後も維持させるものであり、その発行は、直接的外資規制への代替措置とみることもできる。かかる事業の特徴から、原告は欧州委員会、他方、被告は加盟国であり、いずれも義務不履行請訴[4]として提起されている。

政府持株に付与される「特権」は、後述するように、事業毎に異なり、また同一事業においても異なる権利が複合されていることが多い。従来の事例研究では、ECJは政府等の持株への「特権」付与の根拠規定について個別に判断を加えているにもかかわらず、政府等の持株に付与されたこの多様性とかかる多様性がECJの資本の自由移動との抵触の有無および抵触がある場合の正当化の可否の判断にもたらす影響については必ずしも精緻ではなかったように思われる[5]。折から、わが国においても、2011年3月の東日本一円における大震災

---

[1] 欧州委員会は、公式にはspecial rights（特殊な権利）という語を用いている。European Commission (Staff Working Document), *Special Rights in Privatised Companies in the Enlarged Union—A Decade Full of Developments* (Brussels, 22 July 2005)。ECJの英語版判決文においては、「黄金株」(golden shares)という語も散見するが、このような特殊な権利が付与された株式の総称・俗称である。本稿が、「黄金株」と表記するのはこのような考慮に基づいているからである。なお、用語については、小塚荘一郎「公益を理由とした株主の権利の制約――黄金株に関する欧州裁判所判決の教訓――」上法52巻1・2号 (2008年) 12頁注 (4)。

[2] わが国においてもそれらを巡る事例研究はすでに複数公刊されている。たとえば、池田良一「欧州司法裁判所におけるフランス・ポルトガルの「黄金株」のEU法抵触判決」国際商事法務30巻11号 (2002年) 1494頁、今野裕之「ECにおける資本移動の自由の原則といわゆる「黄金株」」国際商事32巻1号 (2004年) 80頁 (以下、今野 a)、由布節子「黄金株付与と資本の自由移動の制限」貿易と関税54巻4号 (2006年) 75頁、上田廣美「域内市場における企業再編――資本の自由移動と開業の自由の原則との関係――」日本EU学会年報27号 (2007年) 148頁、小塚・同上9頁、今野裕之「いわゆる「黄金株」に基づく権利の行使と資本移動の自由の原則」国際商38巻12号 (2010年) 1730頁 (以下、今野 b)。

[3] 日欧における黄金株の概念の相違に積極的意味づけをするものとして、由布・同上72頁。

[4] TFEU258条、参照。

[5] とはいえ、小塚・前掲注 (1) 14頁、今野 b・1730頁はこの相違に着目した分析をしている。小塚論文では、政府が株主の構成な議決権の割合に介入するものなのを「株主規制型」、政府が経営上の意思決定について承認権または拒否権をもつものを「経営事項型」と呼んでいる。後者については、株式の移転が妨げられるわけではないので、そもそも資本の自由移動との抵触の問題は生じないではないかという考えもあろう。後者のような類型付を行った株主の問題としてとらえるようとする欧州司法裁判所の論法が、「黄金株」と表記するのはこのような考慮に基づいているからである。後述するように、他の一般株主との関係については、政府系持株は会社法によって付与された特殊の権利外にあり、投資とのバランスをとる原則外にあり、比例平等原則を理由とした株主の権利の制約――黄金株に関する欧州裁判所判決の教訓――」（今野 b・1732頁、参照）。

を機として、危機時の電力産業の管理のありかたが問われており、細かな類型化の下に今一度 ECJ 判例に現れた一連の「黄金株」とそれに対する判決とを見直すことにより、一国の公共の安全や公益に直結する産業の特殊性を一株式会社のガバナンスにどう反映すべきかについて、一定の示唆を得ることができるのではないかと思われる。

本稿では上記関心に基づき、第1節では、「黄金株」に関する一連の ECJ 判決を概観する。第2節では、認定事実の細かな相違に配慮しつつ、「黄金株」の類型化と判決内容の対比、および、その背後にある論点を検討することとともに、これらの個別論点は多岐にわたるため、本稿では整理を試みるに留めざるをえないが、結びにおいて、論点を絞り、掘り下げることを予定している。

なお、以下、TFEU とは、欧州連合運営条約 (Treaty on the Functioning of the European Union) の略記である。

1. 欧州司法裁判所における一連の「黄金株」事件

本節では、第2節および結びにおける検討に先立ち、筆者が渉猟しえた、「黄金株」に関連する13事件(併合事案1件を含む)について、事実の概要と判旨をまとめることとする。

1-1. 対イタリア事件 Case C-58/99 Commission v. Italy[6](以下、イタリア第一事件)

一連の「黄金株」事件の嚆矢となったのは、1999年に欧州委員会から提訴された対イタリア事件である。もっとも、被告イタリア政府は、本件では、指摘された EC 条約違反を自認し、それを前提とした主張を繰り広げた。しかも、ECJ はかかる主張を手続的に採用することができなかったため、欧州委員会の主張がその実質的意義は大きいといってよい。

[事実の概要]

イタリアの1994年デクレ第332号は、その後1994年法律第474号となり、イタリアにおける国や公共部門の持株の売却を促進する目的で制定され、その会社における株式の売却について詳細な定めを置いていた。たとえば、主1条は、当該持株の引受けの準備および履行の目的のため、企業年数や操業能力のある国内または外国会社や、専門家としての登録年数が5年以上の専門家に、所定の職務(調査、助言、評価等)を課すことができる旨を、主務官庁は、(イタリア国内の)閣僚理事会議長は、デクレにより、国防、運輸、通信、エネルギー資源、その他公共部門に携わる会社のうちとこの会社を国有化するかを決めることができ、かかる会社の支配権を失う措置が採択される前に、定款において、臨時株主総会の決議により国の意思決定により、所定の特殊な権限を付与する規定が挿入されなければならない旨を、それぞれ定めていた。財務大臣の特殊な権限には、所定の割合の議決権保有への承認、所定の事項に対する議決権監査役員の選任権、および、所定の事項について拒否権が含まれていた。かかる定めに基づき、1995年に閣僚理事会議長デクレにより、エネルギー・石油事業を営む ENI SpA の定款規定にかかる特殊な権限が導入されたほか、1997年に2つのデクレにより、Telecom Italia SpA の定款に同様の規定が挿入された。2つのデクレのうち一方は特殊な権限の内容を定め、他方は3パーセント以上の議決権の取得について財務大臣の承認権を付与するものであった。

欧州委員会は、以下の見解および理由によりその措置をイタリア政府に正当化する旨をとる旨および是正措置をとる方向で、その後関連規定の改正を行ったが、期限内に国会への改正法案の提出がなされなかったため、欧州委員会、ECJ への提訴に踏み切った。

欧州委員会は、かかる特殊な権限を定める措置は、①非差別的措置でなければならず、②一般的利益保護にかかる不可避的要請により正当化されず、③かかる措置の目的の達成のため適切でなければならず、おおよび、④かかる措置の目的の達成のため必要な範囲を超えてはならない、との4基準を定立したうえで、イタリアが定立した、恣意的差別を構成する可能

性があり、EC条約52条（TFEU49条：域内開業の自由の保障）、59条（TFEU56条：域内サービスの自由移動の保障）、および73b条（TFEU63条：域内資本の自由移動の保障）に違反するものと主張した。イタリア政府はEC条約違反についてのみであった。EC条約違反の可能性を指摘された議長デクレとして、1999年5月4日に同年12月23日付法律第488号に際して財務省令閣僚理事会議長デクレとして改正することとなった。イタリア政府は本件審理に際し、当該改正内容及び改正の趣旨を提示し、その後の一連のデクレの改正および改正アクトの法律化により、欧州委員会からの指摘事項はすべて是正された旨を主張した。

【判旨】

欧州委員会の請求認容

義務不履行訴訟における加盟国の義務不履行は、欧州委員会が意見書に記載された是正期限の満了時における加盟国の状況によって判断され、それ以降の変更を考慮することができない。したがって、イタリア政府は、ENI SpAおよびTelecom Italia SpAの民営化に際し財務大臣に特殊な権限を付与することにより、EC条約52条（TFEU49条）、59条（TFEU56条）、および73b条（TFEU63条）に規定された義務を履行していないと結論する。

1-2. 対ポルトガル、フランス、およびベルギー事件

1-1でみたイタリア第一事件は、「黄金株」に付与された特殊な権利とEC条約上の基本的自由との関係について全く判断していないため、実際には、次の2002年の3判決[7]でもって「黄金株」に関するECJの立場が固められたということができよう。これらの3判決は、同一裁判官構成により同一日になされていることから、ここでまとめて概観することとする。

1-2-1. Case C-367/98 Commission v. Portugal[8]（以下、ポルトガル第一事件）

【事実の概要】

EC条約73b条（判決時56条：TFEU63条）1項および73d条（判決時58条：TFEU65条）1項は、次のような定めを置いていた。「本章の規定の枠組みにおいて、加盟国間および第三国間の資本の自由移動へのあらゆる制限は禁止される。73b条の規定は、加盟国の以下の権利を侵害するものであってはならない。…b）とりわけ、租税・金融機関に対するプルーデンス監督分野における加盟国法規則違反を防止するため、資本の移動の見地から正当化される措置をとる権利、行政的もしくは統計的情報目的で、資本の移動の申告手続を定める権利、または、公序もしくは公共の安全の見地から正当化される措置をとる権利。…」

派生法として、EC条約67条[9]の履行に関する1988年6月24日付第361号指令は、その附属書Ⅰにおいて、資本の移動を構成しうる具体的行為を掲げ、それには直接投資や非居住者による上場、非上場の証券取得などが含まれていた（この点については、後述、結びに代えて）、参照）。

ポルトガルは、国営会社の再民営化（もともと民間会社であったものが、1974年4月25日のクーデターにより国営会社となり、再び民間資本に返還されるもの）に関し、1990年法律、民営化に関する1993年および1994年のデクレを定めた。1990年法は、かかる制限においては、外国会社の持株比率には制限が課せられる旨、および、かかる制限を超える部分については、超過部分について、売却、議決権の剥奪、または譲渡および引受けが無効の定めがなされ、さらに、1993年デクレによりかかる持株比率の上限は原則として25パーセントとする旨が、1994年デクレでは、自然人もしくは法人単体での保有制限が定められた。

---

7 判決日は、2002年6月4日。

8 [2002] ECR I-4731.

9 旧EEC条約67条（判決時はすでに削除されていた）は、1項において、移行期中、かつ、共同市場の適切な機能を確保するために必要な範囲で、加盟国は加盟国の居住者に帰属する資本の移動への制限、および当事者の居住地、または投資地国を理由とする差別を進んで廃止しなければならない、および、2項において、加盟国間の資本の移動に関連する現時の支払いは、第一段階終了後はあらゆる制約から解放されなければならない、と定めていた。

1-2-2. Case C-483/99 Commission v. France[13] (以下、フランス事件)

[事実の概要]

フランスの1993年第1298号デクレは、2条1項において、Société National Elf-Aquitaine社における政府保有株に次のような権利（条件）を付与していた。①自然人または法人による株式総数または議決権の10分の1、5分の1、3分の1超の単独または共同での直接・間接保有に経済大臣の承認を要し、かかる承認は、他者との共同取得、支配権の移転、または、保有者集団の個々の構成員の変動の際には常に必要である（たとえば、10分の1超過時に承認を受け、さらに5分の1超過時における個々の保有者集団にも承認を受けなければならないということ）。さらに、保有者集団承認に際しては事前承認に基づき、②経済大臣および2名を取締役会での議決権のない取締役に選任し、かつ、③附則に列挙する4つの子会社の資産の過半数の譲渡または担保権の設定への決定への異議申立てをすることができる。

欧州委員会は、フランスの当該デクレ規定につき、上記1997年コミュニケーション基準に反し、かつ、EC条約52条（判決時43条：TFEU49条）ないし58条（判決時48条：TFEU54条）、および、73b条（判決時56条：TFEU63条）に違反すること、および、55条（判決時45条：TFEU51条）、56条（判決時58条：TFEU52条）、73d条（判決時58条：TFEU65条）の除外事由に該当せず、また不可欠な政府裁量権の範囲に関する周知の基準によっても正当化できない旨を主張した。フランス政府は、これに対し、当該措置は、第一に、EC条約56条（判決時46条：TFEU52条）および73d条（判決時58条：TFEU65条）1項bの除外事由のうち公共の安全保護（国外の原油備蓄施設からの調達と国内の経営意思決定機関からの授権手続により供給する石油危機の際の公共の安全の維持は、公共の保護に関わる）から、正当化される（内外無差別供給は同義である）と考えられる。一般的利益保護に関する不可避的措置（overriding requirements）とともに、比例性原則を満たす（石油危機に際し国内供給をそれ以上維持する手段はない）と答弁した。

---

[10] Communication of the Commission on certain legal aspects concerning intra-EU investment [1997] OJ C 220/06 (1997年6月19日付).
[11] 次のフランス事件では、overriding requirements との用語で表現されているが、これらや mandatory requirements は同義であると考えられる。
[12] Para. 27 of the judgment.
[13] [2002] ECR I-4781.

が10パーセントを超えることとなる民営化発効後の株式の取得には、財務大臣の事前の承認が必要である旨が、それぞれ定められた。

欧州委員会は、1997年のコミュニケーション[10]において、公的機関による承認手続や拒否権行使などにより、他の加盟国投資家による域内投資に対し制限的性質を有する措置は、EC条約73b条および52条に違反する差別的措置であって、EC条約内の資本の自由移動および開業の自由に関する諸措置に該当する除外事由に該当されえず、他方、非差別的措置については、不可避的要請 (imperative requirements)[11]により正当化されうるが、公的機関による権利による権利の裁量的行使を行使者に事前に知悉されなければならず[12]、さらに、安定的基準が適用会社に事前に知悉されていないならない、各客観的、かつ、非差別措置・比例性原則が尊重されるべきことを明らかにしており、ポルトガルの1990年法および1994年デクレおよび1994年デクレおよびコミュニケーション基準に抵触する1993年および1994年デクレはいずれも、コミュニケーション基準に抵触するものと主張した。これに対し、ポルトガル政府は、①政策判断により、共同体法の直接効果に基づき、国内関連規定はもっぱら域外投資家に対して適用されること、②関連規定は、内外差別なく適用される、および、③いずれにせよ、関連規定は民営化後の企業体における市場競争力強化、生産手段の効率化の要請により、正当化される、と争った。なお、ポルトガル政府は、EC条約222条（判決時295条：TFEU345条）の生産財保有制度を反論の論拠としても制への EC 条約の不介入を反論の論拠（この点については、後述 Colomer 法務官意見参照）、同様の主張は、後述の1-2-2および1-2-3事件でも加盟国政府からなされている。

1-2-3. Case C-503/99 Commission v. Belgium[14] (以下、ベルギー事件)

[事実の概要]

ベルギーの1994年6月10日デクレは、Société nationale de transport par canalisations (SNTC) 社の政府特別株について、以下の権利が付与される旨を定めていた。①エネルギーの国内輸送の重要な幹線・支線（いわゆるパイプライン）における譲渡、担保権の設定、または変更には、主務大臣（エネルギー大臣）への事前の通知が要求され、主務大臣は、かかる行為が国のエネルギー部門への不利益をもたらすおそれとの判断のもとに、かかる行為に対し通知受領後21日以内に異議を申し立てることができる。②主務大臣は、会社の議決権のない取締役に連邦政府の代表2名を選任することができる。当該2名の取締役は、国のエネルギー政策に反する取締役会決定の取消しを主務大臣に諮ることができる（取消しの付議は、政府代表取締役の取締役会に出席していれば、当該取締役会決定日から起算して、他方、政府代表取締役の付議のいずれかが欠けていた日から起算して、4営業日以内にされなければならず、主務大臣が政府代表取締役の付議に係る取締役会決定の取消しに付議すれば、当該決議は確定しない）。もっとも、政府代表取締役がかかる期間計算について中断することができる。さらに、1994年6月16日デクレは、Distrigaz社の政府特別株について、ほぼ同様の権限を付与した。

欧州委員会は、次のように主張した。ベルギーのデクレは、エネルギー大臣のガス幹線等の譲渡等の行為への異議申立権、および、国のエネルギー政策に反するガス取締役会決議の取消権の取消権限において、他の加盟国市民の自由移動への障害であるとしても、1997年のコミュニケーション基準に合致しないため、EC条約52条（判決時58条：TFEU49条）および73b条（判決時56条：TFEU63条）に違反する。かかる違反が、正当化されるのは、EC条約55条（判決時45条：TFEU51条）、56条（判決時46条：TFEU52条）、および73d条（判決時58条：TFEU65条）の除外事由に該当するか、一般的利益保護の観点から不可避的に要請され、かつ、かかる措置が相当なる裁量を最低限に制限する安定する客観的かつ周知基準を有している（異議申立権のような積極的措置は長期的供給計画や供給源の多元化のような消極的措置に比べ、天然ガスの適切な供給の確保に資するとはいえない。欧州委員会は、さらに、天然ガスに関する1998年第30号指令の趣旨から、天然ガス事業分野における企業間の競争と供給確保の目的とのバランスが必要である旨を付言した。

これに対し、ベルギー政府は、デクレの規定がEC条約上の開業の自由および資本の自由移動を制限するとしても、次の諸点から正当化されると争った。関連規定は、①EC条約56条（TFEU46条）、および73d条（判決時58条）、②一般的除外事由のうち公共の安全の保障に該当する、さらに、一般的利益保護のための不可避的要請がある。③当該措置によって達成しようとする目的に鑑みて当該措置の手段は均衡であり適正である。①について、国のエネルギー供給の保障は、不可避的要請である。②SNTC社とDistrigaz社は、他国のエネルギー資源に依存せざるをえないベルギー当局における戦略的地位を保持し、両社に対するデクレを通じたエネルギー当局の中断効果はやむをえない。また、手続的にも、ベルギー大臣への事前通知には期間計算の限りがあり、大臣の権限行使は、単に大臣に対するデクレに対する情報提供の意味を有するにすぎず、大臣の決定的基準を持って、所定の場合に所定の期間に限って認められ、大臣の決定には書面での理由が付せて通知されなければならない。したがって、デクレ規定は、実体・手続の双方において、規制の目的に比し均衡のとれ、さらに、かかる措置は、EC条約56条（判決時46条：TFEU52条）1項bの除外事由に該当する。ベルギー政府は、付加的に、当該措置は競争規定の適用除外を定めるEC条約90条（判決時86条：TFEU106条）2項によって正当化される旨を主張した。

[判旨]

ポルトガル事件　欧州委員会の請求認容
フランス事件　欧州委員会の請求認容

---
14 [2002] ECR I-4809.

ベルギー事件 欧州委員会の請求棄却

ベルギー事件では、ECJは、他の加盟国の投資家に所定の割合を超える株式保有を認めない措置は、それ自体でEC条約73b条(判決時56条：TFEU63条)に違反するとした。仮に非差別措置であるとしても、他の加盟国からの投資を委縮させ、資本の自由移動を「幻想」に帰せしめるもの[15]というのが、その論拠である。

ECJは、ポルトガルの1990年法およびデクレ規定のすべてについて必ずしも差別措置と断じてはいない[16]。73d条(判決時58条：TFEU65条)1項の除外事由にあたるかのみならず、不可避的要請があるか否かの判断が必要性をも選択的に示したうえで、さらに、これらの基準を満たしたとしても比例性テストを満たさねばならないと同旨に言及したのも、あからさまな外資規制とはいえないデクレ規定に配慮したものと考えられる。

ECJは、上記デクレ規定のうち、①については、否定し、②については明言せず、③については、一加盟国の財政上の利益の保護は、73d条(判決時58条：TFEU65条)1項の除外事由(不可避的要請)からも正当化されない(不可避的要請からも正当化されうる場合まで正当化されない)、とした。ECJの先例からすれば、欧州委員会が主張していた開業の自由の諸規定との関係については、開業の自由に関する諸規定の違反は資本の自由移動の違反と同様の直接的帰結としてもたらされるものであり、73b条(判決時56条：TFEU63条)違反が認定されることをもって足りるとされた[17]。

フランス事件 欧州委員会の請求棄却

フランス事件では、ECJは、まず、フランスのデクレが形式的には非差別措置であっても他の加盟国からの投資を委縮させる効果を有する以上、資本の自由移動の規定に抵触しうる規範として、除外事由にあたるかにかかわらず当該措置が正当化されうる場合まで、比例性原則を満たしかつ当該事業に知悉している者にも非差別的・客観的基準と当該措置から不利益を受ける者すべ

てに法的救済措置が用意されているか否か、を設定した[18]。そのうえで、非差別措置である1993年第1298号デクレ2条1項について、①国家の危急に存亡の石油供給の確保は不可避的要請としての正当な公益保護にあたり、また、73d条(判決時58条：TFEU65条)1項b号の除外事由を構成する、②資本の自由移動を後難しうる「公共の安全」は厳格に解釈されなければならず、共同体諸機関の介入なく加盟国が一方的に定めうる性格のものではなく、社会の基本的利益への「十分に重大な(sufficiently serious)」危険がなければならない。ECJは、比例性原則の具体的適用について、比例性テストと狭義の比例性テストを区別せず[19]、かつ、③比例性原則が満たされなければならないとし、先例に従い、同一目的がより制限的でない手段により達成されうるかの判断であると客観化した[20]。

ECJは結論的に、フランスのデクレは、比例性を有しないと判示したが、その論拠は、かかる規定は承認基準を設定しておらず経済大臣は自由に裁量権を行使でき、その結果、投資家は承認が得られるか否かについての見通しを持つことができず、このことは、経済大臣の事前承認であろうと、異議申立権であろうと変わるところはない[22]、というものであった。ポルトガル事件における当該規定の違反への結論も、開業の自由委員会は、当該措置における開業の自由規定の違反を主張してはいたが、ベルギー事件と同様の理由から、審査されていない。

ベルギー事件では、ベルギー政府はデクレ規定が資本の自由移動を制限する効果を有することについて前置きなく争っていないため、ECJは当該措置の正当化可否について争点なく判断した。加盟国におけるエネルギー供給の安定化、不可避的要請にあたり、かつ、資本の自由移動違反の除外事由のひとつ、公共の安全(EC条約73d条(判決時58条：TFEU65条)1項b)にも該当することを確認し、さらに、資本の自由移動違反の除外事由である公共の安全は「真の、かつ重大な危険時の最低限のエネルギー確保

---

15 Para. 44 of the judgment.
16 池田・前掲注(2)149頁、上田・前掲注(2)160頁、本件アクレ規定は差別的措置にあたり、そもそも例外規定適用の前提要件を満たしていないとする。
17 Paras. 40-42 of the judgment.
18 Paras. 45 and 46 of the judgment.
19 Para. 48 of the judgment.
20 Para. 49 of the judgment.
21 Para. 46 of the judgment.
22 Para. 52 of the judgment.

適用されるとしてほとんど言及されていないが、法務官意見では、同条が規定する条約の中立性から、企業を国営とするか民営とするかの選択は加盟国権限に属し、非差別措置に関する限り、EC条約222条（判決時295条：TFEU345条）の適用の可能性が検討されている。法務官意見は、EC条約295条、史的・目的論的解釈から各事案への適用の可否を論じるべきとし、その「生い立ち」、および、立法者意思解釈の必要性と同条約の経済的意義・事実上の効果について考察している。ポルトガル政府の措置が差別的であるという点について、フランスおよびベルギー事案については同様に論ずるべきであるとした。上記から明らかなように、判決はベルギー事案以外は法務官意見に従っておらず、また、同事案について、法務官意見は異なる論理構成によっている。詳言すれば、222条（判決時295条：TFEU345条）の射程に関する詳細な考察に基づいており、①EC条約第6編の総則規定として置かれており、無条件の規範である。②EC条約222条（判決時295条：TFEU345条）の所有権とは厳密に法律的な所有ではなく、加盟国権限に対し何らかの影響をうるという程度の経済的実態に即した概念である。③加えて、私的所有権のみを捕捉するものでもない、③事案における件の措置は、いずれも、形式的には株主の権利行使として会社の意思決定に関与するものの、実体としては公的監督と何ら変わるところがない（いわゆる官民混合形態）、⑤3事案（判決時295条：TFEU345条）により100パーセント加盟国権限に属し、加盟国による企業の経営管理まではそのような権限の専有には強い不適法性の推定が働く、⑥政府保持株に特権を付与することにより、特定の企業経営に政府が介入する措置は、EC条約222条（判決時295条：TFEU345条）によって加盟国権限とされる企業組織の生産財保有制度にはからず、したがって加盟国の規定は、EC条約222条（判決時295条：TFEU345条）にとって保護され、EC条約上の基本的自由には抵触しない。[24]

であること、および、当該目的に必要な範囲を超えて規制していないこと（上記フランス事件判旨、参照）を満たす必要があるとの規範定立を行った。そのうえで、①主務大臣のイニシアティヴに基づいて異議申立手続が開始されるわけではない、②事前承認ではなく、事後の異議権の付与のみである、③エネルギー大臣以外のはねの国のエネルギー政策に重大な危険が迫ったとき SNRC社のみの決定について書面により理由書を作成し、かつ、Distrigaz社の取締役会に通告しなければならず、比例性原則にも抵触せず、正当化しうるとした。なお、ベルギー政府は、加盟国における一般的経済的利益のための事業の優越性に関するEC条約90条（判決時86条：TFEU106条）2項も引用していたが、本件措置は同条による保護の対象ではありえず、さらに、欧州委員会が主張していたEC条約52条（判決時43条：TFEU49条）（開業の自由）違反については、資本の自由移動における例外事由が定められており、同様の理由で正当化されるとして、欧州委員会の請求を棄却した。

ECJは、ポルトガルないしフランス事案で加盟国側から主張された、加盟国の生産財保有制度への条約の不可侵性・中立性なり可能性、とするColomer法務官意見[23]主張を除き欧州委員会の請求を棄却すべき、とするColomer法務官意見[23]を根拠とするEC条約222条（判決時295条：TFEU345条）を根拠とする上記3判決について、法務官意見をも紹介することとする。

上記ECJ3判決では、加盟国における生産財所有制度への条約の不介入に関するEC条約222条（判決時295条：TFEU345条）は、本件の論点には抵

[法務官意見]

後掲する各事案とは異なり、上記ECJ3判決は、ポルトガル事件の一部

---

[23] Opinion of Advocate General Ruiz-Jarabo Colomer delivered on 3 July 2001.

1-3. 対スペイン事件　Case C-463/00 Commission v. Spain[25]（以下、スペイン事件）

[事実の概要]

スペインの公共部門における事業の民営化に関する1995年の法律は、①所定の条件を満たし、国が直接・間接に総株式数の25パーセント超を保有し、商事立法に規定される方法により閣僚による事業であって、②単発または数個の取引において、総株式数の10パーセント以上にあたる閣僚保有株式の処分行為（処分後の国の直接・間接保有割合が50パーセント未満となる場合を除く）、または、行為もしくは取引の直接的もしくは間接的結果として、閣僚保有株式数が総株式数の15パーセント未満にまで減少する場合に適用され、③会社の所定の経営意思決定や取引に行政の事前承認が必要である。所定の経営意思決定事項として、a) 資産の継続・維持に関わるもの、事業目的だか任意清算、分割、合併、b) 事業目的または事業目的であってそれらへの担保のいかんを問わず、事業目的であったあらゆる資産の処分行為、もしくは所有されもしくは数個の株式取引の目的組織の目的変更、または、c) 事業組織の目的変更、また、所定の取引として、a) 単発または数個の株式取引によって国の保有割合が10パーセント以上減少する場合、および、b) 株式その他の証券の直接・間接の取得により総資本の10パーセント以上を有することとなる場合が列挙されていた。アクレはさらに事前承認の内容や、事前承認に服する取引、承認権を有する機関、および、事前承認について定めを置き、1990年代後半には、相次ぐアクレの発布により、石油、通信、銀行、タバコ、電力の各企業が事前承認手続に服する旨が定められた。

欧州委員会は、「所定の会社支配株式の取得、議決権の無制限の行使、または、事業組織の運営に事前承認を要するスペインのアクレ規定は、直接投資およびポートフォリオ投資の双方を抑制し、1997年のコミュニケーションの総旨に従わず、EC条約43条（TFEU49条）および56条（TFEU63条）に違反する。したがって、公序、公共の安全、公衆衛生などの一般的利益保護に基づく公的権力行使の正当化は、厳格な解釈のもとに、必要な限度を欠き、タバコや銀行のように純粋に経済的・行政的性質を有する事業は、正当化の前提を欠き、また、一般利益保護の要請があるとしても、Telefónica de España SA や Telefónica Servicios Móviles SA のような当該会社が国境を越えて企業活動している場合には、そもそも加盟国経済の戦略的役務確保に貢献しないゆえ、加盟国の一般的利益保護の要請は、関連アクレ規定は政府に無条件の裁量権行使の保障はない。いずれにせよ、関連規定はそれ自体の比例性原則を満たさない。」と主張した。

他方、スペイン政府は、①1995年アクレ前文では、EC条約上の資本の自由移動と開業の自由の諸規定に従う旨が置かれている、②関連規定は、EC条約295条（TFEU345条）から正当化される、③事前承認が必要なので、事業の存続確保の観点から正当化される、④民営化会社に投資する者を国籍により差別するものではない、⑤アクレ関連規定は、供給の保障、経済・社会の安定、および消費者利益の保護のための国の介入を認めるものであり、いずれにせよ、不可避的基準を具備し、比例性原則を満たす、⑥かかる規定は、行使条件等の基準を具備しており、比例性原則を満たす、および、⑦関連規定は、EC条約86条（TFEU106条）2項から基本的自由に関する英国アクレが正当化される。なお、本件被告側に訴訟参加していた英国アクレの非差別措置について、市場アクセスを阻害せず、Keck 基準からEC条約56条（TFEU63条）1項の射程外と判断されると主張した（この点について、英国が次に掲げる事件において詳細に展開しており、この点に関するECJの判断も同事件において明確に示されているので、割愛する）。

[判旨]

欧州委員会の請求容認

ECJは、スペイン政府の非差別措置であるという主張に対しては、EC条約56条（TFEU63条）は単に国籍による不平等取扱いをしないということを要求することにとどまらず、非差別措置であるということのみをもって56条（TFEU63条）1項違反を構成しないということはできない。

24　Para. 91 of the Opinion.
25　[2003] ECR I-4581.

1-4. 対英国事件　Case C-98/01 Commission v. The United Kingdom[26]（以下、英国事件）

[事実の概要]

英国航空局（British Airports Authority）は、英国の7つの国際空港の所有と管理を行っていたが、1987年にBAAという民営化会社に承継された。主務大臣はBAA社の額面1ポンドの特殊株式1株を保有し、BAA社の附属定款10条には、特殊株式の①他の国務大臣等のみへの譲渡、②所定の事項への特殊株主の書面による同意等、が規定されていた。所定の事項には、所定の定款規定の変更、指定空港を保有する子会社の総議決権の過半数を保有する子会社の権利の放棄、会社または指定空港を保有する子会社の再建・再生（これにより、会社または他の子会社が当該指定空港の操業者でなくなるもの）（これにより、会社または子会社が当該指定空港の操業者でなくなるもの）の合意の締結が列挙されていた。もっとも、主務大臣の特殊株式には、株主総会および種類株主総会の通知受領権、出席権、および、発言権はあるものの、議決権はない。優先的残余財産分配請求権としては額面での株式の償還を請求することができるとされた。さらに、附属定款40条は、BAA社の定款の所定の者以外の者による総議決権の15パーセント超の議決権保有の防止を目的に、所定の者以外の者による総議決権の15パーセント超の議決権保有の防止を目的にあることを明確に規定していた。

欧州委員会は、BAA社の附属定款40条およびEC条約43条（TFEU49条）および56条（TFEU63条）に違反するとともに、EC条約43条（TFEU49条）および56条（TFEU63条）に違反すると主張し、他方、英国政府は、次の2点を主張して争った。①会社法上種類株式の発行は可能であり、特殊株式は種類株式のひとつにすぎない。また、実務上も無議決権株式として差別的としても用いられている。②あらゆる加盟国市民を国籍により差別せず、市場アクセスを制限するものではない。したがって、BAA社附属定款規定のEC条約違反はなく、正当化事由や比例性原則への適合の判断は必要ない。

[26] [2003] ECR I-4641.

とし、むしろ、①株式取得制限に制限を設ける規定は、資本の自由移動に対する制限を構成する、②EC条約295条（TFEU345条）は、基本的自由への例外措置として加盟国の生産財所有制度を保護しているわけではない、③事前承認制度は、同等の目的により達成されうる他の手段により達成されてはならないことに加え、当該制度は客観的、非差別的で、かつ、あらかじめ知悉されており、また、当該制度の影響を受けうるすべての者が経済的用意を整えていなければならない。スペインの事前承認制度は、タバコや銀行を含む広範な分野で措置されており、まず、これらの分野すべてに一般的利益保護の要請が働くのかが疑われる。タバコと銀行については、かつて国営産業であったとしても、事業自体の性質から公的役務提供を目的とするとはいえない。その他の石油、通信、電力についていえば、一般的利益保護の要請に例外的に優位される一般的利益は存在するが、EC条約上の基本的自由に対して真の、十分重大な危険が存在する場合でなければならず、社会の基本的利益に対して真の、十分重大な危険が存在する場合でなければならず、スペインの1995年法における事前承認が必要な事項のうち、[名称の如何を問わず、事業目的にかかわるあらゆる会社の株式はまたはそれらの担保づけを行っているアクト]の定義づけがあまりに広すぎて、かく定義されるのかについてみても、閣僚等の権限行使は無条件で認められ、テクノ規定について子見できる何らの具体的・客観的手がかりも用意されていない。以上から、石油、通信、電力については、EC法の一般原則である法的安定性の原則に反し、当該措置は当該規定が達成しようとする目的の必要な範囲を超えている。EC条約86条（TFEU106条）2項による正当化可能性については、スペイン政府が当該規定の適用によって正当化されうるとする根拠について十分立証を尽くしていないことから否定され、欧州委員会が主張していたEC条約43条（TFEU49条）違反については、他の事案における主張と同様に、独立別個の判断を要しないとして審理されていない。

[判旨]

欧州委員会の請求認容

ECJは、①加盟国市民間の非差別措置であっても、資本の自由移動規定に違反しうる。②物の自由移動に関するKeck基準（selling arrangements）に関する措置は市場アクセスを阻害せずEC条約28条（TFEU34条）に違反とはならない、本件英国会社法に基づく定款規定は、居住者にも非居住者にも同等に適用されるが、市場アクセスを取得しようとする他の加盟国の投資家の行動を委縮させ、市場アクセスに影響を与えうるといえる。③国内会社のみに主張できるという英国の主張も首肯できない。BAAの定款規定は、私法上のメカニズムに従うのみであるから公的監督機序に服するといえるかであるから、このような場合には、英国の定款規定が、資本の自由移動を制限するといえる。結論として、英国BAA社に依拠する必要性はないと主張するが、ECJは他の事件とは異なり正当化の可否に関する判断を行っていない。なお、欧州委員会が主張していた開業の自由への抵触に関する判断については、1-2の各事例における同様に、開業の自由がもたらされる以上、資本の自由移動への制限の直接的帰結としてもたらされるため、独立の判断は不要とされている。

1-5. 対イタリア事件　Case C-174/04 Commission v. Italy[28]（イタリア第二事件）

[事実の概要]

イタリアの2001年第192デクレは、「電力およびガス部門の市場開放が完了するまでは、当時進行中であった自由化と民営化のプロセスを保障するため、当該部門の事業会社の資本の2パーセントを超えて、政府が保有し、公共部門が支配し、国内市場で圧倒的地位を有し、公開取引所に株式を公募している会社については、事業の承認または認可の付与もしくは譲渡はデクレに定める条件に従う」……上記2パーセントの上限を超えた場合には、承認または認可の付与もしくは譲渡の手続きから、上限を超えた部分の株式の議決権は停止し、株主総会等の定足数に算入されない。また、2パーセントを超える新株予約権も行使できない」との定めを置いていた。

欧州委員会は、上記デクレ規定について、特定の類型の投資家の投資によるイタリアの電力・ガス部門の株式の保有を抑制するため、共同体内の資本の自由移動を阻害する、と主張した。イタリア政府は、これに対し、①内国公共企業と他の加盟国の公共企業とを差別するものではない、②新規上場や金融商品取引等に関連する指令[29]によっても、議決権制限株式の発行は認められている。③加盟国の電力・ガス部門に上方裁量が認められたため、各加盟国に加盟国間で規格差が生じ、イタリアのデクレは、イタリア市場が他の加盟国の公共企業から投機的に反競争的な妨害を受けないための手段であった、④イタリアの本件デクレは、他の「黄金株」先例とは異なり、時限措置である、と反論した。

[判旨]

欧州委員会の請求認容

所定の要件を満たす公共企業はイタリアの電力・ガス事業の経営および支配に効果的に関与することができ、イタリア政府が主張するデクレの目的が他の加盟国の同業の公共事業からの反競争を回避するということにあるならば、イタリア政府は、当該措置によって他の加盟国の公共事業のイタリアにおける株式取得が抑制されていることに等しい。したがって、本件デクレは、EC条約56条（TFEU63条）に抵触する。なお、イタリア政府が参照した指令は議決権制限株式を認めているものの、法律上の開示義務等に違反した場合の制裁として認めているにすぎ

---

[27] Joined Cases C-267/91 and 268/91 Criminal Proceedings against Keck and Mithouard [1993] ECR I-6097, [1995] 1 CMLR 101 (Keck).

[28] [2005] ECR I-4933.

[29] Directive 96/92/EC concerning common rules for the internal market in electricity [1997] OJ L 27/20; Directive 98/30/EC concerning common rules for the internal market in natural gas [1998] OJ L 204/1; Directive 2003/54/EC concerning common rules for the internal market in electricity and repealing directive 96/92/EC [2003] OJ L 176/37; Directive 2003/55/EC concerning common rules for the internal market in natural gas and repealing directive 98/30/EC [2003] OJ L 176/57.

ず、本件には該当しない。最後に、上記違反が正当化されるか否かについて、ECJは、「一般的に市場の競争構造を強化するというのみでは、基本的自由に優越する一般的利益とは認められない。資本の自由移動の阻害を正当化しうる一般的利益にあたるとしても、イタリア政府の目的的型の公共事業株の議決権制限が当該エネルギー供給確保の目的のため必要であること(逆に、私人や取引所で公募している公共事業株の無制限の株式保有が当該目的のため必要であること)の立証をしていない。以上から、イタリアの関連アクト規定のEC条約56条(TFEU63条)違反は正当化できず、確定する。」とした。

1-6. 対オランダ事件 Joined Cases C-282/04 and C-283/04 Commission v. The Netherlands[30] (以下、オランダ事件)

[事実の概要]

1989年、オランダの国営電信電話・郵政会社が民営化され、PTT Nederland NV (PTT) 社となった。その後1998年にPTT社はさらにその電信電話部門と郵政部門とが分割され、Koninklijke KPN NV (KPN) とTNT Post Groep NV (TPG) の2社になった。附属定款上、オランダ政府が保有する両社の株式には、次の事項に関する会社の意思決定への事前同意権が付与されていた。すなわち、①新株の発行、②普通株主の優先権の制限または消却、③普通株式の1パーセント超の取得でオランダ政府保有の特殊株式が両社保有する株式の議決権15パーセント未満にあるとき株式投資、⑦株式配当および/または準備金を財源とする配当、⑧合併または分割、⑨解散、および、⑩会社の目的等にかかるオランダ政府との協定変更。加えて、KPNおよびTPGとオランダ政府の利益に合致すると認めるとき、または、郵便サービスの保障のためにKPNおよびTPGの利益に合致すると認めるとき、または、大株主としてTPGの利益保障のための特殊株式の確保のため必要とされるときのみ特殊株式にかかる権利を行使し、敵対的買収への防衛策としてかかる権利を行使してはならない旨が合意されていた。

1998年以降、欧州委員会からオランダ政府に宛てて条約違反の疑義の意見書が送付され、かかる意見書に記載された是正期限までの間、両社における政府特殊株割合は急激に減少したが、KPNとTPGにおける政府特殊株の「黄金株」事件に付合審理された。

欧州委員会は、両社定款によりオランダ政府の同意権等の特権を付与することは、EC条約56条 (TFEU63条) 1項および43条 (TFEU49条) に違反し、一般的利益の保護の趣旨からの措置であるとしても、比例性原則を到底満たさないと主張し、他方、オランダ政府は、①関連諸国の措置ではない(一会社の株式のEC条約56条 (TFEU63条) 1項の射程に属する国の措置ではない、②分割民営化2社の定款上の措置により、特殊株式の投資家の投資にあいまいかつ間接的であり、資本の自由移動への障壁が存在するとしても、③仮にEC条約56条 (TFEU63条) 1項違反が成立するとしても、一般利益保護の要請から正当化される、と争った。

[判旨]

欧州委員会の請求認容

ECJは、①KPNおよびTPG両社の定款規定は、民営化の過程でオランダ政府の決定により導入されたものであるから、EC条約56条 (TFEU63条) 1項の射程内にある、②会社の基本的意思決定にかかるオランダ政府の事前同意権は、その投資額(の低さ)により正当化できず、他方、付与される権利は、普通株主が通常保有する権限に比べはるかに大きいゆえ、他の株主のKPNおよびTPGの株式保有する影響力を制限する、③特殊株式はオランダ政府の同意がなければ消却することができない、両社への株式投資の魅力を減殺する、他の株主の株式の価値を下落させ、両社への株式投資の魅力を減殺する、として、オランダ政府の特殊株式の定款規定のEC56条 (TFEU63条) 1項違反を認めた。そのうえで、かかる措置は、自由移動を阻害するしうる正当な利益保護のためのEC条約58条 (TFEU65条)、または、一般的利益保護

---

[30] [2006] I-9141.

の要請から正当化される余地はあるとの規範を定立し、オランダ政府は、①KPN社については一般的利益保護の目的を主張立証しておらず、KPN社の定款規定についてはEC条約56条（TFEU63条）1項違反が維持される、②TPG社については、郵便事業サービスの普遍性確保およびTPGの財務の健全性および継続性という不可避的要請はあるといえるが、比例性原則を満たさない（政府の事前同意権は、厳密な行使要件を欠き、同意しない場合の理由説明などもなされない）、としたが、欧州委員会が主張していたEC条約43条（TFEU49条）違反については、上述の各事件における同様の理由により判断の必要はないとされている。

1-7. 対ドイツ事件　Case C-112/05 Commission v. Germany[31]（以下、ドイツ事件）

[事実の概要]

ドイツのフォルクスワーゲンヴェルク社の民営化に関する法律（Gesetz über die Überführung der Anteilsrechte an der Volkswagenwerk Gesellschaft mit beschränkter Haftung in private Hand[32]、以下、VW法という）は、1960年目的で立法された。VW法は、総株式数の5分の1を超える額面株式を保有する議決権を1つとする旨、何人も総株式数の5分の1超の議決権を行使することはできない旨、連邦およびニーダーザクセン州より選任される監査役（株主代表監査役）を各2名（合計4名）選任することができる旨、および、株式法上では5分の4超の賛否を要するものとする旨が定められていた。

欧州委員会は、VW法上の議決権行使制限規定については、株式法上の特別決議成立に関する75パーセント以上要件は、一般株主に賃否の選択の余地を残しているが、VW法の80パーセント超要件は、主要株主が20パー

セントまでの議決化により、常にブロッキング・マイノリティとなりうることを意味すると主張した。また、連邦およびニーダーザクセン州の監査役選任権については、株主代表監査役員の2分の1、すなわち、員選任権の場合は10名のみであり、そのうちの4名が連邦およびニーダーザクセン州の選任にかかることになり、一般株主の監査役選任権およびニーダーザクセン州の選任にかかることになり、一般株主の選任権はEC条約上保障されることとなり、したがって、かかる規定はEC条約上保障されるべき資本の自由移動を阻害する。これに対し、ドイツ政府は、まず、VW法はVolkswagenwerk社の労働組合およびニーダーザクセン州との協定主張した。すなわち、VW法はVolkswagenwerk社の労働組合およびニーダーザクセン州の協定が会社に対する自己の請求権を放棄する代償として支配株主からの安定的保護を受ける趣旨で1959年に締結され1960年5月に「Volkswagenwerk社の法的地位に関する法律」（Staatsvertrag）に端を発し、それが1960年7月に同月にVW法として立法化にいたまま、かかる定款規定はVW法の定款規定が加盟国措置であり、EC条約56条（TFEU63条）1項との関係が問題となる加盟国措置にはあたらない。次に、上述の議決権行使制限規定は、もともと一般株主の議決権行使が0.01パーセントまでに制限されていたところ、連邦とニーダーザクセン州の持株にのみ認められていたものが他の株主にも平等に開放されるようになったことの歴史的経緯によるもので、国や州の持株に特別な権限を付与するものではない旨、また、株式法上の規定により厳格な決議要件を各会社の定款により設けることができる旨、特定の会社に関し加盟国法は原則として自由にかかる特別な法の定めを置くことができる旨、および、実際にVolkswagen社の株式は欧州市場で最も多く取引が高い人気銘柄のひとつであり、他の加盟国からの投資も多い旨を主張した。連邦およびニーダーザクセン州の監査役選任権とEC条約規定との関係については、監査役会は経営意思決定機関ではなく、また、その選任員数も、連邦の場合はは少ないくらいであり、VW法の関連規定は出資の多寡とは無関係であるのなお、ドイツ政府は、子備的にVW法関連規定の正当化事由についても主張している。すなわち、VW法は、先述の歴史的経緯から明らかなように、VW法は、もともと労働者およびマネル株主保

---

[31] [2007] ECR I-8995.
[32] BGBI, 1960 I, p. 585 and BGBI, 1960 III, p. 641-1-1.

護の観点から設けられたものであり、かかる立法には社会経済政策上の不可避的要請がある。

[判旨]

欧州委員会の請求一部認容（欧州委員会、行政的段階においては、EC条約43条（TFEU49条）違反をも主張していたが、提訴段階では同条違反の議論を展開していないため、ECJはEC条約56条（TFEU63条）1項のみを認定した）

ECJは、VW法が加盟国措置ではないとのドイツ政府の主張については、VW法が現実に法律として施行され、当事者の意思のみで変更できない以上、受容できないとしたうえで、VW法上の議決権行使制限とEC条約56条（TFEU63条）1項の関係については、①ドイツ株式法上の特別決議できる要件の引上げのための定款を変更であれば一般株主は賛否の選択ができるが、VW法によって当該要件が付与とされている本事例の場合には根本的に異なる。すなわち、欧州委員会が主張するように、20パーセントの議決権行使により、決議は常にブロックされる。1960年にVW法が制定されて以来、連邦と下ザクセン州は各々恒常的に20パーセント程度の株式を保有するVolkswagen社の2大株主である。②本件は、ポートフォリオ投資というよりむしろVW社への直接投資の事例である。上記VW法規定はVolkswagen社の経営および維持を目的でVolkswagen社への直接的投資関係を確立・維持する上で決議に参入するものとする者の投資意欲に明らかに負に影響するものである、として、EC条約56条（TFEU63条）1項違反を認定した。VW法上の連邦および下ザクセン州の比例平等原則からいえば、VW法上の選任権規定は、両者の選任員数について最大3名までとすべきであり、監査会は、取締役の選解任権を認定するのほか、一定の重要な取引を承認する権利などを保有するものである。監査会は、株式法上、優先的権利などを付与することはないが、ドイツ政府が主張するように単なる加盟国の継続的投資家を確立Volkswagen社の経営または支配のための継続的直接経済的を維持しようとする（とりわけ他の加盟国の継続的直接経済的を維持しようとする）ことは明らかである。かくして、VW法は支配のための加盟国のEC条約56

条（TFEU63条）1項違反を認定したうえで、ECJは、当該規定の正当化の可能性について次のように判示した。労働者保護および少数株主保護が一般的利益を構成しうることは否定しないが、①ドイツ政府は、Volkswagen社の株主および下ザクセン州の連邦がその地位を強化することによって、同社労働者保護が実現できるとする根拠を説明できていない。そもそも、共同決定制度に基づく労働参加により労働者の保護は図られているはずである。②少数株主保護についても同様のこととがいえる。ドイツ政府は、連邦および州への優先権付与少数株主保護との関係を立証できていない。Volkswagen社の規模の会社では社会保護の公器としての役割が期待され、一般株主の利益のために行動する会社を保護する動機づけが働くとしても、ドイツ政府はVW法上の関連規定のかかる目的との適合性・必要性を立証できていない。

1-8. 対イタリア事件　Case C-326/07 Commission v. Italy[33]（以下、イタリア第三事件）

[事実の概要]

イタリアの1994年第332号デクリトは、防衛、運輸、通信、エネルギー資源等の分野の事業を営み、国に直接・間接に支配されている会社について、国の支配権が喪失することとなる措置の採択に際し、経済・財務大臣が生産大臣との諮問のうえ行使することができる所定の特別な権限を臨時株主総会の決議でもって附属定款に挿入するものとする旨を、所定の手続きを経たうえで財務・財務大臣の提案により採択されるデクリトにより決定しなければならないとしていた。所定の特別権限は当該デクリトにより列挙されており、①ある者は、かかる会社における総議決権の5パーセントまたは経済・財務大臣デクリトにより規定されるそれよりも少ない割合の保有を目的とした経済・財務大臣デクリトにより規定されるそれよりも少ない割合の取得への異議申立て、②かかる会社における総議決権の5パーセントまたは経済・財務大臣デクリトにより規定されるそれよりも少ない割合の合意申立て、③かかる会社の解散、事業譲渡、合併、分割、会社の本店の外国への移転、会社の目的の変更、および特別権

[33] [2009] ECR I-2291.

限の剥奪または修正にかかる決議への拒否権行使、ならびに、④取締役会において議決権を有しない取締役の選任権行使、であった。これらの権限行使の相手方は、かかる権限行使することを争うことが可能であるが行使日から90日以内に、後に定められた2003年の財務法は、当該法の財務規定の存在に関わる利益を害する場合に限り上記特別権限の行使を認めるものとする旨を規定していた。

2004年デクレは、上記特別権限は、公序、公衆の安全、公衆衛生、防衛などの公益のために正当化されえない事由により行使される場合にのみ行使され、適切な期間内に、国内法・共同体法の諸原則、とりわけ無差別原則を遵守しつつ、それらの公益保護に適切かつ均衡な措置をとるものとし、さらに、特別権行使事由などを列挙していた。ちなみに、1994年デクレが具体化された2003年財務法および2004年デクレは、国のエネルギー・石油製品最低供給への真のかつ重大な危険などを列挙していた。

欧州委員会は、1994年デクレを補足する2003年財務法およびEC条約43条（TFEU49条）および56条（TFEU63条）に違反する疑いがあることを2004年デクレをイタリア政府の意見書をイタリア政府に送付した後に採択されたものである。

欧州委員会は、次のように主張した。すなわち、2004年デクレが財務大臣の特別権限行使条件が十分明確に規定されていないことから、（真のかつ重大な危険）に該当する場合は無数にあって、あいまいであり、結果的に、かかる会社の経営に影響を与えるうえ、EC条約43条（TFEU49条）および56条（TFEU63条）違反を構成する。かかる違反は、EC条約46条（TFEU52条）および58条（TFEU65条）の除外事由により、または、一般的利益保護の要請から正当化されうる。問題となっている公益分野の規制は、電力、天然ガス、および電子通信ネットワークに関しては指令があり、イタリア政府はこれら関連指令に則った規定ではなぜ小国内供給が保障されないのか、また、このような共同体法がない分野について、なぜかかるイタリア基準が必要なのかは特別権限の要否に関する1994年デクレの導入にほとんどかかわらず、EC条約43条（TFEU49条）および56条（TFEU63条）違反とされているのは、特別権限行使に関する争点を資するにおいて、②開業の自由に関することはできない、③国家の基幹部門について指令の保護規定以上の保護策を策定することに何ら支障はない、④補完性原則から、加盟国のほうが国の存在に関わるリスクを適切・適時に評価しえ、また、共同体法がない分野に関しては、共有財産に重大な侵害が及ぶ可能性がある場合は加盟国は独自の措置をとりうる、⑤1994年デクレが可能にした場合となる場合となる条件を正確に画定することはできない、と手続・実体の両側面から反論を展開した。

[判旨]

欧州委員会の請求認容

ECJは、イタリア政府が喚起した手続的な議論を採用せず、本案について、まず、資本の自由移動の規定が適用されうるものの、本件のような会社の意思決定に決定的影響を保持する場合はEC条約56条（TFEU63条）の射程内にあるとの前提を確認し、上記規定に関する①②については、EC条約56条（TFEU63条）のみならず43条（TFEU49条）をも重量的に適用する必要があり（株式が分散保有されている場合は、少数割合の株式を制約する措置であり同時に開業の自由をも制約しうる措置であるため、資本の自由移動のみ問題となる）、③については、もっぱら、EC条約43条（TFEU49条）との関係のみ問題となる（EC条約56条（TFEU63条）違反はEC条約43条（TFEU49条）違反の結果として不可避である）[34]との解釈を示した。

そうして、上記関連デクレ規定のうち、①ないし③のすべてに関わるEC条約56条との関係については、当該規定の趣旨に、エネルギー一貫[35]

---

[34] Paras. 36-38 of the judgment.
[35] Para. 39 of the judgment.

源の最低供給の確保、国防や公序のためといった一般的利益に関わる措置として正当化事由を有するが、比例性原則を満たさないと判断した。すなわち、2004年デクレは、当該行使条件と行使権限との間に相関性がなかったが、比例性原則適用過程における第一テストである、当該措置が当該措置の達成目的に適合的であるかどうか、の審査を通過し得しえない。さまざまな公益保護に関わる規定であっても、一般的かつ広範囲にわたって、経済・財務大臣に広範な裁量権行使を認めており、かかる広範性は、当該措置の目的に照らし、不均衡である。権限行使の相手方は、それのみで、それについて司法審査を求めることとしても、EC条約遵反行為が治癒されるわけではない。したがって、①②③すべてについて、EC条約56条（TFEU63条）違反である（もっとも、③については、もっぱらEC条約43条（TFEU49条）が適用されるとの前提に立っているため関係からも、結論的にEC条約56条（TFEU63条）遵反の宣言がなされたのは、上記デクレ規定のうち①②のみである）。さらに、①②については、EC条約56条（TFEU63条）との適合性に関して提示した理由から同様にあたはまり、EC条約43条（TFEU49条）違反が重畳する。

③とEC条約43条（TFEU49条）との関係については、行使条件と特別権限との関連性はあるものの、行使事由があいまいであり（列挙された公益保護の要請が具体的にいかなる場合に生ずるかは投資家に予見できない）、比例性原則を満たさない。指針が存在することも、電信電話、および電力部門については、基本的自由の除外事由にあたるか否かの判断は、きわめて厳格になされるべきである。

1-9. 2010年の2つの対ポルトガル事件判決

1-9-1. Case C-171/08 Commission v. Portugal[36]（以下、ポルトガル第二事件）

2010年にはポルトガル政府に対し欧州委員会から提起されていた義務不履行訴訟2件に対する判決が下された。Portugal Telecom SGPS SAおよびEnergias de Portugalに対する判決は異なる会社史を有するものの、いずれも民営化会社であるが、2009年6月11日付で、欧州委員会からポルトガル政府に対し、石油・ガス会社の政府黄金株に関する義務不履行訴訟が提起されており、現在ECJに係属中である[38]。

[事実の概要]

ポルトガルの1990年民営化基本法は、民営化後の会社における「黄金株」創設の可能性について次のように規定していた。すなわち、民営化により公開株式会社に組織変更された会社の附属定款において、国営保護の要請により、例外的に、附属定款に定めることにより定款変更および他の特定の決定について国の拒否権を付与した。Portugal Telecom SGPS SA社（以下、PTという）の1995年の同法の附属定款によれば、国の配当優先権以外の特殊な株式上の権利が付与された株式数は、一般また他の公共部門により保有されなければならない。A種類株式以下のような株主への譲渡は国または公共部門の保有に属し、これを受け、PTの附属定款は、A種類株式の過半数は国または公共部門の保有に属する旨を定めていた。A種類株主は以下のような特殊な権利が付与される旨を定めていた。①取締役（取締役会議長を含む）の3分の1以上は、A種類株主総会の総議決権の過半数の賛成をもって選任される、②取締役会委員である5名もしくは7名で構成される経営委員会のうち1名（5名の場合）もしくは2名（7名の場合）はA種類株主総会の総議決権の過半数をもって選任する、③業務執行取締役の指名はA種類株主の過半数の株主総会決議の同意でもってなる、①定款変更や優先的権利の制限・廃止などのA種類株主総会決議には、A種類株主決議権の過半数が賛成しなければならない、さらに、⑤④に掲げられた事項以外の株主による事前の授権が必要な事項（会社の目的の変更、会社また関連会社株式の取得や処分に関する基本方針の策定など）の決定に際し、A種類株式の総議決権の過半数の同意を必要とした。EC条約への適合性が

---

[36] CELEX: 62008J0171（ECR未登載）.
[37] 再民営化という語は、1974年のクーデター (Revolução dos Cravos) によって国営化された企業に対しては用いられており、民営化という語とは使い分けられているようである。
[38] Case C-212/09 Commission v. Portugal, [2009] OJ C 180/36.

欧州委員会は立証責任を尽くしておらず、欧州委員会は立証責任を尽くしていない。②欧州委員会の意見書は、本訴において、司法手続上前提されるべき行政段階における意見書に記載されていない請求をしており、本訴訟要件を満たさず、却下されるべきである。ECJは、①については、立証責任は欧州委員会にあるが、行政的段階では、欧州委員会の存在を争っていない。また、ポルトガル政府はかかる規定の存在を開示している。②については、行政的段階で欧州委員会から送付される通知と義務不履行訴訟の争点は同一のものである必要はなく、この点においてが提訴許可命令請求書の逸脱ではない、として本案審理を行った。

実質的論点として、欧州委員会に割り当てられる附属定款によって割り当てられるものの、ポルトガル政府の黄金株は、PT社の附属定款に基づいて策定された附属定款規定を有するものとは言えない。したがって、EC条約295条（TFEU345条）における「加盟国生産財保有制度」が問題となる場合にはあたらず、当該「黄金株」の存在および権利行使により、保有株式の割合に応じて認められた株主の経営参加・支配の可能性は狭められ、基本的意思決定に関与する権利を剥奪され、他の加盟国の株主による支配株式の取得が妨害される。EC条約56条（TFEU63条）および43条（TFEU49条）に違反するものと言える。①ポルトガル政府は、「社会の正当化の可否について、欧州委員会は、十分に重大な危険への真の、十分に重大な危険（a certain degree of competition）を維持するためにポルトガル政府との抵触を正当化するものではなく、EC条約上の基本的自由への制限は、ECJの先例は、民営化するものの自己矛盾を来していない、いずれにせよ、ECJの先例は、経済的事由を根拠に正当化を認めていない。A種類株式における特殊な権利の行使は、比例性原則を満たしていない。「国益保護の要請がある場合」という条件は事実上無制限である。かかる政府による株式発行、当該定款の付与は公共部門の目的に照らし必要な範囲を超

えている。」と主張し、他方、ポルトガル政府は、「①デクレは、PTにおける特殊な権利が付いた株式発行の可能性を規定しているのみに基づく（附属定款により当該権利が付いた株式発行の可能性を規定しているのみに基づく）。②かかる株式は純然たる私的性質を有しており、EC条約295条（TFEU345条）により国や公共部門による保有は保護される[39]。③当該措置は非差別措置であり、通商を規制する加盟国措置そのものではないため、EC条約56条（TFEU63条）および43条（TFEU49条）の射程外である。④仮にEC条約56条（TFEU63条）および43条（TFEU49条）違反であるとしても、国家が危機に瀕した際の通信サービスという公共の確保および公序の要請から正当化される。さらに、通信市場における競争の確保という観点からも正当化される。」と反論した。

[判旨]

欧州委員会の請求認容

ECJは、大要、次のように判示した。①ポルトガルのデクレは黄金株発行の可能性をとどめているのみであり、実際に黄金株に関する定款規定を導入を決定したのはPTであるが、民営化に当該定款規定を導入した際PTの株式の過半数を制限していたのはポルトガル政府であり、民営化基本法やデクレにより「黄金株」のPTにおける「黄金株」の付与、およびそれら特殊な権利の画定は、ポルトガル政府自身によるものと同視しうる。EC条約56条（TFEU63条）1項における「資本の移動」の射程にある。②ポルトガル政府が保有する「黄金株」は、その株式保有の大きさゆえに正当化されない限り、持株増加に応じて経営・支配決定に参画する会社の意思決定にポルトガル政府の直接投資を妨げる[40]。また、会社の利益に合致する会社の意思決定にポルトガル政府の承認を要することは、株式の価値を低め、ポートフォリオ投資のポルトガル政府の魅力を減殺することになる[41]。したがって、PTにおけるポルトガル政府への「黄金株」付与は、EC条約56条（TFEU63条）1項に違反する。かかる違反は、EC条約

---

[39] Para. 42 of the judgment.
[40] Para. 60 of the judgment.
[41] Para. 61 of the judgment.

295条（TFEU345条）の適用により治癒することができず、また、ポルトガル政府が援用するKeck基準の適用にも服しない。EC条約295条（TFEU345条）は、基本的自由への侵害を免除する効果を有せず、また、非差別的措置であるとはいえ、他の加盟国の投資家の投資行動を抑制する、もしくは市場アクセスを自国民以上に制限するゆえ、そもそもKeck基準の適用基盤を有していない。③経済的事由は不可避的要請たる一般的利益とは解されないし、国家が危殆に瀕した際の通信サービスの確保たる公共の安全にEC条約58条（TFEU65条）の除外事由を構成する。もっとも、公共の安全は、「社会の基本的利益に真の、十分に重大な危険」が存在するときにのみ依拠されうる。ポルトガル政府は、国への「黄金株」の付与が社会の基本的利益への侵害を防止することができるとする理由を説明できていない。さらに、ポルトガル政府の特殊な権利の行使条件は、「国益保護の要請」という他は、基本法や定款によっても規定されておらず、当該権利行使につき無制限の裁量権を国に付与するに等しく、比例原則を満たさない。なお、欧州委員会が範囲を超える手段といえ、比例原則の達成たりえない。なお、欧州委員会がEC条約43条（TFEU49条）違反をも主張していた上記ポルトガルの事件における主張と同様の理由から、独立判断はなされていない。

1-9-2. Case C-543/08 Commission v. Portugal[42] 第三事件

[事実の概要]

ポルトガルの電力会社 Energias de Portugal（以下、EDPという）は、もともとは民営企業であったが、1974年のクーデター後の1976年にテクノクラートによって公営企業となった（ポルトガルの再民営化の経緯については、上述ポルトガル第一事件、参照）。ポルトガルにおける1990年代初頭からの電力産業再編により、同社は1991年から公開株式会社として段階的に再民営化された。

ポルトガルの1990年民営化基本法には、公的競争入札、証券取引所にお

ける取引、または公募による再民営化においては、いかなる者も所定の割合を超えて株式を取得しましたまたは引き受けしまたは違反した場合には、超過株式の強制売却、取得または引き受け株式にかかる議決権の剥奪、もしくは、取得または引受けによる無効の制裁があるりつつも規定されていた。第四次再民営化に際して制定されたデクレは、何人もEDPの総株式の5パーセント超保有することを禁じ、5パーセント超の取得提案は、5パーセントまでの取得に減じられる旨が規定された。また、同法には、上記のポルトガル第二事件で紹介したように、民営化会社の定款によって「黄金株」の創設の可能性を認める旨の規定があり、EDP社の場合、2000年第141号デクレにより、①定款変更、②グループ会社の構成員および支配の5パーセント契約の締結、③資本増加に際してなされる株式の優先的権利の廃止または制限について、国による賛成決議の行使の要件とされた。さらに、民営化基本法により、再民営化会社の附属定款の策定に関し、公益保護のため、特定の事項の決定には国によって選任される取締役の承認を要する旨を規定することができるとされた。これに基づき、上述の2000年デクレは、選任決議が否決された取締役候補者について、国により選任された取締役と交代させることができることとし、EDPの附属定款には、次のような規定が置かれた。①原則的な規定として、1株1議決権であるうち所定数を超えられていたものの、B種類株式のうち代理行使であろうが、総議決権の5パーセントに服しないとされ、②A種類株式については、総議決権の5パーセントを超える議決権は、本人行使であろうが代理行使であろうが、数に入れない。③会社またはその従属会社の戦略的計画の採択や所定の事項の決定には監査会の承認が必要であるとして、所定の事項には、a) 資産、権利、または株式の取得や処分、b) 多額の借財、c) 営業所の全部もしくは大部分の開設・閉鎖、d) 金銭的価値または戦略的関係が高い取引、e) 営業活動の拡大・縮小、f) 価値が高い営業または組織関係の協業関係の廃止、合併または組織変更、および、g) 附属定款の変更が列挙されている。

ポルトガル政府は、上記ポルトガル第二事件における主張と同様に、欧州委員会主張の条約違反（提訴後新たな主張を追加）をも争ったが、ECJはこれを

---

[42] CELEX: 62008J0543（ECR 未登載）.

認めず本案審理に入った。

欧州委員会は、①ポルトガル政府の「黄金株」は、立法により付与されるものであり、私的措置とはいえず、EC条約56条（TFEU63条）1項、43条（TFEU49条）の射程にある。したがって、②政府による拒否権付与により、他の一般株主の持株に応じた意思決定支配変動への発言権が封じられる。また、拒否権付株式の発行は、投資行動へ明らかに影響し、他の加盟国からの投資を委縮させる。③ポルトガル政府への拒否権付与は、認可制をとるに等しく、開業の自由を阻害し、また、民営化基本法は、答観的かつ事前に関連会社に同知された拒否権行使要件を規定していない、と主張した。他方、ポルトガル政府は、①EDPの政府黄金株が問題とするEC条約43条（TFEU49条）および56条（TFEU63条）が問題となるのは、他の加盟国措置とはいえない、②非差別措置が制限措置にあたるのは、他の加盟国の投資家の市場アクセスを自国投資家のそれ以上に阻害する場合に限る（Keck基準）。③政府の拒否権は、国家の安全を危うくに瀕した場合に例外的に行使されるのみであり、したがって、他の株主の経営戦略的権限に関する意思決定権を剥奪するものではない。④政府役選任責任については、2006年の商事会社法改正以降[45]は監査役選任責任として理解されており、にせよ他の加盟国からのいかなる影響ももたらさない。また、本件については、一定割合の株式を保有するEC条約56条（TFEU63条）は無関係である。さらに、仮にEC条約との抵触があったとしても、当該措置には公共の安全確保の目的があり、一般的利益または58条（TFEU52条）1項bまたは46条（TFEU65条）1項のb除外事由にあたり、あるいは、一般的経済的利益を有する自国事業の保護のための加盟国措置を認めるEC条約86条（TFEU106条）2項から、正当化されうる。

[43] Para. 27 of the judgment.
[44] Paras. 27-30 of the judgment.
[45] もっとも、いかなる改正がなされ、当該改正が政府黄金株に付与された取締役選任権の解釈にどのような影響を与えるのかは判旨からは不明である。

欧州委員会の請求認容

[判旨]

ECJは、本案について、まず、本件は、EC条約56条（TFEU63条）、43条（TFEU49条）の問題なのかを判断した。基本的自由のいずれに関するのかは、立法目的に照らして判断されるべきとしつつ、資本の自由移動と開業の自由との関係について論じた。会社への出資により出資者間に経済的関係の継続的・直接的関係を構築・維持する目的でなされる投資はEC条約63条（TFEU63条）の問題となる。本件ポルトガルの措置は、EDPの経営および事業に関連に決定的影響を及ぼそうとする意図を有する株の経営に決定的影響を及ぼそうとする意図を有するまた潜在的株主のみに影響するわけではなく、株式保有の大きさに関わらず全ての潜在的株主を含めすべての株主に影響するので、EC条約43条（TFEU49条）のみならず56条（TFEU63条）の問題でもある。[46]

A種類株式における議決権行使の5パーセント制限規定は、再民営化第一段階終了前に政府の支配的持株をEDPの附属定款に導入され、さらに、その後政府持株割合が減少すると再民営化が立法され当該立法規定によりEDPにおける政府持株に特殊な権利が付与されることとなったものである。かくして、5パーセント制限規定は、政府の同意なく廃止できなくなった。続いて、上述のポルトガル第二事件における議論と同様の議論を展開し、ECJは、かかる措置は加盟国措置であるかか、譲渡不能であることとも補強論拠としている。政府「黄金株」の拒否権について、ECJは、政府「黄金株」が加盟国固有の独占的論拠を用い、EC条約56条（TFEU63条）1項違反にあたるとした。[47]5パーセントの議決権制限についても、議決権は株主の経営・支配に参画する手段であり、議決権行使を阻止しないし条件付きとするような措置は他の加盟国の投資家の投資を委縮させ、資本の自由移動に対する公共の利益を構成する。直接投資を阻害することも明らかである。政府「黄金株」にもとづくポルトガル政府の主張する商事会社法の解釈「取締役選任権」ではなく

[46] Paras. 41-44 of the judgment.
[47] Paras. 56-57 of the judgment.

に、額面1ポンドの名目株式の保有により、政府は民営化後も当該企業に自在に介入することができた。欧州委員会が1997年にコミュニケーション[49]を公表して以降は、欧州委員会と加盟国との協議やト記のような相次ぐ義務不履行訴訟の提起を背景に、民営国等への「黄金株」付与の事例は著しく減少した[50]ものの、EUの拡大に伴い、新規加盟諸国における国営企業の民営化の過程で、黄金株を付与する動きは再び顕著となった[51]。もっとも、これらの後発加盟国に対して提起された義務不履行訴訟は未だないようである。本節では、上記の一連の事業における「黄金株」をめぐる論理に反ばす影響を検討しつつ、「黄金株」の内容の相違が明旨論理に反ばす影響を検討する。

2-1. 対象となりうる産業

まず、法令上の根拠に基づく（強制的な）「黄金株」の発行は、冒頭で述べたように、民営化会社にはほぼ限定されている。ECJの認定事実によれば、業種としては、電力、ガス、石油等のエネルギー産業（イタリア第一、フランス、ベルギー、スペイン、イタリア第二、イタリア第三、ポルトガル第三）、電信電話・郵政（スペイン、オランダ、イタリア第三、ポルトガル第二）、銀行（スペイン）、タバコ（イタリア第三）、国際空港管理（英国）、自動車（ドイツ）、防衛（イタリア第三）、および、運輸（イタリア第三）などの基幹部門に関する。

ECJは、純然たる経済的・行政的性質の事業については、EC条約上の基本的自由への制限を正当化しうる一般的利益を有しないとの解釈を示している[52]。したがって、エネルギーや通信に関わる産業などとは異なり、タバコや銀行などの産業については、そもそも正当な前提となる一般的利益保護の要請がないこととになる[53]。また、エネルギーや通信などの

-----

[48] 欧州における黄金株形成の過程については、小塚・前掲注（1）11頁。
[49] 野村宗訓「イギリス民営化企業に対する政府介入 ―「黄金株」の問題を中心として―」「名学」28巻1号（1991年）31頁。
[50] European Commission, supra note 1, p. 16ff.
[51] たとえば、欧州委員会の2004年の調査では、域内141社が政府黄金株を有している実態が明らかになった。Ibid., p. 19 and Annex 3.
[52] たとえば、Case C-463/00 Commission v. Spain, supra note 25, para. 70.

「監査役員」の選任役員の選任権はすべての株主に保障されるべきであって国がそれを覆してはならない。かかる措置は、会社の経営・支配を決める、他の加盟国の投資家の関係構築を国以外の株主が行うような機会を求める。本事件では、他の加盟国の投資家の関係構築を国以外の株主が行うような機会を求める。本事件では、直接的関係構築を国以外の株主が行うような機会を求める。本事件では、阻害され、したがって、Keck基準の適用前提を欠く。

次に、ECJは、EDPにおける政府への「黄金株」付与が、一般利益保護の要請から正当化されるか否かに、さらに、比例性原則を満たすか否かについて次のように判示した。①EC条約56条（TFEU63条）違反が問題となる場合、②同58条（TFEU65条）の除外事由に該当する場合、または、公益上の必要な範囲内に正当化されうる。②公共の安全は「社会の基本的利益に真の、十分に重大な危険」がなければ満たされない、③ポルトガル政府がその予見できないエネルギー危機に、当該措置を用いていかに迅速かつ効果的に対応し供給を確保するかのメカニズムを立証すべきである。また、本件ポルトガルのエネルギー供給確保との関係を立証すべきである。また、EDPの事業の目的は、立法およびEDPの定款規定の目的は、EDPの事業を保護するために特殊な権利を付与するという点において、本件とEC条約86条2項とは無関係である点において、本件とEC条約86条2項とは無関係である（TFEU106条）2項とは無関係である。④政府持株の特殊な権利の行使要件は、いずれも、法律および EDPの定款において何ら規定されておらず、比例性原則に反する。かつ速やかな文言以上に何ら規定されておらず、比例性原則に反する。かつ、欧州委員会が主張していたEC条約43条（TFEU49条）違反の点については、上述の先例における同様に、56条（TFEU63条）違反の結果として不可分かにもたらされるので審理の必要なしとされている。

2. 「黄金株」と公共の安全ないし公益の保護

「黄金株」は、英国においてサッチャー政権時に国営会社の民営化が積極的に進められ、その過程で民営化後も政府支配を確保するべく考案されたものといわれている[48]。上記英国事件における英国航空空局の黄金株を有している実態が浮き彫りにされた BAA社の附属定款にもあったような争点が浮き彫りにされた。

国家のインフラに関わる基盤産業であったとしても、かかる民営化会社が、単体または子会社やグループ会社等を通じていわゆる多国籍企業化している場合にも、加盟国経済に関する戦略的役務提供の維持に関わらないので、正当化の前提を欠く[54]。

2-2. 一連の事件における「黄金株」上の優先的権利

次に、問題となった「黄金株」をみてみると、明らかな内外差別を伴うものはポルトガル第一事件のみであるが、イタリア第二事件と、他の「黄金株」事件とは逆に、公共部門に対し議決権取得制限を課すものであり、自国への外国公共投資の抑制を図るものでない。その他の事案ではいずれも形式的には内外差別を伴わない。その優先的権利は、大きく、a) 株式譲渡および議決権取得に関するもの、b) 役員の選任に関するもの、ならびに、c) b) 以外の会社の基本的意思決定に関するもの、の3つに分けられるように思われる。a) はある加盟国の支配株主市場への投資家の参画そのものをブロックするものであり、資本の自由移動の文脈からは、b) およびc) とは決定的に異なる。a) ないしc) は複合的に用いられていることが多いが、ECJは、その権利内容に応じて個別的に検討を加えており、基本的自由への抵触を導く論理自体は各々若干異なるといえる。そこで、a) ないしc) について、さらに細分化を試みる。

a) 株式譲渡および議決権取得に関するもの

事前措置として、所定の割合を超える株式譲渡や議決権の取得等を処分、または、所定の議決権取得を目的とする株主間契約の締結に政府の事前承認（「黄金株」保有者）の事前承認（実態としては許認可）を要するもの（イタリア第一、ポルトガル第二、フランス、スペイン、イタリア第三、オランダ）、および、閣僚保有株式による単発または複数の株式処分であって所定の持株割合の減少に帰結する場合に政府の事前承認（譲渡制限）（スペイン）がある。また、「黄金株」に関する政府の事前承認（譲渡の相手方を

国務大臣等に限るなど）の規定（英国、ポルトガル第二）も、事前措置のひとつに数えられよう。

事後措置としては、所定の割合を超える議決権取得等への政府の異議申立て（イタリア第三）、所定の割合を超える株式の強制売却（ポルトガル第一、ポルトガル第二）、所定の割合を超える議決権の不算入（ドイツ）、所定の割合を超える議決権の割合を超える議決権の割合を定める例がある。もっとも、所定の割合を超える事後措置に関する措置の多くは、法令上引受けの無効（ポルトガル第一、ポルトガル第三、イタリア第三）、議決権行使に関するものであって、必ずしも黄金株の権利内容が実効措置として強制されるものではない。「黄金株」を随意償還条項として措置されているわけではない。なお、自国権に関し無議決権優先株式とする例があり（英国）、自国権に関しても特殊な権利が付与されていることが実際には多いと思われる。

b) 役員の選任に関するもの

「黄金株」には役員の選任権が付与されていることが多い。所定の員数の議決権のない取締役の選任権（フランス、ベルギー、イタリア第三）、議決権のある取締役・監査役員の選任（ポルトガル第三）、監査役員の選任（ドイツ）、取締役・監査役員会委員の選任（イタリア第一）、経営委員会委員の選任（ポルトガル第一）、取締役の事後的差替選任権（ポルトガル第三）、業務執行取締役の指名同意権（ポルトガル第二）などである。さらに、ベルギー一事件のように、「黄金株」の権利行使により選任された取締役に、取締役会の議決権決議取消しの付議を認めるものもある。「黄金株」によって選任された取締役に議決権を認めるか、あるいは、監査役員の選任権に留めるかは、一民間企業体としての経営裁量を尊重しつつ、公的な監視を反しばす趣旨であろう。

c) その他の会社の基本的意思決定に関するもの

「黄金株」による会社の意思決定への政府等の介入は、最もよくみられるものであり、対象となる意思決定事項も多岐にわたる。まず、一般的な会社の基本的意思決定への介入として、所定の割合を超える議決権行使の制限（ドイツ）や所定の事項（解散）に関する持株会社の議決権行使の制限

---

[53] Ibid.
[54] Ibid.

(オランダ)、あるいは、特別決議要件の加重（ドイツ）などが挙げられよう。また、投資と支配に関する制約をも可能とすべく、新株発行（オランダ第二）、普通株主の優先権利の制限や剥奪（オランダ）、「黄金株」の優先権利の制限・廃止（ポルトガル第三）などがある。そのほか、一連の所定の割合を超える資産取引（譲渡、担保権設定・変更等）、会社または子会社の任意清算（スペイン、オランダ）、合併（スペイン、オランダ）、事業譲渡（スペイン）、本店の外国への移転（イタリア第三）、グループ会社化に関する契約の締結（ポルトガル第三）、会社の目的の変更（スペイン、オランダ）、所定の定款規定の変更（英国）、所定の株式配当・無償割当（オランダ）、所定の株式投資（オランダ）、所定の株式取消（オランダ第二）への事前承認または当該取締役会決議申立ての異議取消に所定の決議申立に議決権を付与する「黄金株」について上述した。

d）「黄金株」に随伴する権利行使の条件

閣僚等が「黄金株」上の権利行使をする際には、行使条件が定められている場合が多い。行使条件の有無、その内容は比例性テストを通過するか否かの判断を左右する（この点については、後述、結びにて加えて）。参照）。少なくとも、2002年の3判決以降、閣僚等に無制限の裁量権を付与すれば、違反措置は、たとえ例外事由を有していたとしても比例性テストを通過しえないものが多い。加盟国において自主的に行使条件を定める例が多くなっているのも、そのため、と思われる。もっとも、「国家の危急存亡時に（オランダ、ポルトガル第三）、「国のエネルギー・石油製品最低供給への真の重大な危険がある場合（ポルトガル第二）、「国益保護の要請がある場合（イタリア第三）」といった抽象的な行使条件のみの措置では足りず、具体的かつ詳細な行使条件が定められる必要がある。

たとえば、スペイン事件では、法律上事前承認事項のひとつとして列挙されている「各称の如何を問わず、事業目的、事業分野もしくは株式の所有または取得にかかるあらゆる資産もしくはその担保への方針が、かく定義されるものの正確な定義が、限られたテクニックにとらわれているにはすぎないこと（権利行使事由の抽象性）を挙げ、他方、「黄金株」の行使に関し、法律により、事前承認権の対象取引、承認機関、および承認期間の定めるデクレに委任していたもの、かかる点に何ら言及せずに比例性原則違反が帰結されていることから、かかる委任規定が存在するのみでは、比例性テストを通過しえないことが合意されていると思われる。「黄金株」の判決において唯一加盟国が勝訴したベルギーの事件では、上の権利行使によって選任された取締役の事後の異議申立の付議に従い異議申立の期間において限ってを行使することに留まり、かかる決議がなされる点が評価された。事後承認等の事前承認より制限的でないECJの先例が、取締役の異議申立の事例が取締役の決議を争うことを前提とする限り、取締役会の先例であり、取締役会の場合に所定の主務大臣の事前承認等よりに比例ヘ事前承認を与えるタイプの黄金株が比例性テストを通過することは困難である。また、事後措置であっても、かかる場合、会社の意思決定の効力発生に「黄金株」保有者の同意を条件とする場合（拒否権付の「黄金株」）は、あくまでもかかる意思決定権の行使申立権と同じであって、比例性原則の適用にあたっては事前承認権が付与される場合と同視しうるのではないかと思われる。

2-3. 普遍化と示唆

「黄金株」に関する一連のECJ判決は、主に、EC条約上の基本的自由との適合性の文脈において争われているため、当該産業分野に関する国内法の存否に特段影響されることなく、加盟国法に基づく「黄金株」付与は、加盟国措置の条約上の除外事由をのひとつとして、EU法の解釈や一般原則視しうるのではないかと思われる。

[55] Case C-515/99, C-519/99 to C-524/99 and C-526/99 to Case C-540/99 Reich and Others [2002] ECR I-2157, para. 37.

等の適用を通じた正当化に関する先例群を形成するに留まり、それ以上の意義はないようにもみえる。にもかかわらず、ここではEU固有の事情があらわれ、それ以上の意義を見出すことに意を注ぐのである。その普遍化には自ずと限界はあろうから、以下では、国家の基幹産業を担う株式会社のガバナンスの点に絞って、EU「黄金株」事件が眺める点にしたい。

上記において整理した各種「黄金株」は、いずれも、その根拠規定の定款の一規定にあるにせよ、各会社の定款規定の挿入を拘束する法律等によって強制されるに限り、各会社の定款自治の挿入の地位を通じ、株主の地位を利用して行う特殊な権利の付与によって措置を通じ、株主の地位を利用して行う特殊な権利の付与によってきた（この点につき、後述、結びに代えて c）、参照）。財務基盤の効率化を図りつつ、国営会社から民営会社への過渡期のみならず、基幹産業の危機時にはなおそうすべき業種が限定されて然るべきように思われる。これは、経営者のひとつであるように思われる。これは、経営者のひとつであるとっても、EU立法における裁判所[56]や国務大臣等[57]の監視の枠組みとのいずれが望ましいかが絡み、十分重大な危険に瀕したときに監視されるべき業種を依存する。一連の判旨であるが、上記のひとつであるに、そしが一般に、十分重大な危険に瀕する業種を依存する。したがって、一般会社規制には馴染まず、須らく業種を依存する。一連の判旨であるように、純然たる経済的・行政的な国民の生命・身体の安全に関わる産業との必要かが断たれれば国民の生命・身体の安全に関わる産業との必要かが断たれれば国民の生命・身体の安全に関わる産業との必要があるとされている。この点は、EU域内の自由移動を維持するという判断であるので、どこまで一般化しうるのかという問題はある。いずれにせよ、エネルギー産業に、EUの文脈においても、自由移動

2-2において、一連の事業から「黄金株」の多様な改善策を設計してみた。そこでは、完全なる国有化への普遍化を辿れ、それ以上の意義を見出すことなく、電力会社等の定款を変更し、政府「黄金株」を導入することが示唆されるように思われる。「黄金株」保有者による無議決権取得議案や監査役（員）の選任権、あるいは、経営者の意思決定への異議申立権などを、行使条件を明示したうえで付与するガバナンス・モデルは、寄しくもECJ判決においても支持されたおそれがあるが、最小限の公的監督のありかたとして、わが国においても参照されてよい。

政府がまとまった割合の議決権付株式を常に保有するならば、一定の割合の議決権を「黄金株」により阻止することでもっても足りており、国有化を選択しない場合には、政府の議決権の譲渡は常に過半数に反ることもなくなる。外資規制に代えとかかる定款規定を置くことといずれが望ましいかは、実際の運用如何にも絡み、非常に悩ましい問題である。この点については、別途考察の機会を持ちたい。

結びに代えて ― 抽出される論点 ―

以上、本稿では、ECJの「黄金株」判決をもとに、社会の基本的利益を維持すべく、かかる利益に直結する産業におけるガバナンスのありかたを検討してきた。最後に、EU立法との関係で一連の判決が提示する論点を取り上げ、本稿の結びに代えることとしたい。なお、ここでは論点を整理するに止まる。

---

[56] たとえば、わが国の会社法について言えば、明文上の制度として、裁判所による株主総会の招集（307条）、裁判所による検査役の選任（33条、207条、284条、306条2項、325条、358条）、一時役員ならびに代表取締役の職務代行者の選任（346条、352条）、所定の場合の清算人の選任（478条、479条）、特別清算（510条）、および、個別的の非訟（訴訟事件を通じての事件を除くことなかが挙げられる。

[57] わが国の会社法においては、法務大臣による解散命令の申立て（824条）、外国会社の取引継続禁止・営業所閉鎖命令の申立て（827条）、登記（907条以下）などのほか、会社の機関である会計参与会計監査人に一定の国家資格を有する者のみの選任を認める（333条1項、337条1項）こととされている。

[58] 譲渡前の会社への承認請求（譲渡の相手方は政府等が指定する者に限る）を譲渡要件とすることや譲渡の相手方（たとえば、政府等、政府等が指定する者、または会社）を定款で定めることができる場合には、承認機関（譲渡人の議決権行使を認める定款規定はあるか）が、株主総会、代表取締役などのどれが望ましいかが論じられる。

[59] たとえば、2008年4月16日に、「外国為替及び外国貿易法」に基づき、経済産業等審議会の答申を慎重に考慮したうえ、英国投資ファンドによる電源開発株式会社株式の買い増しを中止勧告令を出した例は記憶に新しい。

である。[64]

資本の移動について以上のように概念づけるとき、なぜ「黄金株」は資本の域内自由移動を阻害しうるのか。投資家は、たとえ個別企業に「黄金株」が存在していたとしても、なお当該企業に投資するか否かの選択権を有している。したがって、ある企業が「黄金株」を政府等の特定の者に付与していることが、ただちに資本移動の自由の禁止規定の者に結しうるのかとの疑問は当然ありうるであろう。[65] この点におけるECJの論理から、直接投資に関しては、「その持株制合の多寡に関わらず国からその会社の経営への影響力を与えず、他の一般投資家は株式価値に比例した当該会社の経営・支配への参画ができない」[66] ことを、他方、ポートフォリオ投資に関しても、会社の重要な意思決定について会社の利益に合致するとの意思決定機関が判断しているにもかかわらず、国が当該判断に対し拒合権を行使する可能性があるならば、当該会社の株式への投資の魅力は低く評価される可能性がある、かかる株式への投資の魅力は減殺される[67] として、いずれにせよ、「黄金株」の存在および付与に関わる特殊権利の行使の可能性により、他の加盟国の投資行動が抑制される可能性があることに資本の自由移動との抵触の根拠を見出している。欧州委員会は、上記一連の「黄金株」事件のなかで、たびたびこのような主張を繰り返しており、[68] その立場は、2005年の欧州委員会職員作業部会文書に凝縮されている。[69] TFEU63条に加

留めることとし、個別論点の深化については別の機会に議る。

〈規範化の前提となる概念・定義または条件等に関する論点〉

a) 資本の自由移動の意味

TFEU63条１項は、「加盟国間および加盟国と第三国間の資本の移動へのあらゆる制限は禁止される」と、また、同65条１項は、かかる禁止規定の除外事由を定め、域内自由移動を尊重しつつ、加盟国の以下の権利を侵害してはならないとされる。すなわち、①居住地または投資地の相違により納税者を区別する租税法規定を適用する権利、②租税、金融機関のプルーデンス監督分野における租税法規定への違反を防止するべく必要なあらゆる措置をとる権利、行政的もしくは統計的情報のための宣言手続を定める権利、または、公序もしくは公共の安全の見地から正当化される措置をとる権利、である。同条３項により、資本の自由移動に関する除外事由とされる措置および上記２項にとされている「これらの措置および手続は偽装制限に該当してはならないとされる。

資本の自由移動は、EC条約または、TFEU上の基本的自由のうち、最も後発的に、他のEU上の基本的自由の機能に必要な範囲で段階的に推進されてきた。[60] 資本の自由移動を性急に進めれば、加盟国の経済政策や通貨政策を損なって損なうこととなり、国際収支の不均衡を招くおそれがあったからといわれる。[61] 事上記事実において触れられているように、TFEU58条１項（EC条約56条）１項は「資本の移動 (movement of capital)」という文言を有しながら、その定義を行なっていない。ECJは、当時のEC条約67条（アムステルダム条約により削除）の履行に関して採択された1988年第361号指令の付属書[62] をより所として、「資本の移動」には、経営支配権の取得を直接の目的とした投資とポートフォリオの運用を目的とした投資とを合むと解釈してきた。前者は、投資先の会社の経営・支配への関与の明確な意図を合むものであって株式等を保有するものであり、[63] 後者はそのような意図を欠く財の投資

---

[60] 旧EEC条約67条１項。今野a・82頁。
[61] 今野a・同上。
[62] Annex I to Council Directive 88/361/EEC of 24 June 1988 for the implementation of Article 67 of the Treaty.
[63] 1988年第361号指令第一附属書末尾の注記 (explanatory notes) によれば、直接投資とは「自然人、または、商工業もしくは金融業によるあらゆる種類の投資であって、資本を拠出する者と経済活動を遂行するための資本を保有する企業もしくは事業組織とのあいだに継続的・直接的関係を確立または維持するものとされ、また、資本市場における証券取引（市場取引と市場外取引の双方を含む）も資本の移動に合まれるとされている。
[64] See, e.g., Joined Cases C-282/04 and 283/04 Commission v. Netherlands, supra note 30, para.19 and cited cases therein. なお、池田・前掲注 (2) 1496頁が邦語で詳細に紹介している。
[65] 小塚・前掲注 (1) 19頁。
[66] たとえば、Case C-112/05 Commission v. Germany, supra note 31, paras. 50-52.
[67] たとえば、Joined Cases C-282/04 and 283/04 Commission v. Netherlands, supra note 30, para. 27; Case C-171/08 Commission v. Portugal, supra note 36, para. 61; Case C-543/08 Commission v. Portugal, supra note 42, para. 57.
[68] たとえば、Case C-543/08 Commission v. Portugal, ibid, paras. 27-30.

盟国市民間、および加盟国と第三国の市民間の平等性を担保するに留まらないというのがECJ判例法であり、かかる立場を前提とする限り、外国からの投資を正面から排除しない、いわゆる間接差別にあたりうる上記事案の多くにおいて、同条違反が認定されたことは驚くに値しない。もっとも、間接差別にあたりうるか否かの評価は容易ではなく、上記事案の多くが真に間接差別にあたるといえるのかについては、疑われるべきである。

b) 資本の自由移動と開業の自由との関係

上記事案において、資本の自由移動単独の問題とされたのは、イタリア第二事案およびドイツ事件のみであり、他の事案では、すべてが資本の自由移動および開業の自由の両者を阻害しうるとされている。

両者の切り分けについて、ECJは、投資家による投資のうち、投資先会社の経営や支配に影響をしうるものはより開業の自由にかかるところとしてきた。たとえば、イタリア第三事件では、資本の自由移動に関するいくつかのデクレの関連規定と開業の自由に関するEC条約との整合性が問題とされたが、判旨は、政府持株の議決権の所定の割合の保有を目的とする株主間契約取得への異議申立権および開業の自由との関係のみならず、資本の自由移動と開業の自由との両者を阻害する旨のデクレ規定については、もっぱら開業の自由との関連でのみ判断されるべきとした[71]。前者については、「小資本割合であっても当該会社の経営に決定的影響を与え、会社の諸活動を決定しうる」[72]ため、資本の自由移動を阻害しうることはもちろんであるが、

TFEU49条の開業の自由との抵触もまた問題となる。他方、会社の所定の意思決定事項に対する政府の拒否権割合については、議決権割合とは無関係であり、政府による一方的な会社への経営・支配への介入として、TFEU49条の開業の自由との抵触のみを検討すれば足りる[73]。もちろん、かかる措置についても、資本の自由移動を制限する効果はないわけではない。ECJは、当該効果を副次的効果にすぎないとして、TFEU63条単独の問題とみなかったのである[74]。この副次的効果として現れるポルトガル投資抑制効果は、先述した2005年の欧州委員会の文書やそれを踏襲するECJの判旨によれば、かかる拒否権付株式の発行によって、一般株主の株式価値の歪曲が生じ、投資家の投資行動を抑制する点に求められるのであるが、少なくとも、イタリア第三事件では、ECJはかかる効果の存否についてそれ以上の詳細な分析を行っていない。他方、より最近のポルトガル第三事件においては、イタリア第三事件におけるポルトガルを有する投資家のみ影響するわけではない決定的株式を有すると意図する投資家のみ影響するわけではない点を挙げ、イタリア第三事件と異なる点として、ECJは、ボルトガル政府の判断を進めた[75]。イタリア第三事件と異なるのは、TFEU63条の整合性を判断している点であり、この文脈において、上記欧州委員会の主張を採用している[76]。両判決の重要かつ基本的な会社の意思決定への政府からの自由を認めるタイプの「黄金株」に関しては、ECJの判断にも揺れがあるということになろう[77]。実務的には、いずれかの基本的自由との抵触を明らかにすれば、加盟国の義務不履行を導くかもしれないが、論

---

69 European Commission, supra note 1. なお、supra note 36, para. 34.
70 たとえば、Case C-367/98 Commission v. Portugal, supra note 8, para. 44; Case C-483/99 Commission v. France, supra note 13, para. 40; Case C-463/00 Commission v. Spain, supra note 25, para. 56.
71 Case C-326/07 Commission v. Italy, supra note 33, paras. 38-39.
72 Ibid, para. 38.
73 Ibid, para. 39.
74 Ibid. なお、Case C-196/04 Cadbury Schweppes and Cadbury Schweppes Overseas v. Commissioners of Inland Revenue [2008] ECR II-3643, para. 33.
75 Case C-543/08 Commission v. Portugal, supra note 42, paras. 41-44.
76 Ibid, para. 72.
77 Ibid, paras. 56-57.

理の詰めにやや欠けるという問題が残ることになる。

釈には、実効性に欠けるという問題がある。

＜規範の適用を巡る論点＞

d)「黄金株」と Keck 基準との関係

EC 条約上の物の自由移動に関しては、EC 条約上の基本的自由のなかで最も規定が整備されており、すでに相当量の ECJ の判例の蓄積がある[80]。ECJ は、加盟国における数量制限同等措置の物の自由移動への制約を定める TFEU34条およびでの例外事由を定める同36条に関し、いくつかの注目すべき規範を定立してきた[81]。そのうち、1993年に ECJ が Keck と Mithouard の両名に対する刑事訴訟に関する先決裁定において示したいわゆる Keck 基準とは、次のようなものである。

「……かかる立法〔フランスの不当廉売に関する罰則—筆者注〕は、商人から販売促進の手段を奪う限り、売上高、したがって、他の加盟国からの商品の売上高を抑制する…他の加盟国からの商品に販売条件[82]を制限しましたは禁止する国内立法規定を適用することは、ダッソンヴィル判決の意味における加盟国間の通商を直接的・間接的・明示的・黙示的に阻害するものではない……ただし、かかる規定は、影響しなければならない……かかる条件が充足される場合、かかる規定は他の加盟国商品の市場アクセスを阻害せず、または、内国商品の市場アクセス以上に阻害するものとはいえない。かか

c) State measure としての「黄金株」

一連の黄金株事件は、民営化の過程で導入されたものであり、多くは国家の基幹産業に関わり、公共性がきわめて高い目的で創設されたものである。他方、黄金株の根拠規定は、形式的には会社法上に見出され、上記の多くの事案で、TFEU63条を適用する怒口上として、黄金株は加盟国措置とはいえないとの主張が加盟国により展開されている。確かに、上述したように、資本の自由移動をも含め、TFEU 上の基本的自由に関する諸規定は、いずれも加盟国措置との関係で自由を保障するものである。実態としては、ECJ が指摘するように、政府主導で定められた諸規定の導入であり、加盟国措置に等しく、加盟国には会社法上の措置であったとしても、民営化会社についてのみ特別にかかる定款規定を置く旨の立法的措置が背後にあってのことではある。この点については、異論はないものの、そもそも、EC 条約上の諸自由の名宛人（国家対私人）のみならず水平的（私人間）関係においても直接効果を有すると解釈されてきた[79]。仮に、諸事件で問題となった措置等を直接的私人との抵触はやはり問題になるようにも思われる。もっとも、各企業が任意に導入した定款等の規定ではなく、加盟国措置である以上、EU 諸条約および派生法上の義務の履行確保の対象外となる。義務の名宛人は、あくまでも加盟国である。欧州委員会の強権的介入による、私人による EC への自発的提訴を促すことはかなうとすれば、仮に政府等への黄金株の付与が望ましくないという価値判断に立つならば、かかる解

---

[78] もっぱら、開業の自由の問題とする判断、または、開業の自由と資本の自由移動の双方の適用があるとする判断が多方の可能性において、ポートフォリオ投資への抑制効果を明らかにし、それを直視するならば、後者の判断に迫り着く。後者を前提とすれば、上記の多くの事案で採用されているように、実態的には、もっぱら資本の自由移動との抵触のみを判断し、開業の自由との関係については、判断の必要はないとして判断しないことになる。

[79] M. Andenas and F. Wooldridge, *European Comparative Company Law* (Cambridge: Cambridge UP, 2009), p. 20.

[80] EC 条約上、基本的自由は、「物の自由移動（TFEU28〜37条）」「人の自由移動（TFEU45条〜48条）」「開業の自由（TFEU49条〜55条）」「サービスの自由移動（TFEU56条〜62条）」および「資本の自由移動（TFEU63条〜66条、75条）」の5つがある。基本的自由間の制度比較として、J. Snell, *Goods and Services in EC Law: A Study of the Relationship Between the Freedoms* (Oxford: Oxford UP, 2002).

[81] たとえば、Case 8/74 Procureur du Roi v. Benoit and Gustave Dassonville [1974] ECR 837, [1974] 2 CMLR 436 (Dassonville); Case 120/78 Rewe-Zentrale AG v. Bundesmonopolverwaltung für Branntwein [1979] ECR 649, [1979] 3 CMLR 494 (Cassis); Joined Cases C-267/91 and 268/91 Keck and Mithouard, supra note 27.

[82]「販売条件」について、学説により、その概念の明確化が検討されてきた。たとえば、営業時間、労働条件、あるいは、店舗規制などは「静的販売条件」に、広告、営業形態、おまけの提供などは「動的販売条件」に、TFEU34条の射程内にあるとの見解が提示されている。E.g., P. Craig and de Búrca, *EU Law, 4th Edition* (Oxford: Oxford UP, 2008), pp. 686-687.

続く4項において、「比例性原則の下では、連合の行為の内容と形式は、本条約およびTFEUの目的の達成に必要な範囲を超えてはならない。連合の諸機関は、補完性原則および比例性原則の適用に関する議定書の規定に従い、比例性原則を適用しなければならない」としての比例性原則を定めている。ECJは、これまで、EC条約上の基本的自由との抵触が問題となった多くの判例においてこの一般条項との整合性を判断するために比例性原則を適用してきた。[84]

比例性原則との整合性の判断は次の3つの段階を経なければならないとされる。[85] 第一段階は、いわゆる適合性（suitability）の審査に関わる。そこでは、問題とされる措置がその目的の達成のために適切であるか否かが判断される。第二段階は、いわゆる必要性（necessity）の審査に関し、当該措置が達成しようとする目的に鑑みて必要であるか否かが判断される。第三段階では、いわゆる狭義の比例性（Proportionality Stricto Sensu）の審査がなされ、当該措置の目的との適合性および必要性、あるいは、当該措置の負の影響と負の影響とを衡量して、その目的の達成に比例的であるか否かが判断される。

ECJの裁判実務においては、第二段階と第三段階とを厳密には区別しておらず、当該措置の目的との適合性と必要性のみに、あるいは、必要性と比例性とを互換的概念と捉え、適用してきた。[86] また、現実の適用に際しては、狭義の比例性テストは、同等の効果を達成しうるより制限的でない手段であるか否かの判断基準としてのみ機能化されてきた。

e）「黄金株」事件と比例性原則

比例性原則は、欧州連合条約（以下、TEUという）5条4項および「補完性原則および比例性原則の適用に関するアムステルダム条約議定書（Protocol on the Application of the Principles of Subsidiarity and Proportionality）」を根拠とする。TEU 4条、3項において補完性原則を、

続く4項および5条4項および「補

ECJは、関連規定に他の加盟国からの投資を抑制しうる効果があるということと他の加盟国からの投資家の市場アクセスが阻害される（あるいは、内国投資家の市場アクセス以上に他の加盟国投資家の市場アクセスを阻害する）こととを同視して、Keck基準の適用を否定している。もっとも両者を同視しうるのか、そうであるとするならば、詳細な事実認定および事実に関する法的評価の問題なのかもしれないが、事実認定および事実に関する評価の問題ならば、その分析が加えられるべきであろう。

仮に、上記イタリア第二事件のように、株式保有の制限を受けないとしても、自国投資家の市場アクセスを阻害するといっているのか、他の加盟国の投資家の市場アクセスを阻害するといっているのかについては、疑問なしとしない。ただ、そのような規定が、他の加盟国からの投資家の議決権保有を排除するためのものであり、そのような明らかな目的と効果があるといえる。

Keck基準に照らしたとしても、40条は、所定の割合を超える公的機関以外の議決権保有を排除するという定めの投資を明示したものではなく、その加盟国からの投資が全てに適用できる可能性はある。

英国事件およびポルトガル第三事件において、加盟国は、Keck基準に依拠した議論を展開している。両事件（家）を別異に扱うのではなかった。もっ的には、他の加盟国からの投資、少なくとも形式

異なる株式の権利内容で特定の者にのみ認めること、いわゆるKeck判決のいう「販売条件」に相当する投資条件とみることもできるとすれば、Keck基準の下、資本の自由移動の阻害の局面にも適用できる可能性はある。

る規定は、EC条約30条（TFEU34条）の適用を受けない……」[83]

---

[83] Cases 267/91 and 268/91 Keck and Mithouard, supra note 27, paras. 13-16.

[84] もともとは、古代ギリシアの法格言に端を発し、加盟国における法の基本原則に発展したのち、加盟国法との相互作用を通じてEU法上の一般原則として明文化されるに至ったとされる。See, e.g., T. Tridimas, *The General Principles of EC Law* (Oxford: Oxford UP, 1999), p. 89.

[85] E.g., G. de Búrca, 'The Principle of Proportionality and Its Application in EC Law', (1993) 13 Yearbook of European Law 109. なお、警察比例に関心を置く研究ではあるが、ドイツを中心とする欧州における比例性原則を巡る議論状況については、須藤陽子『比例原則の現代的意義と機能』法律文化社（2010年）第6章。

[86] M. P. Maduro, *We, The Court: The European Court of Justice and European Economic Constitution* (Oxford: Hart, 1999), p. 57; T. Tridimas, 'Proportionality in Community Law: Searching for the Appropriate Standard of Scrutiny', in E. Ellis (ed.), *The Principle of Proportionality in the Laws of Europe* (Oxford: Hart, 1999), p. 68. なお、Case C-483/99 Commission v. France, supra note 13, para. 46.

[87] Case C-483/99 Commission v. France, ibid.

ECJは、前述の通り唯一加盟国の主張を認めたベルギー事件について も、資本の自由移動への抵触を前提としたうえで（ベルギー政府が当該抵 触を争わなかったからでもあるが、あくまで、正当化の過程で比例性原 則のフィルターを通すことによって、当該措置が許容されているか一般的 利益とのバランスにおいて例外をなすにすぎない。ECJの立場を 前提とする限り、黄金株付与に伴って権利化された直接投資ではあっても、かかる権 利行使の可能性は、域内における直接投資または／およびポートフォリオ 投資に制限的効果を有し、いずれも、資本の自由移動または／およびその開業 の自由に抵触すると捉えられ、その前提に立っても、TFEU345条のECJの 解釈に制限的な可能性があると捉えると、かかる措置がその達成しようとする目的 に鑑みて比例的でない限り、問題となったECJが黄金株付与するものの、ベルキー事件では、事実上、ECJが異議申立権を付与されていることが比例性原則の画定に偏らしていると解することは不可能であり、事後的措置ではなく、その裁量権が抽象的に画定されるのみで事実上無制限にかかる政府に付与される場合に は、比例性原則を満たさず、基本的自由への侵害が確定することとはいえ ないことない（この点について、前述、2-2d)、参照）[89]。

f）「黄金株」に対するTFEU345条の適用の可否

1-2の各事案に関する法務官意見は、TFEU345条からの正当化を試みた。 TFEU345条は、「本条約はならない」と定めるのみである。財産所有制度の諸規 則を侵害してはならない。問題とされた加盟国の諸規定が、「財産所有制 度を司る加盟国の諸規則」に依拠したにあたるからである。ECJは、こ こでの加盟国における財産所有制度規整は、あくまでも私的所有にかかる ものとの「黄金株」の付与を、一貫して保護してきた。c) でみたように、政府等 への「黄金株」の付与を、State measure と解する以上、ECJとしては、 TFEU345条は私的所有制度に関わるもののみに適用はな

いとしなければ、論理破綻を来すこととなる。他方、1-2においては明され れた法務官意見では、一連の政府等への「黄金株」付与の諸制度について、 いわば官民混合の中間的過程で関わるものとみているようである。TFEU345条が適用される「財産所有制度」については、私的所有制度のような 有形をするものではないと、このような中間的企業所 有形態への同条の適用の布石として提示されているようにも読める。c) での議論にも関わる黄金株付与について各事会社の定款を通じた純 然たる私的措置と捉えられ、仮に黄金株付与にTFEU345条のECJの 解釈が認められる可能性があるとすると、ポルトガル事件における同条の射程が及ぶことをこの点を自国措置の正当化の論拠のひ とつとしたが、この解釈はまさにこの点を自国措置の正当化の論拠のひ とつとした[90]。このような解釈の可能性を提示していて、ポルトガル第二事件に おいては、非差別措置における一般的利益保護による不可減的要件と差別措置 における条約上の除外事由によるTFEU345条による正当化の可能 性の途が開けることを意味する。

原稿受理：2011年5月13日
掲載承認：2011年6月15日

---

88 On this point, see, Joined Cases C-515/99 and 519/99 to 524/99 and 526/99 to 540/99 Reisch and Others, supra note 55, para. 37; Case C-463/00 Commission v. Spain, supra note 25, para. 78.

89 Case C-503/99 Commission v. Belgium, supra note 14, para. 52.

90 Case C-171/08 Commission v. Portugal, supra note 36, para. 42.

金融商品取引法研究会名簿

(令和元年5月28日現在)

会　　長	神　作　裕　之	東京大学大学院法学政治学研究科教授	
会長代理	弥　永　真　生	筑波大学ビジネスサイエンス系 　　　　　　　　ビジネス科学研究科教授	
委　　員	飯　田　秀　総	東京大学大学院法学政治学研究科准教授	
〃	大　崎　貞　和	野村総合研究所未来創発センターフェロー	
〃	尾　崎　悠　一	首都大学東京大学院法学政治学研究科准教授	
〃	加　藤　貴　仁	東京大学大学院法学政治学研究科教授	
〃	河　村　賢　治	立教大学大学院法務研究科教授	
〃	小　出　　　篤	学習院大学法学部教授	
〃	後　藤　　　元	東京大学大学院法学政治学研究科教授	
〃	武　井　一　浩	西村あさひ法律事務所パートナー弁護士	
〃	中　東　正　文	名古屋大学大学院法学研究科教授	
〃	藤　田　友　敬	東京大学大学院法学政治学研究科教授	
〃	松　井　智　予	上智大学大学院法学研究科教授	
〃	松　井　秀　征	立教大学法学部教授	
〃	松　尾　健　一	大阪大学大学院高等司法研究科教授	
〃	松　尾　直　彦	松尾国際法律事務所弁護士	
〃	宮　下　　　央	ＴＭＩ総合法律事務所弁護士	
オブザーバー	小　森　卓　郎	金融庁企画市場局市場課長	
〃	岸　田　吉　史	野村ホールディングスグループ執行役員	
〃	森　　　忠　之	大和証券グループ本社経営企画部担当部長兼法務課長	
〃	森　　　正　孝	ＳＭＢＣ日興証券法務部長	
〃	陶　山　健　二	みずほ証券法務部長	
〃	本　井　孝　洋	三菱ＵＦＪモルガン・スタンレー証券法務部長	
〃	山　内　公　明	日本証券業協会常務執行役自主規制本部長	
〃	島　村　昌　征	日本証券業協会執行役政策本部共同本部長	
〃	内　田　直　樹	日本証券業協会自主規制本部自主規制企画部長	
〃	塚　﨑　由　寛	日本取引所グループ総務部法務グループ課長	
研 究 所	増　井　喜一郎	日本証券経済研究所理事長	
〃	大　前　　　忠	日本証券経済研究所常務理事	

(敬称略)

[参考]　既に公表した「金融商品取引法研究会（証券取引法研究会）研究記録」

第1号「裁判外紛争処理制度の構築と問題点」　　　　　　2003年11月
　　　　　報告者　森田章同志社大学教授

第2号「システム障害と損失補償問題」　　　　　　　　　2004年1月
　　　　　報告者　山下友信東京大学教授

第3号「会社法の大改正と証券規制への影響」　　　　　　2004年3月
　　　　　報告者　前田雅弘京都大学教授

第4号「証券化の進展に伴う諸問題(倒産隔離の明確化等)」　2004年6月
　　　　　報告者　浜田道代名古屋大学教授

第5号「EUにおける資本市場法の統合の動向　　　　　　2005年7月
　　　　　　―投資商品、証券業務の範囲を中心として―」
　　　　　報告者　神作裕之東京大学教授

第6号「近時の企業情報開示を巡る課題　　　　　　　　　2005年7月
　　　　　　―実効性確保の観点を中心に―」
　　　　　報告者　山田剛志新潟大学助教授

第7号「プロ・アマ投資者の区分―金融商品・　　　　　　2005年9月
　　　　　販売方法等の変化に伴うリテール規制の再編―」
　　　　　報告者　青木浩子千葉大学助教授

第8号「目論見書制度の改革」　　　　　　　　　　　　　2005年11月
　　　　　報告者　黒沼悦郎早稲田大学教授

第9号「投資サービス法(仮称)について」　　　　　　　　2005年11月
　　　　　報告者　三井秀範金融庁総務企画局市場課長
　　　　　　　　　松尾直彦金融庁総務企画局
　　　　　　　　　　　投資サービス法(仮称)法令準備室長

第10号「委任状勧誘に関する実務上の諸問題　　　　　　2005年11月
　　　　　　―委任状争奪戦（proxy fight）の文脈を中心に―」
　　　　　報告者　太田洋 西村ときわ法律事務所パートナー・弁護士

第11号「集団投資スキームに関する規制について　　　　2005年12月
　　　　　　―組合型ファンドを中心に―」
　　　　　報告者　中村聡 森・濱田松本法律事務所パートナー・弁護士

第12号「証券仲介業」　　　　　　　　　　　　　　　　2006年3月
　　　　　報告者　川口恭弘同志社大学教授

第13号「敵対的買収に関する法規制」　　　　　　　　　　2006年5月
　　　　報告者　中東正文名古屋大学教授

第14号「証券アナリスト規制と強制情報開示・不公正取引規制」　2006年7月
　　　　報告者　戸田暁京都大学助教授

第15号「新会社法のもとでの株式買取請求権制度」　　　　2006年9月
　　　　報告者　藤田友敬東京大学教授

第16号「証券取引法改正に係る政令等について」　　　　　2006年12月
　　　（ＴＯＢ、大量保有報告関係、内部統制報告関係）
　　　　報告者　池田唯一　金融庁総務企画局企業開示課長

第17号「間接保有証券に関するユニドロア条約策定作業の状況」　2007年5月
　　　　報告者　神田秀樹　東京大学大学院法学政治学研究科教授

第18号「金融商品取引法の政令・内閣府令について」　　　2007年6月
　　　　報告者　三井秀範　金融庁総務企画局市場課長

第19号「特定投資家・一般投資家について―自主規制業務を中心に―」　2007年9月
　　　　報告者　青木浩子　千葉大学大学院専門法務研究科教授

第20号「金融商品取引所について」　　　　　　　　　　　2007年10月
　　　　報告者　前田雅弘　京都大学大学院法学研究科教授

第21号「不公正取引について－村上ファンド事件を中心に－」　2008年1月
　　　　報告者　太田　洋 西村あさひ法律事務所パートナー・弁護士

第22号「大量保有報告制度」　　　　　　　　　　　　　　2008年3月
　　　　報告者　神作裕之　東京大学大学院法学政治学研究科教授

第23号「開示制度（Ⅰ）―企業再編成に係る開示制度および　　2008年4月
　　　　集団投資スキーム持分等の開示制度―」
　　　　報告者　川口恭弘 同志社大学大学院法学研究科教授

第24号「開示制度（Ⅱ）―確認書、内部統制報告書、四半期報告書―」　2008年7月
　　　　報告者　戸田　暁　京都大学大学院法学研究科准教授

第25号「有価証券の範囲」　　　　　　　　　　　　　　　2008年7月
　　　　報告者　藤田友敬　東京大学大学院法学政治学研究科教授

第26号「民事責任規定・エンフォースメント」　　　　　　2008年10月
　　　　報告者　近藤光男　神戸大学大学院法学研究科教授

第27号「金融機関による説明義務・適合性の原則と金融商品販売法」2009年1月
　　　　報告者　山田剛志　新潟大学大学院実務法学研究科准教授

第28号「集団投資スキーム（ファンド）規制」　　　　　　2009年3月
　　　　報告者　中村聡 森・濱田松本法律事務所パートナー・弁護士

第29号「金融商品取引業の業規制」　　　　　　　　　　2009年4月
　　　　　報告者　黒沼悦郎　早稲田大学大学院法務研究科教授

第30号「公開買付け制度」　　　　　　　　　　　　　　2009年7月
　　　　　報告者　中東正文　名古屋大学大学院法学研究科教授

第31号「最近の金融商品取引法の改正について」　　　　2011年3月
　　　　　報告者　藤本拓資　金融庁総務企画局市場課長

第32号「金融商品取引業における利益相反　　　　　　　2011年6月
　　　　─利益相反管理体制の整備業務を中心として─」
　　　　　報告者　神作裕之　東京大学大学院法学政治学研究科教授

第33号「顧客との個別の取引条件における特別の利益提供に関する問題」2011年9月
　　　　　報告者　青木浩子　千葉大学大学院専門法務研究科教授
　　　　　　　　　松本譲治　ＳＭＢＣ日興証券　法務部長

第34号「ライツ・オファリングの円滑な利用に向けた制度整備と課題」2011年11月
　　　　　報告者　前田雅弘　京都大学大学院法学研究科教授

第35号「公開買付規制を巡る近時の諸問題」　　　　　　2012年2月
　　　　　報告者　太田　洋　西村あさひ法律事務所弁護士・NY州弁護士

第36号「格付会社への規制」　　　　　　　　　　　　　2012年6月
　　　　　報告者　山田剛志　成城大学法学部教授

第37号「金商法第6章の不公正取引規制の体系」　　　　 2012年7月
　　　　　報告者　松尾直彦　東京大学大学院法学政治学研究科客員
　　　　　　　　　教授・西村あさひ法律事務所弁護士

第38号「キャッシュ・アウト法制」　　　　　　　　　　2012年10月
　　　　　報告者　中東正文　名古屋大学大学院法学研究科教授

第39号「デリバティブに関する規制」　　　　　　　　　2012年11月
　　　　　報告者　神田秀樹　東京大学大学院法学政治学研究科教授

第40号「米国JOBS法による証券規制の変革」　　　　　　2013年1月
　　　　　報告者　中村聡　森・濱田松本法律事務所パートナー・弁護士

第41号「金融商品取引法の役員の責任と会社法の役員の責任　2013年3月
　　　　─虚偽記載をめぐる役員の責任を中心に─」
　　　　　報告者　近藤光男　神戸大学大学院法学研究科教授

第42号「ドッド＝フランク法における信用リスクの保持ルールについて」2013年4月
　　　　　報告者　黒沼悦郎　早稲田大学大学院法務研究科教授

第43号「相場操縦の規制」　　　　　　　　　　　　　　2013年8月
　　　　　報告者　藤田友敬　東京大学大学院法学政治学研究科教授

第44号「法人関係情報」 2013年10月
　　　報告者　川口恭弘　同志社大学大学院法学研究科教授
　　　　　　　平田公一　日本証券業協会常務執行役

第45号「最近の金融商品取引法の改正について」 2014年6月
　　　報告者　藤本拓資　金融庁総務企画局企画課長

第46号「リテール顧客向けデリバティブ関連商品販売における民事責任 2014年9月
　　　　―「新規な説明義務」を中心として―」
　　　報告者　青木浩子　千葉大学大学院専門法務研究科教授

第47号「投資者保護基金制度」 2014年10月
　　　報告者　神田秀樹　東京大学大学院法学政治学研究科教授

第48号「市場に対する詐欺に関する米国判例の動向について」 2015年1月
　　　報告者　黒沼悦郎　早稲田大学大学院法務研究科教授

第49号「継続開示義務者の範囲―アメリカ法を中心に―」 2015年3月
　　　報告者　飯田秀総　神戸大学大学院法学研究科准教授

第50号「証券会社の破綻と投資者保護基金 2015年5月
　　　　―金融商品取引法と預金保険法の交錯―」
　　　報告者　山田剛志　成城大学大学院法学研究科教授

第51号「インサイダー取引規制と自己株式」 2015年7月
　　　報告者　前田雅弘　京都大学大学院法学研究科教授

第52号「金商法において利用されない制度と利用される制度の制限」 2015年8月
　　　報告者　松尾直彦　東京大学大学院法学政治学研究科
　　　　　　　　　　　　客員教授・弁護士

第53号「証券訴訟を巡る近時の諸問題 2015年10月
　　　　―流通市場において不実開示を行った提出会社の責任を中心に―」
　　　報告者　太田洋　西村あさひ法律事務所パートナー・弁護士

第54号「適合性の原則」 2016年3月
　　　報告者　川口恭弘　同志社大学大学院法学研究科教授

第55号「金商法の観点から見たコーポレートガバナンス・コード」 2016年5月
　　　報告者　神作裕之　東京大学大学院法学政治学研究科教授

第56号「EUにおける投資型クラウドファンディング規制」 2016年7月
　　　報告者　松尾健一　大阪大学大学院法学研究科准教授

第57号「上場会社による種類株式の利用」 2016年9月
　　　報告者　加藤貴仁　東京大学大学院法学政治学研究科准教授

第58号「公開買付前置型キャッシュアウトにおける　　　　2016年11月
　　　　価格決定請求と公正な対価」
　　　　　　報告者　藤田友敬　東京大学大学院法学政治学研究科教授

第59号「平成26年会社法改正後のキャッシュ・アウト法制」2017年1月
　　　　　　報告者　中東正文　名古屋大学大学院法学研究科教授

第60号「流通市場の投資家による発行会社に対する証券訴訟の実態」2017年3月
　　　　　　報告者　後藤　元　東京大学大学院法学政治学研究科准教授

第61号「米国における投資助言業者（investment adviser）　2017年5月
　　　　の負う信認義務」
　　　　　　報告者　萬澤陽子　専修大学法学部准教授・当研究所客員研究員

第62号「最近の金融商品取引法の改正について」　　　　　2018年2月
　　　　　　報告者　小森卓郎　金融庁総務企画局市場課長

第63号「監査報告書の見直し」　　　　　　　　　　　　　2018年3月
　　　　　　報告者　弥永真生　筑波大学ビジネスサイエンス系
　　　　　　　　　　　　　　　ビジネス科学研究科教授

第64号「フェア・ディスクロージャー・ルールについて」　2018年6月
　　　　　　報告者　大崎貞和　野村総合研究所未来創発センターフェロー

第65号「外国為替証拠金取引のレバレッジ規制」　　　　　2018年8月
　　　　　　報告者　飯田秀総　東京大学大学院法学政治学研究科准教授

第66号「一般的不公正取引規制に関する一考察」　　　　　2018年12月
　　　　　　報告者　松井秀征　立教大学法学部教授

第67号「仮想通貨・ＩＣＯに関する法規制・自主規制」　　2019年3月
　　　　　　報告者　河村賢治　立教大学大学院法務研究科教授

第68号「投資信託・投資法人関連法制に関する問題意識について」2019年5月
　　　　　　報告者　松尾直彦　東京大学大学院法学政治学研究科
　　　　　　　　　　　　　　　客員教授・弁護士

第69号「「政策保有株式」に関する開示規制の再構築について」2019年7月
　　　　　　報告者　加藤貴仁　東京大学大学院法学政治学研究科教授

購入を希望される方は、一般書店または当研究所までお申し込み下さい。
当研究所の出版物案内は研究所のホームページ http://www.jsri.or.jp/ にてご覧いただけます。

金融商品取引法研究会研究記録　第70号
複数議決権株式を用いた株主構造の
コントロール
　　令和元年11月11日

定価（本体500円＋税）

編　者　　金融商品取引法研究会
発行者　　公益財団法人　日本証券経済研究所
東京都中央区日本橋2-11-2
〒103-0027
電話　03（6225）2326代表
URL: http://www.jsri.or.jp

ISBN978-4-89032-686-0　C3032　¥500E